MORE ENCOUNTERS WITH STAR PEOPLE:

URBAN AMERICAN INDIANS TELL THEIR STORIES

ARDY SIXKILLER CLARKE

ANOMALIST BOOKS
San Antonio * Charlottesville

An Original Publication of ANOMALIST BOOKS
More Encounters with Star People
Copyright © 2016 Ardy Sixkiller Clarke
ISBN: 978-1-938398-62-9

Cover photo by Seale Studios

Book design by Seale Studios

For information, go to AnomalistBooks.com, or write to:
Anomalist Books, 5150 Broadway #108, San Antonio, TX 78209

TABLE OF CONTENTS

FOR KIP

"Yours is the light by which my spirit's born:
you are my sun, my moon, and all my stars." — E.E.Cummings

A NOTE FROM THE AUTHOR

Since I published my first book, *Encounters with Star People*, I have had many individuals ask me where I get my stories. The simplest answer is that "I ask." Amazing stories often become known during casual conversation.

I believe that most people know someone who has had an encounter. If you do not think so, bring the subject up in a group and "ask" if anyone has had an encounter. I think you will be surprised at the degree to which the UFO phenomenon has infiltrated the lives of your friends and acquaintances. It is no longer possible to ignore that something is happening, that millions of individuals are involved in something that does not fit the western worldview.

I was recently at a barbecue with ten people in attendance. An out-of-state individual at the party asked me about the subject of my book. When I told him, almost instantly six of the ten people at the party, one an author and retired educator and five others, two in the medical profession, a graduate student and her husband, and a geologist who traveled the world in search of unexplored oil locations, spoke about their personal experiences with UFOs. In other words, sixty percent of the group had had an encounter.

I began my research years ago among American Indians. My social group, my relatives, and many of my professional colleagues came from tribes throughout the country, and I felt safe with that group, and they with me. Aware that indigenous people had ancient stories of Star People combined with my personal experience, I was a believer. As a result, and tons of coffee later, I decided to record their stories for my own personal interest. In this book, as in my previous books, I have attempted to give the reader a realistic description of the settings (although disguised to protect the participants) and how the interview took place. Some readers will no doubt notice just how often coffee drinking is mentioned in these stories. When you are invited into an American Indian home, it is considered appropriate to offer food and drink. In most Indian homes, the coffee pot is on 24/7, and the poorest families will offer you what they have available. More often than not, it will be coffee—the stronger and blacker, the better.

I approached my inquiries from a nonjudgmental, insider viewpoint. I was interested in the stories. I was not interested in asking questions to influence the direction of the stories, nor was I interested in maligning the individuals who had stories to tell because they had no material proof or witnesses to the encounter. This provided me with unequalled access to people, who I believe are representative of millions of individuals who have stories to tell, but remain silent. I took notes and taped all interviews. In some cases I have taken the liberty to clean up the transcribed dialogue enough to be readable, but not so much that it changed the meaning.

As word of my work spread in the rural communities and reservations where I worked or traveled, individuals who had stories to tell began to approach me. Some of my critics suggested that too many of my stories happened by chance or fate. My response is that I pride myself on being approachable. I hope that today, tomorrow, or ten thousand tomorrows from now individuals with stories to tell will always feel comfortable in approaching me. If someone indicates they have a story to tell, I will always "ask." And if not, I will likely "ask" anyway.

Once *Encounters with Star People* was published, individuals with stories approached me. I received countless emails from readers who had encounters. I answered every email and asked to hear their stories.

This approach was recently brought home to me when I was visiting a Mayan culture specialist and historian in Guatemala. The conversation turned to Eric von Däniken's ancient astronaut theory. When I asked him his reaction to von Däniken's work, he said, "He didn't ask us."

Since childhood, I have watched the sky. There is not a night when I stand under the Montana sky, that I do not "ask" myself: which of these stars above me serve as home to the Star People? It is not difficult for me to imagine that civilizations exist in the universe that are perhaps a million years old, and to think of what they may have accomplished when I consider what humans have accomplished in a few hundred years. We have visited the Moon and now have Mars in our sight. It is not hard to accept the fact that older civilizations are sufficiently advanced to have colonized other planets and sent spaceships to the far ends of the universe.

For the nonbelievers, they await the discovery of those planets or for some kind of proof that aliens exist, but for those of us who are believers or experiencers, we already know they exist. We know there are many galaxies far beyond the reach of telescopes. We know that extraterrestrial life is real. We know that these entities travel to Earth. These beliefs are not confined to the indigenous people of the Americas, but are commonly held among all people of planet Earth. It is only that we forget "to ask."

In this book, you will meet individuals who have had encounters. All are stories collected from American Indians or Alaskan Natives. I have presented their stories as they were told to me.

* * *

As with my first book, I have chosen to use the term "American Indian" instead of "Native American." Here is why. A number of years ago, a group of American Indian researchers, came together and decided that, in writing and research, we would refer to tribal groups in general as American Indians rather than Native Americans. We made this decision based upon the fact that the use of the term "Native American" was increasingly claimed by those individuals born within the United States regardless of ethnicity. Our position was further validated by award-winning journalist Tim Giago, founder/editor/publisher of the *Lakota Times, Indian Country Today*, and *Native Sun News*, who stated: "We realize the word 'Indian' is a misnomer, but for generic purposes, we are forced to use it when speaking of many different tribes… Any politically correct thinker who believes Native American is the preferred identification tag for the Lakota or any other tribe is wrong. Most of us do not object to the use of Indian or American Indian. And as I said, Native American can be used by any American native to this land." I agree with Tim Giago and other American Indian researchers on this matter.

INTRODUCTION

Unlike *Encounters with Star People: Untold Stories of American Indians* that dealt with stories of American Indians on reservations, this book will concentrate on stories of American Indians who live off reservations. There are five hundred and seventy-six federally recognized American Indian tribes living on three hundred and twenty-four Indian reservations in the United States. Of the five million full bloods or mixed race American Indians, seventy-eight percent live among the public. The majority of full-blooded Indians live on their reservations.

The term most often applied to those American Indians who live in small towns and cities throughout the United States is "urban Indians." The National Urban Indian Family Coalition applies the term urban Indians to "individuals of American Indian and Alaska Native ancestry who may or may not have active ties with a particular tribe, but who identify with and are active in the Native community."

The number of Indians living in urban settings accelerated in the 1950s and 1960s because of the Indian termination policy of the United States government. Imbedded in the policy was the intent to terminate the tribes and end the reservation system. At the same time, the Bureau of Indian Affairs (BIA) developed a "relocation" program that encouraged Indian people to move to urban areas. The program was abolished in the 1970s, but it had a profound impact on those involved. Some were never able to adjust to life in urban areas and returned to the reservation. For others, a job, steady income, or other opportunities led to a disenfranchisement from the reservation. Most learned to navigate two worlds.

Today many Indian people have moved to urban areas without any assistance from the BIA. Much of the personal relocation

was a result of the opportunities afforded American Indian youth
to obtain college degrees through Pell grant programs and other
scholarship assistance. Once students completed their education,
it was difficult to find jobs on the reservation, and they moved to
rural areas, small towns, and cities for employment. Others moved
for more personal reasons such as marriage to a non-Indian. Many
who were drafted in the 1950s through 1970s became familiar
with mainstream society and chose not to return to their reservations. Others were adopted as children by non-Indian families and
grew up far removed from their relatives.

Anthropologist James Clifford points out that while many
American Indians live in urban settings away from their ancestral
homelands, this does not necessarily mean that their connection
to those lands are severed. He points out that many American
Indians travel back and forth between their homes off the reservation to their ancestral communities, and maintain active ties to
their ancestral lands even while not living there fulltime. Cherokee
scholar Russell Thornton maintains that American Indians tend to
intermarry with non-Indians at an increasing rate. He attributes
this, in part, to the increased urbanization of the American Indian
population and predicts increased intermarriage as more and more
American Indians meet non-Native people.

While American Indians live in every state in the United
States, the metropolitan areas with the highest percentage of
American Indians include New York City, Minneapolis, Phoenix,
Los Angeles, Cleveland, and Chicago. These cities were the most
popular sites for the government relocation program.

Many of the participants in this book demonstrated a connection with their ancestral heritage and the ancient star stories
of their people, and often returned to the reservation to visit relatives or participate in ceremonies. Some lived in cities and often
worked with Native populations in their respective cities. Others
had lost connection with their tribe and reservation for various
reasons. Some owned land or ranches that bordered the reservation. There were elders who were forced to leave the reservation to

live with relatives once they could no longer care for themselves. A few grew up knowing very little about their heritage other than the fact that they were American Indian. These few had little connection with the reservation, and all reported a feeling of sadness for their alienation from their tribal roots.

The individuals who told the stories you will read come from all walks of life. Many had college degrees; some even had advanced degrees. There were doctors, teachers, administrators, businessmen, veterans, entrepreneurs, nurses, police officers, and even college students. Others, particularly the elders, had limited formal education.

Many of the participants pointed out an early knowledge of the Star People from stories learned from grandparents, parents, or holy men. Unlike those who lived on the reservation, there was a greater concern about the intention of the extraterrestrials. Another difference that occurred included more detailed communication about their purposes, their planets, and life in the universe. There were also more descriptions of different types of aliens. These issues may be the result of the increased educational level of the participants and their need to question and collect information to explain their experience.

None of the participants were seeking notoriety, and if anything, were more insistent about protecting their anonymity. Almost all voiced a concern that their disclosure might affect their jobs, in that they could be considered psychologically unfit. Others believed their stories might decrease their opportunities for job advancement. Several admitted that their biggest fear is that their encounter might appear on Facebook or other forms of social media. In order to protect them from public harassment or any damaging effect on their lives, pseudonyms have been used and locations disguised.

When I questioned them about the possibility of the influence of media on their experiences, the majority regarded the question as absurd. While most of the group had the financial means to own televisions, thirty-three percent did not own a TV. For the males who owned a TV, the majority used it for viewing basketball and football games. For the females, the favorite shows were *Dancing with the Stars* and *The Bachelor*.

As an American Indian researcher, I have always walked in two worlds. It is a world where you can find yourself as a "token Indian" in an environment where others expect you to be the voice of all Indians. In the Indian world, you can find yourself suspect because you are not "Indian enough" or because you live off the reservation. It is not an easy road to walk. To compensate for any such shortcomings on the reservation, it is necessary to become imbedded within the community over time to gain trust. When interviewing individuals off the reservation, this was not the case.

As a university professor trained in both qualitative and quantitative research methodology, there is an expectation that you will approach any research project searching for the empirical truth. Among American Indians, you are expected to conduct research that allows the narrative to supersede the statistics. Facts and statistics are not nearly as important as the story. Using a qualitative approach, which is not always embraced by academia, the goal was to ensure that my research did not influence the individuals who related the accounts. Consequently, every effort was made to avoid leading questions or making inferences or suggestions.

Some social science researchers have suggested that there are two perspectives ("etic" and "emic") that can be employed in qualitative research. The etic perspective is an outsider's interpretation of the experiences of that culture. In contrast, an emic perspective refers to the way the members of the culture envision their world. In other words, the emic perspective is an insider's point of view. Thus, as an American Indian researcher, I chose to approach the research from an insider's perspective, an emic viewpoint. In doing so, I never questioned the existence of the Star People, nor was I skeptical of the encounters regardless of how unique or outlandish they might appear to an outsider.

My motive in collecting these stories was to preserve the experiences of present-day American Indians and their interaction with the Star People. In the process, I walked with the individuals who told their stories. I listened, I questioned, and in the end, I believed.

CHAPTER 1
TRAVELING THE UNIVERSAL HIGHWAY

Nestled near the border of Montana and Canada is the Writing-on-the-Stone Park, which is located in the Province of Alberta, Canada. The park contains the greatest concentration of rock art on the North American Great Plains. There are over fifty petroglyph sites and thousands of other works that date to 9000 BCE.

The pictographs and petroglyphs of Writing-on-the-Stone are both ceremonial and biographical in nature. Some depict crests, headdresses, and sunbursts, and others display accounts of successful hunts, heroic battles, and fallen enemies. Blackfeet legends suggest the paintings and glyphs are the work of the spirit world.

I first learned of this site from a Blackfeet graduate student who told me about the unique events that often occurred at the site. He said there was one account of an individual who stepped into a time portal, went back in time, and saw a Blackfeet Indian village as it was before the coming of the white man. There have also been reports of frequent UFO sightings in the area.

In this chapter, you will meet Tom, who told me that portals to a universal highway exist in this region.

Last summer I decided to make the trip to the Writing-on-the-Stone Park from my home in southwestern Montana. I had visited other sites where portals to other worlds had been reported and having an alleged portal in my own backyard held a special appeal to me.

The scenery was magnificent. At one spot, I pulled off the road and walked several feet through tumbleweeds and wild raspberries to photograph the captivating desolation of the area. As I stopped to photograph the Indian paintbrush, a plant native to the west, a man suddenly appeared from behind an outcropping of boulders. "My grandmother used to collect the flowers of the Indian paintbrush for her salads," he said. "But only the flowers are edible. The roots and leaves can be quite toxic."

I reached in my pocket, searching for a small container of bear spray while inching slowly backwards toward the highway. When my fingers touched my small tape recorder, I pushed the record button. "I didn't mean to frighten you," he said, as he kept his distance from me. He leaned against a boulder and looked out over the valley. He was tall, standing more than six feet. His broad shoulders stretched his short-sleeve, tight-fitting t-shirt, revealing his muscular frame. Two long, black braids hung down to his mid-chest. A white, two-inch scar sliced his left eyebrow in half making it stand out against his bronze skin. A championship rodeo buckle caught the rays of the sun and glistened and spoke of glory in another time.

"I'm fine," I replied, as I turned to go back to my car. "You just took me by surprise. I thought I was alone. I didn't see any other vehicles."

"My pickup is parked over in those trees. It's not visible from the highway." He paused and pointed beyond the large boulder behind him. "I'm making coffee. You're welcome to join me," he offered.

"No, thanks. I'm sorry I didn't mean to disturb your camp."

"This is the Great Spirit's camp. I'm just fortunate enough to use it. I like to watch the valley at night. This is a sacred place. It's a place of peace, and there aren't too many of those places in the world these days."

"It's very tranquil," I replied.

"Not many people travel this way. You're the first person to stop here in a long time. Mostly, I enjoy this place alone, but I'm willing to share it."

"I'm on my way to the Writing-on-the-Stone Park," I explained, wondering silently why I was explaining my presence to this stranger. "I just stopped to take a photo. I'll be on my way. I didn't realize you were camping here."

"Please, stay. Have a cup of coffee. It's the least I can do after frightening you. Besides, I haven't talked to a real person in a long time."

I hesitated, but found myself yielding to his offer. "Sure. That would be great." I watched him pick up a soot-smudged coffeepot from a Coleman stove that sat on a table rock. He held it aloft and smiled as I took a photo of the hospitable stranger.

"My grandfather would turn over in his grave if he caught me boiling coffee on a butane stove," he said, as he offered a cup of the black brew to me.

"Sorry, no cream. By the way, they call me Tom," he said offering his hand. "I'm a full-blood Indian, but I don't live on a reservation. Since I got back from Iraq, I move around a lot. After the war, it's been difficult to find where I belong."

I introduced myself, explaining that I had heard of the Writing-on-the-Stone from one of my graduate students. "Now that I'm retired, I finally have a chance to visit it."

"Who would have thought that out in the middle of nowhere, I would run onto a professor from Montana State University," he said, shaking his head as if in disbelief. "This must be fate; a sign from the Great Spirit."

"I'm a retired professor," I corrected him, "but if it is a sign, let's hope it's a good one."

"I'm sure it is," he said.

"I'm taking advantage of my freedom to travel the back roads of Montana following up on stories. The stories about this area interested me for some time." He nodded but remained silent for several minutes. I drank my coffee and returned the cup to a rock near the stove.

"The Writing-on-the-Stone Park has a spiritual significance. This whole area is sacred. The traditional culture is based on an intimate relationship with the land; this landscape is still part of that time-honored tradition."

"Are you a practicing holy man?"

"I've studied with some, but I'm not a practicing holy man. I'm still searching for answers."

I looked carefully at the stranger. There was something about him that made me suspect that his search would not end soon. "Thank you for the coffee. I will be on my way now so you can set up camp."

"Tell me, Dr. Clarke, do you believe in UFOs?"

I stopped dead in my tracks at his question. "Why do you ask?"

"You said you traveled the backroads of Montana following up on stories. I thought you'd heard about the UFOs that come here. This is the place where the old ones come and go," he said. "This is a place where you can travel the universal highway."

"Who are the old ones?" I asked.

"There are many stories of the spirits and the Star People who visit this place. People often come here to connect with them."

"Is that why you are here?" I asked.

"I come here for many reasons."

"I have been told there is a portal here and if you walk through it, you travel to another time. Do you know of such a place?" I asked.

"There is such a portal. It's not always open. You have to be in the right place at the right time," Tom replied.

"Do you have a clue when it opens? Is there a pattern?"

"As far as I can determine, there is no pattern. It's random. I come here to see the UFOs. Sometimes they appear, other times they don't appear. They travel the universal highway. One day when the portal appears, I will walk through it."

"Have you seen UFOs here?" I asked.

"Yes. Sometimes they land in the valley below. Sometimes they just come to visit."

"What do you mean, they come to visit?"

"The Star Travelers stop and visit with me."

"And what do they look like?" I asked.

"Like me, but not so Indian," he laughed. "Some look like

Indians though."

"How often do you come here?" I asked.

"I used to come here with my grandfather. He was a spiritual man. Some called him a healer. The Star Men came here to visit him. I was young kid back then and would often fall asleep while they visited. It was normal to me. I knew nothing else." He walked toward his pickup and retrieved two folding camp chairs. He set one down and suggested I should sit. He unfolded the other one and sat down next to me.

"Have you seen UFOs and Star Men lately?" I asked.

"Yes. There are other places like this in the world. There is a place in Peru; I hope to go there one day. There is one in Mexico and one in Bolivia. There is one in Alaska. Several others, but mostly they stay hidden. Only those who have traveled the universal highway know of their existence. There is a place in Iraq. My unit was deployed there, and I came upon it by accident. A star traveler saved my life there."

"I'm not sure I understand. How did a star traveler save your life in Iraq? How did you find the portal?"

"When 9-11 occurred, I was angry. I was living in Los Angeles at the time. I quit my job and joined the Army. I was thirty, single with no real direction. I decided to do something for my country. My friends thought I was crazy, but I believed that our country was at war like the president and his cronies led us to believe. Little did I know that it was all propaganda mixed in with showmanship."

I did not ask him about his last statement. I had heard similar comments from veterans who believed they were misled by the rumors of weapons of mass destruction.

"So you ended up in Iraq."

"A few months later, I was in Iraq. The war had been going on for a few weeks when my unit arrived. We were immediately dispatched to a town in the desert. Word had arrived that Saddam Hussein had been spotted there. When we arrived, it was an ambush. I hunkered down next to an abandoned building when suddenly I was peppered with gunfire from above. As I looked for safety, I stumbled into a corridor of an abandoned building. Suddenly, sand began to swirl from the floor and a tunnel opened. I entered the passageway and was greeted by a human-like being who indicated he could lead me to safety. I followed him down a long, narrow tunnel. We arrived at an underground opening the size of a dozen football fields and in the center of it was a spacecraft. It was wonderful there. The heat of the desert was stifling, but it was cool and clean and clear inside the passageway. I walked forward, and the being said I should go with him, and they would take me to safety.

"Do you mean that he offered to take you away from the war?" I asked.

"Yes, he offered to return me to my home. I told my rescuer that I must return to my unit. My absence would be considered desertion."

"What was his reaction to that?"

"He did not understand why I would voluntarily put myself into harm's way, but he honored my decision. As he left, the Star Man said, they would return the next day at the same time, and wait for me if I changed my mind."

"Did you change your mind?"

"It was tempting," he said, leaning over and picking up a rock from between his feet. I realized at the time, that I had stepped into the portal to the universal highway in the middle of the Iraqi desert. I was not surprised though. All the portals are in desolate places."

"Tell me what you know about the universal highway?"

"It's real. There are places all over the world that are sacred. These places were often the portals to the universal highway, but as centuries passed and populations moved or were destroyed, people forgot about them. They are like a network of invisible sky roads that lead across the Milky Way to other worlds. The Maya knew about these portals, so did the Inca. Many American Indian tribes knew too. That is how the UFOs come here. That is how they leave. Without the highway, they would be unable to travel such long distances in such little time."

"Your story is interesting. I met a man in Hawaii many years ago. He said there was a portal in Maui near a waterfall. He said he had traveled it many times. I went there with him, even camped out a couple of days, but the portal never opened."

"Like I said, you have to be in the right place at the right time. There are portals throughout the world. There is one in Navajo Country. It's near Chinle. There is one in Arkansas and another one in West Virginia. There are three in Nevada near the area known as Area 51, as well as one in Dulce, New Mexico. I've heard there is one near Livingston, Montana. Have you heard of it?"

"No."

"When you travel the universal highway, there is no such thing as time like hours or minutes. You think of your destination and you are there within seconds."

"Have you traveled to all of these portals?"

"Only some of them."

"Can you take me with you?"

"If you are with me when the portal opens, but there is no way to know when they will open. It just happens. It is not like I can get off in Bozeman and pick you up. And, there is no guarantee that you will ever return."

"What does that mean? I may not return?"

"There are times when the portals close and you cannot return to the place of your entry."

"The alien you met in Iraq, what did he look like?" I asked.

"He looked like you and me. They are us. They come to Earth and mingle with the people. I traveled one year after I returned from Iraq with one of them. We hitchhiked all over Montana, Wyoming, and the Dakotas. We were taken in by brothers on several reservations and participated in ceremonies. Everyone understood he was a Star Traveler, but he knew his identity was safe with us."

"Why do they come here?" I asked.

"At one time, the Earth was their home, but they moved onto

other places. Sometimes they come just to visit. They tell me there are hundreds of living stars. Those who went in search of another home are those who travel the universal highway and return to visit us. They walk among us all the time. No one can detect the difference."

"Can you detect any difference?" I asked.

"Let me ask you a question. Have you ever met someone who was calm in the face of adversity; someone who was always kind and looked for good in all situations?"

"Of course, I have met a few."

"Then you've probably met a star traveler."

"What about those who are alleged to have abducted humans and conducted experiments on them? Are they us too?"

"There are many species in this great universe, Dr. Clarke. They, too, travel the universal highway. There is no control over that. Some of the species who visit earth have other agendas."

"So humans are not the only species in the universe capable of horrible deeds."

"According to the Star travelers I have met, that is true."

"Did your grandfather know of this highway?" I asked.

"Yes. He traveled it many times. When I was about eight years old, he took me with him. If it had not been for my grandfather, I probably would never have understood what happened to me in Iraq."

"The traveler who hitchhiked around the Northern Plains with you, where did you meet him?"

"I met him here. He arrived on the universal highway. I was camping at this very same place. I knew he was a Star Man from the beginning. He stayed the night and the next day, we set out on our journey."

"Why did he choose you as a traveling companion?"

"Maybe because I didn't question his existence. Maybe because I knew the truth. Maybe because I accepted him."

I looked at my watch. The sun was moving toward the west, and I wanted to make it to the Glocca Morra Inn at Sweetgrass near the Canadian border.

"Do my stories make you uncomfortable? I assure you I'm not a wacko. Just a common, ordinary Indian with an open mind and an accepting heart."

"No, I don't think you're crazy. It's just that I have a reservation at the Glocca Morra Inn, and I have to arrive by 6 p.m. or I'll lose my reservation. I should've prepaid it, but I was sure I had plenty of time to arrive before six."

"You know, you're welcome to stay in camp tonight. I assure you, I will protect you. I will let no harm come to you. Perhaps they will come tonight. Besides, my campfire hamburgers are the best. You're welcome to sleep in the camper or under the stars with me. You can use my sleeping bag. I prefer a blanket anyway. And tomorrow, if you would like some company, I will go with you to visit the park. Besides, I have revealed secrets to you that I've never told anyone. In return, you should honor me with your company. It is not often I find someone that I feel I can trust."

I took Tom up on his invitation. We sat up until 2 a.m. It was close to midnight when the UFOs appeared. At first I saw a large white ball of light. Within seconds, several smaller balls shot out from the large ball. The small balls became discernable circular crafts that flew in several different formations for the next several minutes. I watched in wonder as they performed maneuvers impossible for any aircraft I had ever seen, and then, they zigzagged across the sky to unknown destinations and the large ball of light vanished before our eyes.

Tom and I sat for the next two hours talking about what we had seen. The next day we drove to the Writing-on-the-Stone Park. We stopped in the Last Chance Cafe in Sunburst for dinner that night. Afterwards, we went to Tom's cousin's house where we talked until three pots of hot, black coffee had been consumed. Later I slept fitfully in a bed at the Glocca Morra Inn, as my dreams were filled with the images of UFOs. I returned home the next day after dropping Tom off at his campsite. Before leaving I explained to him that I was a writer and that I had secretly recorded our conversation the previous night. I explained that I would like to use his story in my next book.

"I knew you were recording me," he said with a broad smile.

"How could you know?"

"The Star People told me. I was waiting to see if you would tell me before you left. My intuition has been confirmed. You're an honorable person."

When I started to apologize for taping him without his consent, he held up his hands to stop me. "It is okay, but if you tell my story, change my name. I want to protect the Star Travelers. And please, don't reveal this location. I like to keep it private."

"You can count on that," I said.

Tom opened his arms, pulled me to him giving me a hug, while reassuring me that my taping our conversation was not offensive. He walked me to my car and stood there while I pulled onto the highway. I knew as I drove away, that Tom would become a permanent fixture in my life.

I have seen Tom many times since that fateful encounter. I have never met a kinder or gentler man. Although we have become good friends, there are times I question who he really is. A part of me believes he is a wandering Indian who calls no place home. But, there is another part that thinks I have met a Star Traveler and he is one of us. One day, I am going to ask him.

CHAPTER 2
ALIENS AND AN ABANDONED
COPPER MINE

In 2013, copper miners at Collahuasi Mine in northern Chile filmed a ten-meter UFO hovering over their excavation complex for about an hour. They kept the footage under wraps for fear of ridicule, until a year later when they showed the recording to a mine official who encouraged the men to turn it over to authorities. Scientists at the Center for the Study of Anomalous Aerial Phenomena, after completing a yearlong investigation, announced the silver disc performed vertical and horizontal movements that no aircraft can do. They reported the mysterious object was not man-made.

In this chapter, a New Mexico mechanic also tells a story about UFOs with an interest in copper.

Beau was a wiry man in his mid-60s, who by his estimates had rescued more than two thousand wayward travelers during his career as an auto mechanic. He chewed tobacco, and as I sat in his garage and watched him repair a fan belt on my Subaru, I marveled at how he could spit tobacco juice at a copper spittoon nearly five feet away. His dark, weathered skin was tattooed on every visible place on his body, except his face. Most of tattoos were Indian designs or historical warriors. The son of a white teacher and a Navajo woman, he spoke of the difficulty of growing up on the reservation. "Kids called me 'Whitey,' 'Wannabee,' and all sorts of things I won't say in front of a lady. My father died in a car wreck when I was in 'Nam; he left a life insurance policy. My mother gave it to me, and I opened this repair shop when I got discharged. Been here ever since."

"Does your mother still live on the reservation?"

"Until she died two years ago. Back when she was alive, I visited her every month, but now I rarely go back. Too many bad memories."

"I understand. I think every person of mixed heritage has suffered similar bullying."

"It's better off the reservation. Mostly I deal with tourists who find me a tourist attraction as well, but they need me to help get their vacations back on track." He paused and laughed at his description of himself. As I watched him, I knew it was his infectious laughter, his affable manner, and his ability to entertain strangers in distress that made him approachable as well as endearing.

"I've seen it all, girlie, in my sixty some years on Earth. Nothing surprises me."

"I asked your wrecker driver, Justin, about the alleged UFO sightings in 1950 in Farmington, and he told me there were current UFO stories that were basically unreported that were far more interesting. He said you were the keeper of that knowledge, and that you have a great story about an incident near Four Corners."

"Well, I don't know if I deserve that much credit, but as for the 1950 sightings, it ain't alleged. I had it on good authority, my own father, God rest his soul, the event happened and every effort was made to cover it up."

"I've not been able to uncover much information about it except what is in the newspaper archives."

"And you won't girlie. The government doesn't want anyone to know the truth. It's all a big government conspiracy. It's called the mushroom effect. Keep us in the dark and eat…well you know what I mean."

I laughed at his comment, amused by both his rancor and humor. "What about a current story? You said you have seen many remarkable things in your life."

"I have at that, girlie."

"Can you tell me about the Four Corners incident?"

He removed the broken fan belt from my Outback and held it up. "Now for the new one. I'll have you on your way in a jiffy."

"I'm not going anywhere until you tell me the Four Corners' story."

"Well then, I expect breakfast as payment," he replied smiling at me.

"Deal."

"And I should warn you, it did not happen at Four Corners. I was on my way to Four Corners for a ceremony honoring veterans when it happened, but for some reason, Justin refers to it as the Four Corners incident."

An hour later, we were sitting in an almost-empty, all-night truck stop. The jukebox was playing an old Elvis Presley song, "Suspicious Minds." A disgruntled truck driver sat at the counter talking loudly on his cellphone. When the waitress brought our breakfast, Beau applied salt to his eggs and hash browns without tasting them.

"Since my wife died, I come here most nights for breakfast. I live alone with Henry, my Labrador. I sold my house after the wife passed. I live at the shop now in the backroom. Henry and I don't need much space. We have a bathroom, a bed, a hot plate, fridge, and a table. I got some land on the reservation I inherited from my mother. A little house there, but I don't go there much anymore."

"Tell me about your UFO story."

"It happened about eleven months ago. After Emily died, I spent a lot of time in the backcountry. Some people need friends around them when their spouse dies. I needed solitude. Henry and I used to close up the shop Friday noon and head for the back-country just to get away from all the well-wishers and do-gooders. I needed to mourn Emily in my own way, so I would go there to be alone, get my head straight and remember the good times we shared."

"Did Emily go with you to the backcountry?"

"When we were first married, we couldn't afford vacations, so we'd go there every few weeks. As my business grew, we could afford to go on real vacations but we preferred the backcountry. We often talked about the old days. The days of our youth." For a moment, I saw tenderness, a softness crossed his face as he remembered the time he had shared with Emily.

"Is that where you saw the UFO?" I asked.

"Yes." He motioned for the waitress to bring him a coffee refill and once she left the table, he continued. "Henry and I arrived at our favorite spot, set up the tent and the cooking table. I checked out the Coleman stove and filled the lantern with kerosene. By evening, we were ready to enjoy a night of watching the stars and singing."

"Singing?"

"I like to sing, the old cowboy songs. It's for my own pleasure. I always carry my guitar with me. Henry and I sit out under the stars, and I play the guitar and sing the old classics. Henry likes the classics, particularly 'Tumbling Tumbleweeds.' Do you know that song?"

I nodded. "It's one of my favorites too." He smiled and embraced his coffee cup with both hands.

"Did you see the UFO that night?" I asked.

He nodded.

"It was a warm night. We had finished our dinner, and I made a pot of coffee. By that time it was dark, we had a fire going, I had my guitar and Henry by my side. It was a perfect evening. Emily used to say about nights like that, 'that it didn't get any better' and she was right." He paused and took a sip of his black coffee.

"What time did your encounter happen?"

"Around midnight, a slight breeze came out of nowhere. I thought it strange. It was a cold breeze like the kind you get when there has been a storm in another town and the breezes are cooled by the storm. Suddenly I became aware that it had grown dark. I looked at the skies and the stars were gone."

"Gone?"

"I first thought it was a cloud cover and that a threatening storm had moved in and blocked out the stars." He shook his head as in disbelief. "How wrong I was."

"Was it a spacecraft?"

"It was the mother of all spacecraft. It covered almost the whole sky. If you can imagine lying flat on your back and staring up at the heavens, and a machine so huge is hovering above you that it blocks out the stars, except for those on the fringes. That was what I was watching. It was incredible."

"How long did it stay above you?"

"A couple of minutes. As it hovered there, I was shocked as balls of light shot out from underneath the craft spreading out across the countryside."

"How many lights did you see?"

"A dozen, maybe more. I'm not sure. I was too excited to count."

"So what happened after that?"

"The mothership slowly moved upward, tilted on its side, and moved off to the west and was gone almost instantly. It went up and up and up until it was no longer visible. The breeze died and the stars returned."

"And Henry?"

"At the first sign of the breeze, Henry began to whimper. He doesn't like storms and is particularly afraid of thunder. He crawled under the truck and stayed there until the coast was clear so to speak."

"Was there thunder that night?"

"None that I heard, but a lot of lightening. A lot. Sometimes I was afraid too. It was very close."

"After the mothership was gone, what happened next?"

"Nothing. Absolutely nothing. We stayed up another hour or so and around about 2 a.m. we went to bed."

"So is that the end of the story?"

"Not at all. It was just the beginning."

"Did you see them again?"

"Early the next morning, Henry and I had our usual campsite breakfast: hot coffee and buttered cinnamon bread that I buy at a local bakery. After we had secured our provisions inside the pickup, we got ready to leave. The veteran's ceremony was scheduled for noon, so we had plenty of time. As we crested a butte on the southern side of the trail, we saw them."

"What did you see?"

"The aliens, girlie. What were you expecting me to see? There were two spaceships parked in the valley below. I'd say they were about forty feet in circumference. About twenty feet high. They were perched on three legs that came out of the bottom of the craft. They were a dull silver. Sounds like the typical UFO of movies, doesn't it?"

I nodded. "I've had others describe similar craft," I said.

"Well, I have my own theories about that. Either the government is feeding Hollywood information about aliens and alien spacecraft so they can lull the public into oblivion, or the Hollywood producers have had experiences themselves. Besides what better way to indoctrinate the public into accepting the presence of aliens than with the movies?" He looked at me and smiled. His gold tooth glistened. "I know. You are thinking more conspiracy theories, but mark my word, girlie; I'm smarter than you might think."

"I'm not questioning your intelligence, Beau. I think you might be onto something."

"Good. Now we are on the same page."

"So did you see any Star People from the spacecraft?"

"Star People? They were aliens. No need to call them fancy names. These were aliens."

"How many did you see?"

"Eleven in all, but there were more over the next ridge. I counted nineteen in all."

"What did they look like?"

"They wore some kind of protective suits, like chemical protective suits. They were covered completely. They had black goggles and boots on their feet that were an extension of their suits and gloves. So I never saw any part of their body. But one thing that I was not used to seeing was that their suits were flexible, not like the suits our astronauts wear, and I didn't see a breathing apparatus."

"Does that mean they were breathing our atmosphere?" I asked.

"Yes. That is exactly what I mean, and in my opinion, that makes them even more dangerous that the little bug-eyed ones.

"How tall were they?"

"There were two different heights. Some appeared average height. Maybe five feet eight or ten. Others were much shorter. No more than four feet tall. They were the little bug-eyed ones, I think."

"What were they doing?"

"They were mining."

"Mining? Can you explain?"

"I saw the small ones enter an abandoned mine and return with chunks of rocks or ore. They loaded them onto a conveyer belt, and then returned to the mine."

"The little ones? How many did you see?"

"There were eight little men. Four at each site. They were helping the taller ones."

"What do you think they were mining?"

"Well, the abandoned mine was likely a copper mine. There's also uranium, but I'm sure this was an old copper mine. There are rumors there are special minerals here. I've heard it is a precious mineral used in modern technology and could bring a boom to the Farmington area, but it is on reservation land I believe."

"You said you saw another group that was at a different location. What were they doing?" I asked.

"They were drilling. They had some kind of machine that came out of the side of the craft and drilled several holes at different depths. They would bring up samples and the little guys would catch the samples, sort through them and choose certain specimens and dump the remaining one."

"How long did you view them?"

"I watched them all day. Needless to say, I missed the ceremony at Four Corners."

"Did you see them leave?"

"I saw them on Sunday. I called Justin and asked him to put a closed sign on my door. It was my intention to stay there until they left. But that night, the mother ship returned. They packed up and left. The next morning, I climbed down the cliff and investigated. Henry and I searched everywhere, but there was no sign they had ever been there."

"What about the mine?"

"I didn't go inside the mine, but the outside appeared as though no one had been there for a century."

"Any idea about what you think they were doing?"

"They were taking samples, perhaps for future mining. Perhaps they have used up the resources on their planet, or maybe they just need certain minerals to run their ships and they were searching for a spare parts shop. I'm just guessing, but it makes me feel uneasy that we are so vulnerable."

"Why does it make you uneasy?" I asked.

"Hells Bells, Girlie, I think they are a threat. First of all, if they can travel to Earth, they are already superior to us. I see them as someone who can take from this planet anything they want, and there ain't nothing we can do about it."

When the waitress brought the bill, Beau quickly retrieved it.

"No," I protested. "I was supposed to buy your breakfast. A breakfast for a story. Remember?"

"I remember, but that was just my way to get an attractive lady to join me for breakfast. I knew you could not resist a challenge."

"And how did you know that?" I asked.

"A friend of mine in Albuquerque saw your book in the library and checked it out. He told me about it and said that I should read it. In fact, I bought it. You confirmed my suspicions when I asked you for your name and address when I wrote out your repair ticket. I knew who you were. A famous writer and you believe in UFOs."

"Not so famous," I said.

"But you are. The government is probably watching your every move. You are dangerous, you know."

"More conspiracy theories?" I asked.

"No theories. Just the facts." He opened the door, and we walked outside. It was 4 a.m.

"Have you told anyone else this story?" I asked.

"Just a couple of friends. We have a neighborhood watch for aliens. We call ourselves the Star Commanders. We watch the skies at night for any anomalies. We follow up on them too. For the time being, we will remain anonymous, but you can tell my story. Perhaps we should use the government tactics and alert the people through books and movies. That way the public will not be so surprised if there is an invasion."

"Why do you think there might be an invasion?"

"I don't think we are going to give up our resources of the planet willingly. They will have to invade."

As we said goodbye, he warned me again. "If you ever need anyone to cover your back, call me. I am only a phone call away." He handed me his business card. "Call me any time of the day or night."

"I have one question, Beau. You observed the aliens during daylight. Why didn't you take any photos?"

"I don't own a camera."

"But you have a cellphone."

He pulled his phone out of his shirt pocket. "It's a TracFone from Wal-Mart. It doesn't take pictures. I don't go in for those newfangled contraptions. I don't text. I don't search the Internet. I don't Facebook. I don't Twitter."

"But you know about those things."

"Well, I ain't no dummy. I see the way it holds kids and their parents hostages when they end up in my shop. Now me, I like to keep things simple."

I unlocked the car door and turned and hugged Beau. I kissed him on the cheek and thanked him for telling me his story.

"I haven't talked to a woman so much since my Emily," he said. "I should thank you."

I climbed in the car, and he closed the door behind me.

"Travel safe, dear lady and keep your eyes open. And whatever you do, keep my card close by. I meant it when I said; I will watch your back."

I blew him a kiss and backed out of the parking lot. He stood there watching me drive away.

I have not seen Beau since that night, when his tow truck driver deposited my injured Subaru and me on his doorstep. While I haven't seen him, that does not mean we are not in touch. Every Friday night he calls me wherever I am. We talk about UFOs and often reminisce about the night he tricked me into buying my breakfast. Through it all, I have come to call Beau one of my dearest friends. On my next trip to the Southwest, I plan to set aside a couple of days to spend with him. He intends to take me to the abandoned copper mine where it all began. He told me he has another story to tell me, but he doesn't trust phones. He suspects he is being monitored.

CHAPTER 3
I MET MY WIFE ON A UFO

Derrel Sims of the Discovery Channel's TV series Uncovering Aliens *believes that one in four people have been abducted by aliens and that alien abduction runs in families. He is also convinced that aliens are not our friends.*

In this chapter you will meet a man who believes that Derrel Sims is correct. He maintains that the first time he saw his wife was on a UFO, and at that moment he decided he would marry her. They were both children at the time.

Colt was a promising doctoral student at a prestigious eastern university. It took him exactly four months to decide that the East Coast was too far from his Montana home, and he packed up and left for his home reservation. In his late twenties, Colt had received both a bachelor's and master's degree from Montana colleges and had been a stand-out student in both programs. I first met Colt when the department head referred him to me to examine his transcripts for transferability into our doctoral program.

While considered good husband material by females on his reservation, Colt surprised everyone when shortly after he returned, he married a girl from another tribe and brought her home to Montana. Until then no one had ever known Colt to be in a serious relationship. Shirline, who stood nearly six feet and was an exceptional beauty with a personality to match, soon won over the skeptics among family and friends.

Colt took a job with a public school district working with high-risk youth in an alternative high school program as a counselor. Sixty-three percent of the students enrolled in the alternative high school were Indian. Our paths frequently crossed since he implemented a two-year, goal-setting experimental program designed to change American Indian students' attitudes about school. I served as the research evaluator. After the students completed the program, they were assessed for a change in attitude and then participated in a two-year follow-up study until they graduated or dropped out. Colt managed the program and frequently met with me to review student progress and to discuss the efficacy of the interventions.

Due to the lack of meeting space in the 200-year-old building designated for the alternative high school, we retreated to the lunchroom for our program reviews. During one of our breaks, Colt turned to me and said, "I met my wife on a UFO." I looked up at him. He shrugged his shoulders and avoided looking at me. "I heard you were interested in UFO encounters. I've had them all my life," he explained.

At first, I was taken back by his declaration, but I noted the genuineness in his voice and expression. He was serious.

"I've never heard about anyone meeting a spouse on a UFO. Would you be willing to tell me about it?"

He nodded and let out a long sigh.

"I was a boy at the time. Eleven, almost twelve." He paused and led me toward an exit door, which opened onto a fenced-in, deserted basketball court. We sat down on a bench that jutted up against a chain-link fence. "I learned to play basketball on a court like this."

I looked at the packed earth, the unevenness of the ground.

He continued: "You know what they say about Indian athletes: that we can't play football, but put us on a basketball court and we're unstoppable. I read where some sportswriter said it was because the Plains Indians never liked contact. Instead they counted coup."

I was familiar with the expression "counting coup." It meant striking or touching an enemy instead of killing him. It was the highest honor earned by warriors participating in intertribal wars on the Great Plains.

Colt picked up a pebble and threw it at the net. It landed in the center and dropped to the packed surface. "Maybe that's true. Maybe we'd rather touch our enemies than kill them. Counting coup was an act of true heroism according to my grandfather."

"You may have a point, but did you bring me out here to talk about basketball or UFOs?" I said, smiling at him. "You said you met your wife on a UFO. Can you think back and tell me your earliest memory of an encounter with the Star People."

"Counting coup is appropriate. I met the enemy. I touched them, but I did not kill," he replied.

I knew he was referring to aliens, not basketball opponents. "Can you start at the beginning?" I asked.

He nodded after checking the time on his watch.

"For as long as I remember, I looked forward to summer. I equated it with freedom. By the time I was eleven, I slipped out the upstairs window and climbed onto the roof of our house, took my sleeping bag and fell asleep watching the stars. Summer days were hot days and no air conditioning on the rez." He paused and laughed. "One night, I saw a UFO circling overhead. When it reached our house, it slowed and just stayed there, suspended in the space above me. Afterwards, it flew away. The next night I waited in anticipation, but it did not come. On the fourth night, it returned."

"So you were not afraid."

"Not at all. I was excited. I don't remember the abduction, but I remember being on a spacecraft with dozens and dozens of other children. I remember seeing the girl I was going to marry."

"And you feel your wife, Shirline, was the girl you saw that night?" I asked.

"She was and is," he said.

"What makes you think the girl of your memory is your wife?"

"I remembered the gap between her teeth when she smiled. I remembered the dress she wore. I remembered everything. She was tall even then. Taller than me." He laughed. "Now I'm taller, but not by much."

"Tell me about that night."

"It was a very hot night. It had been over a hundred degrees during the day. When I climbed onto the roof, the surface was hot. For a moment I thought about going inside, but I unfolded my sleeping bag, took off my shirt and pants, and sat there, waiting for the night air to cool the roof. It wasn't long before I saw a bright ball in the north. It didn't belong there. Not only that, it changed from white to blue, and it kept changing in size, getting bigger and bigger. As it got closer, I knew it was not a star. I knew it was a spacecraft."

"How did you feel once you realized that it was not a star?" I asked.

"Curious. Excited. At an early age, I was convinced the Star People existed. We were told the ancient stories by the Elders-in-the-School Program. I remember talking to some of the elders about it privately. They confirmed my beliefs. They said the Star People had been visiting earth since the beginning of time, and that to deny them was akin to denying our existence."

"Were you ever frightened?"

"Excited, but not frightened."

"So tell me when you realized it was a spacecraft."

"I knew it right away. I had been watching them for a long time. I remember seeing the star and the lights, but I don't remember anything else until I was on board the spacecraft."

"Tell me what was your first memory of the ship?"

"I was in a huge circular area, like an arena. It had a solid dome ceiling. No windows. There was nothing in the room. No chairs, nothing. Just dozens and dozens of children. All about the same age. There was a strange smell in the room, like medicine. It was similar to the smells in the hallway at the hospital. There were three boys sitting in the center of the room. Everyone else was walking back and forth. I remember going over to the three boys. They were the only ones talking. I asked them where we were, and they laughed at me, asking where my pants were. I looked down, and realized I was still in my underwear. Black boxers with red devils on them. A Christmas gag gift from my father." He laughed and stood, looking out toward the street as though remembering that night.

"Were all the children Indian?" I asked.

"No, we were like the rainbow. I remember seeing Chinese or Japanese, maybe they were from some other place. But I had seen pictures of Chinese and Japanese and I knew what they looked like. They could have been Korean. We had a teacher who had an adopted Korean baby. Maybe they were Korean."

"Who else did you see?"

"I saw redheads and blondes and dark-skinned girls and black boys and girls. I saw some Navajos and Hopis. I'm sure of that because their clothing and hair styles. I had seen them at powwows. They were different from us."

"Did you talk with anyone?"

"I only remember the boys who asked about my pants. They were the only others, besides me, who appeared to be awake. Soon, these strange tall men came in and paired us up. I was paired up with a dark-skinned girl with long, black, curly hair, who held my hand but never spoke. I can still feel the sweat from her trembling hand. I told her not to worry. I would take care of her." He paused and laughed. "I guess I was somewhat of a braggart back then…a tough little reservation outlaw." He stood and paced in front of me. "They took us into a small cubicle and attached us to a machine. They had a hand-held machine that stuck our arm. It removed blood because I saw blood."

"Were you afraid?"

"No. They told us not to be afraid, that we were helping them out. I guess I must have believed them because I never remember fighting them or struggling. I was happy to be there. In those days, I had the reputation of being a rebel. I got in trouble sometimes in school because I didn't want any adult telling me what to do. It was a phase I went through, but nothing serious. My dad set me straight and told me he would whip the devil out of me if I didn't change my behavior." He paused for a moment and looked at me reflectively. "But for some reason, I accepted the aliens' authority without question."

"Can you remember anything else?"

"I remember the people who took us were tall, very tall and light-skinned. They had the longest fingers I had ever seen. Our music teacher told us that students with long fingers made good piano players, and I remember thinking that they must be the best piano players in the world. They were dressed in white uniforms with a bright blue patch." He paused and picked up a stick and drew an outline of a circle with three dots in a line. "That is my recollection of the insignia."

"Did you see anyone other than the tall white guys?"

"Do you mean, did I see strange creatures?"

"Yes."

"No, I only saw the tall, white men."

"Tell me about your wife. Where did you see her?"

"I saw her the first time I was on the spaceship. She was standing by herself, away from the group. She wore a lavender flowered dress with a sash in the back. I remember the dress because the flowers looked like those in my mother's garden. When she turned and looked my way, I saw a total lack of expression on her face. I wanted to run to her and tell her everything was going to be okay, but as I stepped forward, they took her away. She never looked in my direction but her face was expressionless as she passed by me."

"Was she from your reservation?"

"No. I thought she was a white girl; it was only later I found out that her mom was white and her dad was part Indian; just like me. My dad is a full blood, but my mom is white. Her hair was blond and she was taller than the other girls in the group. Even then, she stood out. At the time, I didn't know where she was from, but I knew that one day I would marry her. The strangest thing is that I knew the Star People approved."

"So how did you meet Shirline?"

"On Earth?"

"Yes, on Earth."

"I didn't see her again until she was in high school. A bunch of us guys during our senior year in high school decided to go to the Denver Powwow. That's where I saw her. When the rabbit dance was announced, I asked her to dance, and it's all history from there. We kept in touch, met up when we could, saw each other at pow-wows, and got engaged before we graduated from college. She was destined to be mine. The Star People chose her for me."

"Did you ever tell your friends about her?"

"No, she was my secret."

"Did you ever tell Shirline about seeing her on a UFO?"

"I did. I was at her mom's house when I told her. At first she didn't believe me, but when I described the dress she was wearing, she went to a cedar chest in the hall and pulled out the dress I described. It was a dress given to her by her father when she was ten years old. She fell asleep in it that night and I believe that's the night I saw her on the UFO. Her father died shortly after that. She wore the dress twice. The first time was the night of her birthday party; the second time to her father's funeral. She packed it away after that. As she held the dress out for me to examine, I knew she believed me."

"Do the Star People still come for you?" I asked.

"At least once a year."

"What about your wife?"

"If they do, she doesn't remember and I have no recollection of her being missing, but I am a heavy sleeper. It could happen and I wouldn't know."

"Do you have any idea why they are running tests on human beings?"

"It's a part of evolution. They keep exact notes on every form of evolution on the planet. Even the animals and plants. They say humans are getting bigger, not better. They say that humans should be getting better and that everywhere else in the universe, the humanoid inhabitants are getting better."

"How do they define better?" I asked.

"From what I understand, better would be advancement in intellect, longer lifespans. They have said that we should be living longer. Instead we are getting bigger and less intelligent and our lifespan has stagnated. The question they seek to answer: are there situations where evolution is just the opposite of what we expect to happen? Instead of progression we are into regression. It is an interesting question."

"Do you think they care about the human race?"

"No. I think they could wipe us out in a heartbeat. I know they care about their research. Whether they care about the results, I don't know. If they do and they find us unacceptable, I shutter to think about what they might do. They have always been respectful of me. They have never hurt me, and they always ask my permission when taking samples or performing experiments."

"What kind of experiments?"

"Mostly mental. Puzzle solving experiments. Timing experiments. Nothing I can't handle."

"Do you still look forward to your meetings with them," I asked.

"Not anymore. My wife is pregnant now. I don't want them—we are expecting twins—to become their next research subjects."

"How will you stop it?"

"I'm not sure. Until I have to face it, I will count coup," he said winking at me. At that moment, the bell rang and Colt stood. "That's our cue. Are you ready to meet the next group of students?"

I followed him into the school to continue our examination of our experimental program with the students.

I see Colt frequently. He has enrolled in an online doctoral program. I often wonder about the research being conducted on humans by the Star People. As humans we conduct research on other humans, but it is another thing to know that an advanced species is conducting research on us. It is disappointing to know that as a race we are not evolving as expected. I suspect the Star People are disappointed, too.

CHAPTER 4
A UFO CRASH ON A
SOUTHWESTERN RESERVATION

In February 2015, on the Jackhead First Nations Reserve in Manitoba, Canada, reports surfaced about a UFO crash landing into Lake Winnipeg. Several dozen witnesses observed the UFO entering the lake. One individual reportedly took photos of the crash but was detained by the Canadian military and the photos confiscated. Within hours, the military had moved in equipment and blocked any view of the crash site. Tribal members were informed that no one was allowed to enter or leave the reserve. Soldiers reportedly went door-to-door telling the residents they were conducting emergency exercises.

This case is only one of many where the military has been involved in coercing the public and confiscating evidence. In this chapter, you will read a story that has never been told about an event in our own Southwest.

I first heard about the UFO crash and the subsequent military cover-up one night when I attended a high school basketball game. After the game, I joined a group of parents for a dinner to celebrate the end of the season. As we gathered in the parking lot to finalize our plans for the evening, one of the parents reportedly saw a flash in the sky. At that moment, UFOs became the topic of conversation, which continued after we were all seated at a table in the only restaurant in town. One of the parents mentioned a mysterious UFO incident that brought out hundreds of soldiers to the reservation.

"We were told never to talk about it," a man named Donovan said.

I noticed nervousness in his speech, which was unusual for the rowdiest fan of the local team. A single father, Donovan was well known on the reservation as a man who stepped up to the plate when his high school girlfriend became pregnant. Following the baby's birth, his girlfriend announced she had decided on adoption, but Donovan intervened and accepted the responsibility of raising his son alone.

"Can you talk about it now?" I asked.

"We're not supposed to ever talk about it, but perhaps it is time."

"I think we've all had too much excitement for one night," said Bill, another member of our group. "It's time to call it a night." At Bill's declaration, the group agreed, paid the tab, and headed for the door.

In the parking lot, Donovan pulled me aside. "If you get a chance, ask around about the time that a power outage blanketed most of the reservation. You might get some interesting responses."

I never had time to follow up on Donovan's suggestion as I was due to leave the reservation the next morning. Shortly after I wrote my first book, *Encounters with Star People*, I got an email from Donovan asking me if I remembered him. During the next month, we emailed regularly. One morning I opened an email related to the UFO crash that had been brought up at the dinner twenty years ago. He told me if I were ever near his home—he now lived in a small town about fifty miles from the reservation—he would like to meet me. "It is a story that should be told," he said.

Last year I took a trip to the Southwest and stopped along the way to look up Donovan. Shortly after arriving at my hotel, I called him. He suggested we meet for lunch the following day at a rural cafe not far from Route 66. When I entered the cafe, I immediately saw Donovan. He had not changed much; still the tall, lanky man with short-cropped hair. He was sitting in a corner booth with an older man. When he saw me, he stood and waved.

"I would like you to meet my Uncle Ralph," he said, as I sat down. "He was the chief engineer at Tribal Electric the night the UFO crashed and shut off the electricity for half the reservation. He was the first person to discover the crash."

The family resemblance was obvious. Except for his long, white braids, he and Ralph could have passed for brothers, and yet I estimated that he had to be in his eighties.

"Thank you for joining us," Ralph said.

"While it's taken twenty years, I'm anxious to hear your story."

"Not until we have eaten," Donovan said. "Uncle Ralph is diabetic and has to keep to a regular schedule." As we ate, I learned that Donovan's father had accompanied Ralph to the suspected site of the power outage that night; Ralph was living with Donovan and his parents at the time of the incident. "Dad didn't want Uncle Ralph to go out alone that night. Older brother looking out for younger brother. You know how that goes."

I nodded.

"So was your father also witnesses to the incident?" I asked.

"Yes. Unfortunately, my dad passed from cancer when I was in college. He always believed the UFO was responsible."

"What do you mean?"

"He believed he got radiation poisoning or something that created the cancer. Who knows, he could have been right."

"What about you, Ralph. Were you affected in any way?"

"No, my health has been good, but Donovan's father, Hilton, was closer to the object than I was. Hilton was a daredevil of sorts and walked right up to the craft. He even touched it, but I remained about fifty feet away. I was not so brave."

"Uncle Ralph, do you remember that night clearly?" I asked.

"As clear as if it happened yesterday," he began. "As Donovan mentioned, I was living with my brother, Hilton, and his wife, and of course, Donovan, the night the reservation went dark. A call came around midnight. I had just gone to bed and was not asleep. The Tribal Electric hired me the day after I graduated from technical school. I had only been with them about three months. A huge power outage covered most of the reservation. I was told to find the source, evaluate, and report back immediately for the needed resources. Hilton decided to go with me in case I needed help."

"What did you find when you arrived at the site?" I asked.

"We discovered the lines were down, but it didn't take us long to realize it was no ordinary incident," Ralph said. "The lines appeared severed, simply cut. Hilton followed a trench leading from the electric pole, measuring the skid with a tape measure. That's when he discovered the UFO. It was about three hundred feet away from the telephone pole."

"Can you describe the craft?"

"It was shaped like a football, oval in size, with a dome on the top."

"Was there any sign of . . .?"

"Spacemen?" He paused for a moment and Donovan reached out and touched the elderly man's hand. "We saw three outside the craft. One was on the ground and two were crumpled in the doorway. Hilton wanted to go to them and help them. I held him back. I was sure they were dead."

"Can you describe them?" I asked.

"They were small, maybe four or five feet," Ralph said, "but they were thin, almost like they were malnourished. Extremely thin. They wore light colored jumpsuits. They had skullcaps on their heads. I think the two we saw were trying to escape the spaceship. I remember a horrific smell that burned my nostrils even though I was several feet away."

"Would you describe them as human?"

"They had human shape. But I heard one of the soldiers who were on corpse duty say they had six fingers and were bald."

"Corpse duty?" I asked.

"Yes. That's what they called them, but inside the craft, they found five more bodies. They were all dead."

"You mentioned soldiers. When did military get involved?"

"After I assessed the situation, I called the dispatcher and that's when I was told the Army was on its way. That's when I sent Hilton home. I didn't want him to get into trouble for being there and I suspected the Army would detain me and ask a lot of questions. So I told him to go home before they arrived."

"When the Army arrived, what did they do?"

"They immediately quarantined the area for miles. Set up roadblocks in all directions. They took me to an area where tents were being set up and told me to remain there. Two guards accompanied me at all times."

"What about the people in the area? Was there no one else around?" I asked.

"None that I saw. The site was in a rural, hilly area so there would be no reason for anyone to be around. It was late and most people were asleep and wouldn't have even known the power was out. The Army arrived within two hours of the outage. They were well organized. It looked like they had practiced for such an event, or they were experienced. In fact, I think they knew about the crash before Tribal Electric reported the power down. They also closed the school and every business on the reservation and went door-to-door telling people to stay inside their houses."

"How long did this go on?" I asked.

"Three days, as I recall," Uncle Ralph said.

"I remember the superintendent closed the school for a week," Donovan said.

"The Army made up some story about a poison leak from an overturned semi that hit the power lines," said Uncle Ralph. "They told people that breathing the air could cause sickness and possibly death and ordered everyone to stay indoors."

"They even delivered army rations to the people in case they didn't have food," Donovan interjected.

"When did the Army release you, Uncle Ralph?" I asked.

"Not until everything was cleared up. By that time, two flatbed trucks with their contents wrapped in tarpaulins left the area. Bulldozers came in and removed any sign of the trench or the crash site."

"Did you see the trucks?"

"I saw them brought in along with some very heavy equipment. I heard one of the soldiers talking about tarpaulins. They were flown in on a special helicopter and dropped at the site. He said it was to cover the contents of the crash site."

"Did the residents accept the cover story released by the Army?"

"What else could they do? They knew no better."

"When they released you, what did they say to you, or did they just let you walk away?"

"Not at all. They told me if I ever told what I saw that night they would come for me and my family. They said they had their ways and no one would ever know. They would find me wherever I went and would always be watching."

"Did you believe them?"

"Yes."

"How did you first learn about the UFO, Donovan?"

"I was watching all this unfold through the eyes of an eight-year-old. It was a scary night. No lights at all. My mom tried to get me to go to bed, but I insisted on staying up and keeping her company. Finally, we made a bed in front of the wood stove and waited. When Dad returned, he told us what he had seen. I remember how frightened he was. I never saw my father as frightened before. I remember watching him try to light a cigarette. His hands trembled so much that I had to light it for him. I'm not sure I slept that night."

"You mentioned that your father believed the UFO gave him cancer. Did you notice any changes in him?"

"Dad was a devoted Catholic. He believed that God created man in his own image. He could not accept that God might have created other beings on another planet. Now that he knew they existed, it tested his beliefs. He struggled silently with that realization for years. He was never able to rationalize what he had seen and he died an unhappy man."

"What about you?"

"I was a believer in UFOs," said Donovan. "I was weaned on Flash Gordon and the old science fiction movies of the 1950s. I grew up thinking that one day I would travel throughout the universe and meet alien races. It was exciting for me but when Uncle Ralph came home accompanied by three military men, I knew this was something serious."

"What happened?"

"Three men, dressed in military uniforms accompanied Uncle Ralph."

"They drove me home," Uncle Ralph said.

"That's right," Donovan said. "They figured out that Uncle Ralph did not have a vehicle and they put two and two together and realized that someone had driven him to the site. So they came into the house and ordered the four of us: my mom, dad, Uncle Ralph, and me into the living room."

He paused and looked at his uncle. The elderly man appeared lost in thought. Ralph put his arm around his shoulder and said something to him in his native tongue that I did not understand, and Uncle Ralph nodded.

"They told us," said Donovan, "that the object that crashed was a test plane and that we should never talk about it because of national security. And if we ever talked about it, our family would be rubbed out. That's right, isn't it, Uncle Ralph? They said, 'rubbed out'?"

Uncle Ralph nodded but said nothing.

"The oldest man," Donovan continued, "the one in charge looked at me and asked me if I wanted to see my father and uncle dead. I was terrified and started to cry. He said you do not have to worry if you keep your mouth shut, but if you talk, we will find you. So I was silenced and it was a secret I lived with all these years."

"Did you ever tell?"

"I was playing poker one night with some friends, and I asked them if any of them ever heard of a UFO crash that knocked out the electricity for three days. I was surprised. Two of them had heard rumors. Both of their fathers worked for Tribal Electric, so somehow the story had been leaked. One thought it was a military plane that crashed; two others heard it was a UFO. But all they knew was that it happened, and it was a military secret and should never be discussed."

As we left the restaurant, Donovan and his uncle offered to take me to the crash site. "There is nothing there," said Donovan. "No evidence. But if you would like to stand on the site where a UFO crashed, we will take you there."

"It is the same way the Army left it," Uncle Ralph said. "Once the army left, there was no sign that anything had occurred. They brought in their own team to repair the electric lines. Tribal Electric did not do the repairs. They took no chance that anyone else would discover the truth."

When we arrived at the site, we pulled off the main highway onto a dirt road. A mile or so from the main road, Uncle Ralph pointed out the site of the crash.

"It stopped there. I will never forget it," said Ralph. "Donovan and I are the only ones alive who can tell this story. Perhaps some of the soldiers who were there, but none has ever come forward. I am an old man. I wanted to tell this story before I meet my Maker. When Donovan told me you had been in touch with him and that you are writing a book about UFO encounters, I told him I had to meet you. I not only wanted to tell the story, I needed to tell it."

I often think about Uncle Ralph. Even though the military successfully kept the story out of the headlines, there is no doubt in my mind that Uncle Ralph and Donovan spoke the truth. It was not only a story he wanted to tell, but also one that he needed to tell. Perhaps with his telling, others will come forward to validate his encounter. In the meantime, I consider myself fortunate be the one to tell his story.

CHAPTER 5
HE MADE ME FEEL LIKE HE WAS
AN OLD FRIEND

In Strangers from the Skies, *published in 1966, Brad Steiger wrote, "Some scientists are suggesting that not only are we not alone, but we may have been planted here a billion or so years ago by an extraterrestrial expedition. Periodically, the celestial gardeners come back to see how their seedbeds have been progressing."*

In this chapter, you will read the story of a doctor who tells the story of an encounter with an alien who told him about "seeding" planets.

In 2013, I drove to Oklahoma to visit my cousin, Lorna, who had recently relocated there from North Carolina. I called her on the outskirts of the city and learned that she was on duty at the hospital and I should meet her there. When I walked off the elevator, I saw her immediately. After our first greeting, she turned to the staff and introduced me.

"Are you the same Ardy Sixkiller Clarke who wrote *Encounters with Star People?*" a tall, handsome doctor, who introduced himself as Billy, asked.

"Yes. I'm working on a second book. It takes place among the Maya."

"Of Mexico?"

"Including Mexico, but also Belize, Honduras and Guatemala."

"I would think there are plenty of stories in the U.S. that you wouldn't have to go to other countries," he said as he removed the stethoscope around his neck."

"I've been collecting stories from indigenous people from all over the world."

"Do you have any stories from the Southern Cheyenne?" he asked.

"Actually, none."

"Now you do," he said with an open arm gesture. "I am Southern Cheyenne."

"Do you have a story?" I asked.

He pressed his fingers to his lips. "Only for your ears," he whispered. "By the way, I read *Encounters*. In fact, I've read it three times. I've even read it to my ten-year-old son. He's into Star Wars and he loves the stories." He paused and ushered me toward the elevator after telling my cousin that he was taking me to the cafeteria for coffee.

"I need to ask Lorna when her shift is over," I said as the elevator door opened.

"She gets off at 6 p.m. She knows we are going to the cafeteria. She will come there after she checks out."

"Are you sure?"

"I'm sure."

"I had an encounter," Billy said as he sat across from me. "I moved to Oklahoma seven months ago. I thought it would be a good move but I was not prepared for the isolation. My wife hates it. The distances between places are overwhelming and the airline service is miserable. At times, I feel like I've landed on another planet."

"Where did you grow up?" I asked.

"Actually, not too far from here. But I went to a city university where everything is readily available. Here, we are somewhat isolated. My wife hates the lack of the theater and opera, and all the social activities."

"Is she Indian?"

"No, just a blue-eyed southern belle. We met in school. Typical story of Indian boy meets beautiful blonde who steals his heart." He laughed and looked away uncomfortably as if he was not sure why he had made such a comment.

"You said you had an encounter," I said to ease the awkwardness of the moment.

"It's true. I don't know why I'm telling you this. I only have an hour and I'm sure you will have a million questions," he said as he looked at his watch.

"I'm listening," I said. "Please continue."

"One night on my way home from the hospital—I live outside of the town—a deer came out of nowhere and into the path of my car. I swerved, but I hit it anyway. I got out of the car to investigate. Just as I came around the front of the vehicle, the deer suddenly stood up and turned into a person."

"Did I hear you right? Did you say the deer transformed into a person?"

"That's right. I know it sounds ridiculous, but I swear to God, it's the truth. There, in front of me, stood a tall, slender man, dressed in a one-piece suit complete with head covering. He indicated that I should not be afraid. He explained that he often used the form of a deer when he visited Earth. He said deer were faster and more accommodating than the human shape."

"Are you telling me, he was a shape shifter?" I asked.

"Yes. I remember the stories of shape shifters from childhood. I never saw one, but there was an old medicine man who reportedly could turn into all sorts of creatures. I remember accounts of his miraculous feats. But I'm not sure this visitor thought of himself as a shape shifter. That's only an Indian thing, right?"

"I'm not sure. How did he think of himself?" I asked.

"Normal, perhaps. He seemed to think turning into something else was a convenience. Personally, I think they use a cloaking technology to appear anyway they want to appear. I think they use similar technology to appear and disappear at will in the sky and to abduct humans."

"Did he abduct you?"

"No. We stood on the edge of the road and carried on a civilized conversation like two old friends."

"Did he speak?"

"No, not as you and I speak. He was able to communicate with his thoughts. Telepathy."

"Did he say why he was visiting Earth?"

"Not specifically. Only that he liked the planet and the various species found here. He said there were many planets like Earth, but few had the diversity of wildlife."

"Did he reveal if he abducted people and animals?" I asked.

"Not for experimental reasons. He said that they had taken humans to seed other planets, but only with the individuals' permission. He said there are many humans who are willing and enthusiastic about leaving the Earth and starting over. If they meet their rigorous psychological tests and are nonviolent, they can assist them in their desires. He said many planets shared the same atmosphere as Earth, but not in our solar system. If the atmosphere was not conducive to life, but had potential, their scientists were capable of altering the environment."

"Why do you think he told you this?"

"When I hit him, I told him I was a doctor and that he should sit in my car and let me examine him. He told me he was a doctor too on his world and that he was a healer. He said he had already healed himself from the collision. I think he told me because we shared the same profession. One colleague to another."

"Did he tell you how he healed himself?"

"He said that they had perfected the means of healing with the mind. He said that one day humans would be able to do the same. He said there are a few healers on our planet, but most of them are scorned by the medical profession."

"Your story is amazing. Did he tell you anything else that you are willing to share?"

"For your next book?"

"With your permission."

He laughed and nodded.

"As long as you change my name," he said.

"He said his planet was old and in the scheme of things, Earth was not important. He said that he was one of the few from his planet who still came to Earth. He collected animal specimens for seeding other worlds. He claimed that for most of the beings in the universe, he knew of none that wanted to interfere with the planet, despite some of the paths taken by world leaders. He was aware of the abduction experiments. He told me that one group had found human body adrenal glands were a good source of longevity enhancement when mixed with other elements. While they have been encouraged to stop these procedures, there is nothing that we can do to stop them. Their scientists have attempted to develop a means to help them improve their elements without the use of human adrenals, but have been unsuccessful."

"Anything else you remember?"

"One thing, perhaps the most important. He said that there are several thousand intelligent life forms and they do not like the attention that human abduction has brought to the existence of space travelers. He said the intent of his people was to travel and explore, but not to change the culture. Few civilizations that travel the universe have designs on Earth. Many uninhabited worlds are suitable for life where they would meet no resistance. He said they only seed, or colonize, those planets that are uninhabited and they never replace populations."

"But he admitted that they take humans and put them on other planets. Isn't that a form of interfering?"

"Not according to him. The humans chosen for their seed project are ones who have nothing on Earth."

"What does that mean?"

"I asked him the same question. He said some had no family. Others yearned for a new start in life, a different life. In some cases, whole families have willingly uprooted themselves and left Earth."

Suddenly my cousin entered the cafeteria and reminded Billy it was almost time for him to make his rounds.

"Sorry. I must go, but hopefully we will meet again before you leave. It was a pleasure meeting you. As for the alien encounter, please treat it with anonymity if you should decide to use it. I have told you all I learned. Now pass the truth along to the public. Perhaps it will shed light on this whole phenomenon. "

"Before I leave, can you tell me, has your encounter changed your life in any way?"

"Not so much. I read everything I can find on UFOs, which is something I never did before. I study myths and mythology about sky visitors and star people. I have developed an extensive library, much to the chagrin of my wife who does not share my interest, but I have never told her the real story. Even she would have a hard time believing I hit a deer that became a man and we stood beside the road talking like two friends about the life in the universe."

He laughed awkwardly at his comment and then hugged me. "Thank you for listening to me. I will watch for your next book and please keep in touch."

Five months later Dr. Billy relocated to a hospital in Arizona. Although he only stayed in Oklahoma one year, there is no doubt he will ever forget his celestial encounter on the lonely highway. As for the shape-shifting alien, I am a believer. There are many American Indian tribes with stories of shape shifters. I often think of Henrietta Lone Wolf when I hear about shape shifters. She became popular with young men during the Vietnam War. They would seek out her advice as to whether they were being drafted. Inevitably, her response always turned out to be true. When I asked her how she was able to predict the future with such accuracy, she told me she turned herself into a bird and flew to the post office. There she looked for the draft notices. When I questioned her further, she told me she simply went into a trance and became a bird. Years ago, on the Pine Ridge Reservation in South Dakota, I heard stories of a powerful traditional man who had the ability to shape shift into a deer. I never witnessed this transition, but I had friends who testified to his ability. I have never doubted their stories. They are all honest, intelligent, and rational individuals. So, I choose to believe Dr. Billy's story.

CHAPTER 6
THE BROTHERS

Eight years ago, Father Gabriel Funes, a highly respected priest and Vatican official, wrote an article entitled, "Aliens Are My Brother," detailing various extraterrestrial scenarios as they relate to Christian theology.

Father Funes is not the only person to believe that aliens are our brothers. In this chapter, you will read the story of a man who also views the aliens as brothers.

I met John in Washington, D.C. He was employed by the government and worked with American Indian tribes throughout the country. A striking man, he stood over six feet tall with white hair pulled back in a three-inch ponytail at the back of his neck. A beaded bolo tie hung around his neck, breaking the dress code of D.C. professionals who all dressed alike in black suits and silk ties. A monstrous turquoise ring graced his right hand and a large turquoise bracelet circled his left wrist. He often told me that one day he was going to leave the United States and move to Canada.

"My wife is from a First Nations tribe in Canada, and I would like to move there. That's where I feel at home with the brothers."

Since I had heard him speak of "the brothers" several times, I finally asked him what he meant by "the brothers."

As we were walking to lunch one day, he explained what he meant by those words. "I thought you knew. The brothers are Star People."

We stopped at the red light before crossing the street. John took my arm and hustled me across the intersection.

"Can you explain?" I asked.

"Here we are," John said, as we reached the restaurant. He pointed to a doorway below the ground level. "Watch your step."

After being seated, John explained. "The brothers have been coming to me since I was five years old. They were five years old, too. We lived in a small village on the Choctaw Reservation. I use to wander off by myself when I was a small boy. My father was absent most of the time. My mother worked to keep food on the table and a roof over our heads. My older brother, who was twelve, was supposed to take care of me. There was no money for babysitters. In the winter, when he went to school, I stayed at an elderly auntie's house. I remember her fondly. She smelled of cigarettes and cloves."

"So when you first met the brothers, they were five just like you. Where did you meet them?"

"I played with them in the fields and trees. We liked to run and play hide and seek. In the afternoon, when we got tired, we would go to their home. It was cool and relaxing there and we could rest and sleep."

The waiter brought water and asked if we were ready to order.

"Yes," he said looking at me. "The crab cakes are great here."

I nodded and he placed two orders.

"How many brothers did you have?" I asked.

"I had three brothers. Everyone had three brothers as I recall." "Were there other children in the brothers' house?"

"Oh, yes. Sometimes two or three other kids. We were all the same age, I think. They each had three brothers, too."

"So were all the children Choctaw Indians?" I asked.

"I never recognized any of them so I don't know. I remember we were only allowed to play with our three brothers. We weren't allowed to play as a large group."

"How many years did you engage in this activity?"

"Until I left the reservation. They came every summer, several times. In the winter, I seldom saw them."

"Didn't that seem strange to you?"

"When I was five, it didn't seem strange. I was happy to have friends. We loved each other like brothers. We took care of each other. I wasn't lonely when the brothers came."

John leaned back as the waiter placed the crab cakes, assorted sauces, and a large salad bowl on the table. When we assured him we needed nothing else, we continued our conversation.

"Did you ever tell your mother about the brothers?" I asked.

"Oh, yes. She thought they were imaginary friends. I tried to explain that they came from the stars, but she thought my story quaint and imaginative. So I just gave up."

"How old were you when you realized that they were not your brothers?"

"In a way they were my brothers," he said, "but I think I was probably eight when I realized that they really did not live on Earth and that they came from another world far beyond this galaxy."

"How did you come up with that conclusion?" I asked.

"It was when I realized that their home was a spaceship. I know they lived on it but for me, if you lived somewhere, it was a house. I realized they only came to Earth to visit me."

"So how did that make you feel?"

"At first confused. Then special. Now I feel blessed and honored to know I am a part of something much bigger. I look at the world differently now. I can watch these D.C. politicians tell their lies and cover up the truth about UFOs, but I know the truth. They can't fool me."

"Once you realized what was going on and that your brothers were from the stars, did you confront them?"

"Yes. I told them I knew they weren't my real brothers like my brother Jack. They laughed and told me that they were just as related to me as Jack and wanted to know why I felt this way. When I told them they lived on a spaceship, and if they were my real brothers they would live with me in a house."

"That must have been very brave of you to say these things," I said. John toyed with the wedding band on his left hand and stared at his hands. For several minutes he did not speak.

"Anyway, they explained to me that my blood and some of my tissue was taken and they made more of me. My brothers were actually triplets produced from my blood and tissue."

"Were they clones?" I asked.

"I guess that's what you would call them."

"After you knew how the brothers came to be, did the visits stop?"

"Actually, they increased. As I entered high school, they actually became quite frequent."

"What was their purpose on Earth?" I asked.

"These individuals who were created to be my brothers were actually anthropologists. They were chosen at birth to follow this tract and groomed to fulfill this role in life."

"Did they ever reveal to you their mission on Earth?"

"They were doing what all anthropologists do. They were studying human behavior, but as humans."

"Can you explain?"

"Yes. They looked like me. So they could go forth to different locations, blend in with the people and live with them."

"Do you know what aspect of human nature they were studying?" I asked.

"They focused a lot of attention on juvenile violence. They wanted to understand why human males became so violent. They were also interested in the horrible abuse that humans committed against infants and animals."

"When you went to college, what did you study?" I asked.

"Anthropology. I was one of the first Indian anthropologists, but despite having a doctorate in the field, I never practiced. I did not have the patience. I wanted to interfere too much. When I saw a kid in trouble, I was not content just to study him. I wanted to save him. So I was a bad anthropologist."

"From what you have told me over the years, you are still in contact with the brothers, is that correct?"

"Yes, it has been less since I moved to D.C. I own a mountain cabin down in West Virginia near a small town called Summersville. We meet there sometimes where we can talk about their studies and about the universe in general. We still feel like brothers and are happy to see each other. The visits are difficult sometimes, so I want to move to Saskatoon. There it will be much easier. In two more years, I can retire from the federal government with a great retirement. It will be time to move on."

"Is your early retirement motivated by your need to continue your relationship with the brothers?" I asked.

"In part, yes. However, it is impossible to work in a place like D.C. and not become jaded. You only have to look to our leaders to understand why our children are so angry. They have no hope. The star people, my brothers, give me hope. They give me something to believe in."

John retired two years after our visit. We never talked again about the brothers, but when I saw him after that, we both had a connection that only the two of us knew. The last time I saw him, he took me to lunch and we said our goodbyes. He was moving to Saskatoon and had decided to "retire" for at least a year. I have not talked to him since that day but I know that wherever he is, he spends many of his nights with his brothers and his days looking out for children who have no advocate.

CHAPTER 7
A UFO AT THE TOP OF THE WORLD

*In November 1986, a Japanese crew of a jumbo freighter aircraft
reported seeing a UFO. This sighting gained international attention
when the Federal Aviation Administration (FAA) announced that
it was going to investigate this sighting because the Air Route Traffic
Control Center in Anchorage, Alaska, had reported that the UFO had
been detected on radar.*

*In this chapter, you will read about an encounter with a UFO that
did not make the headlines.*

I traveled to Barrow, Alaska in the late 1980s. I was a finalist for
the position of president of the College of the North Slope
and had gone there for an interview. The village lies at the edge
of the Arctic Coastal Plain west of Prudhoe Bay and the Arctic
National Wildlife Reserve. Beyond that, it is a thousand-mile trek
to the North Pole. As fate would have it, a storm hit Barrow on my
scheduled departure day, grounding both incoming and outgoing
planes.

If it had not been for the unexpected weather, I would not have
met Sam. I had gone to Pepe's North of the Border Restaurant
for breakfast, when Sam approached me. He introduced himself
and told me he worked at the college. He explained that he had
overheard an oil worker telling me a story the previous night in
the restaurant about a UFO sighting and suggested that he knew a
real story about UFOs in Barrow. Sam was a small man, about five
foot four inches tall with raven black hair. His round face revealed
dimples when he smiled. He wore hand-carved jewelry from the
tusks of animals.

"UFOs are common in this part of the world," he said. "It's just that they go unreported or even uninvestigated. I can tell you a real story about UFOs. Not some Hollywood story."

I invited him to join me for breakfast. When he was seated across from me, I asked him about his ethnicity.

"Some of our relatives call themselves Inupiat, but we are all Eskimos and I tell everyone I speak Eskimo. So don't worry about using the term. It's not offensive to me but may be to others. The word Eskimo has origins in the Algonquin language and means 'eaters of raw meat,' and that describes my people well."

After we ordered breakfast, I revealed to him my interest in collecting stories about UFOs.

"I suspected that from the evening conversation I overheard," he said.

"So can you tell me, what are the real stories?" I asked.

"My father's grandfather used to tell stories about how the people were originally brought to this part of the earth on silver ships from the sky." Sam paused and put sugar in his hot tea. "My grandfather's stories were those that had been handed down from the beginning of time. Many of those stories are lost today. Alcoholism has entered our culture and many families are affected. We are losing those things that make us unique and even though we are far removed from the rest of the United States, we are gradually losing many of our old ways."

"So are you telling me the Inupiat have had a long history of believing in Star People and space travel?"

"Yes. It is not a well-known fact, but the grandfathers and grandmothers still believe this to be true. I'm not sure about the younger generation. As I said, many things have been lost."

"Have you ever had an encounter with a UFO?" I asked.

"Yes. Four times. The most recent happened only a few weeks ago. I stayed late at the college that night. It was about seventy below zero. A storm had moved in and the visibility was poor. I was using the telephone poles to guide me and keep me on the road, when suddenly I saw lights above me. White lights. Blinding lights. They lit up the whole landscape. They were disorienting. I brought the van to a stop, but I kept it running. You don't turn off an engine in Barrow if you expect it to start again. Suddenly the lights moved upward. I could make out the outline of a UFO as it rose. I saw it make a sharp turn and head out toward the sea."

"Some people say that UFOs stall their vehicles."

"That did not happen to me. Just as I put the van into gear, the UFO came back and hovered in front of my vehicle. For a few seconds, which seemed like minutes, it stayed there, unmoving. Then suddenly, it set down in front of me. A humanlike form appeared in front of the van. It stood there unmoving for a few seconds and then it came toward me. I didn't know what to do. Suddenly, I got the feeling that something was wrong. I kept hearing the word, 'cold' in my head."

"Cold?" I asked.

"Yes, cold. I heard that word in my head many times."

"What can you tell me about the craft?" I asked.

"The best way I could describe it was that it appeared cone-shaped," Sam said.

"Do you mean larger on one end?"

"Yes, like a cone, a parking cone but huge. I could not make out a color. The lights were too bright. There were white lights underneath the craft. When it set down, a white beam came out of the craft. It came from inside the craft, I believe. I saw the outline of a figure approach the van."

"Can you describe the figure?"

"He was taller than an me, but not a giant, maybe six feet tall. I could not see his face, only his form. He was like a silhouette, outlined against the lights. It appeared as though he wore a helmet. As he walked toward me, I saw him stumble, and then he suddenly returned and re-entered the craft. I kept hearing the word, 'cold,' in my head. Once the spaceman was inside, the craft moved away out over the ocean. It was gone in a flash. The strangest thing, once it was gone, I no longer heard the word in my head."

"You said that you have had four encounters."

He nodded. "But never one like this. All the others were sightings. I saw a human form with this one."

"Why do you think the alien returned to his spacecraft?"

"I think it was the cold. I don't think they expected the weather to be that cold. As I said, it was bad weather. The visibility was next to nothing. The wind was blowing the snow sideways. It was a day like today. Sometimes I wonder if they were planning to abduct me and had not anticipated the weather. Have you ever heard of a similar story?"

"No, I haven't. Are there any other instances you can tell me about encounters with Star People?" I asked.

"That was my only experience with an alien. I have heard stories from the grandfathers about such encounters, but this was my first encounter. My uncle tells of a time when he was seal hunting and he came on a craft. He saw aliens. He described them as strange creatures that looked like men at a distance, but they moved strangely. He said they floated over the ice. He was frightened, but when they saw him, they went into their craft and left almost immediately. He was surprised that they did not wear clothes for cold weather."

"Did he tell you what he meant by that?"

"He said they wore thin, silver suits that made his eyes hurt to look at them. He said that silver reflected the sun and would not keep you warm."

"Has anyone you know ever told you about encounters or conversations with the Star People?"

"None. I heard stories of seeing Star People but never conversations. I have a theory though. I think they have a base under the ocean. This is their stopover to other places in the universe. I think the government knows it too, but they are incapable of doing anything about it. How could you possibly deal with a race who is able to travel the universe? We are infants in the world of space, and it will be centuries before we will be able to take our place beside them. Perhaps never."

I learned a great deal about myself in Barrow, Alaska. To live there, you must be able to cope with total isolation and that takes a special person. The darkness is unending and for me it was unbearable. Above all, I learned that strange things do happen in the land of the midnight sun. While I have had no contact with Sam since our breakfast in Pepe's North of the Border Restaurant, I have thought about him many times. When the temperatures drop to thirty below in Montana, I remember those cold nights in Barrow and the story of the spaceman who obviously could not tolerate the cold.

CHAPTER 8
ABDUCTIONS OF AN UNUSUAL KIND

Reports of mutilated horses and cattle began to appear in the news in the late 1960s. While the events occurred mostly in the western states, the reports became the subject of national media coverage by the mid 1970s. Although occasionally connected to reports of UFO sightings, many alternative explanations were offered, including satanic rituals and natural predators. According to investigators, the carcasses were often missing portions of soft tissue and body parts, particularly reproductive organs. Some reports claimed that cuts were made with a precision consistent with surgery.

In 1979, Linda Moulton Howe began working on a film addressing animal mutilation. The film, A Strange Harvest, *was broadcast in 1980. She later stated, "I am convinced that one or more alien intelligences are affecting this planet. I would like to know who they are, what they want and why the government is silent." Howe's film speculated that aliens mutilated cattle to secure body parts or biological substances they needed for their own survival, and the U. S. government was complicit in these efforts.*

In this chapter, you will meet Emory, a retired military officer, who like Howe, believes that animal mutilations have UFO origins.

I met Emory during a visit with my uncle in Montgomery, Alabama. He and my uncle had served in the military together. Later that week, I met him at his office located in the French quarter of Mobile.

"I spent thirty years in the Air Force and thought I'd seen it all," he said. "Even with my experience in communication, I was not prepared for what I learned one night six months ago."

"Can you tell me about your unusual experience?" I asked as I seated myself in a comfortable, leather chair in front of his massive desk.

"Sure thing, but first, I must give you a little background," he said. Emory looked like a military man, not only in the way he carried himself, but also with his crew-cut hair and his faultless dress.

"I was a communication officer in Vietnam," he explained. "I was fresh out of college with a degree in electrical engineering, when I got a draft notice. I signed up for the Air Force to avoid the Army, went to officer's school, and ended up in Vietnam. I met your uncle in the officer's quarters in Saigon."

"Did you see UFOs in Vietnam?" I asked.

"Many times, but only during battle. They were observing, but when our aircraft came near, they disappeared. Sometimes right before our eyes; other times they moved away with incredible speed. The official name for the sightings was 'apparitions of war,' but they were not apparitions. We all knew it was military propaganda."

"When you saw UFOs, what was your reaction?"

"I grew up in North Carolina. I'm Cherokee from my mother and a little bit Choctaw from my father. We saw UFOs frequently when I was a boy growing up in the Smokies. My mother always called them the 'Visitors.' She explained the Star Visitors were part of us. Their blood was in us. Therefore, when I saw them in Nam, I was not afraid. I figured they were looking out for me. At least that is what I told myself. As long as the Star Visitors were there, I felt safe."

"You said, that six months ago you learned something you were unprepared to experience. Can you tell me about that?"

"My most recent job was in Alaska. It was a top secret job so I can't tell you anything about the location."

"Did you encounter a UFO in Alaska?"

He nodded.

"When my mother spoke of the Star Visitors, she spoke of them as those who had gone before. They were friends. I believed they looked out for the Cherokee people and that their visits were timed to make sure we were safe. However, the aliens I saw in Alaska were not looking out for anyone. I sincerely believe we are faced with an incomprehensible enemy."

"Can you explain?" I asked.

"My first encounter happened the second night I was onsite."

"Sorry to interrupt, but did you have more than one encounter?"

"Two in all."

"Please continue with the first one."

"It was dark, very dark, but it is always dark in Alaska in the winter. I was working with a team of engineers and some Alaskan Native electrical power techs brought in to do the grunt work. It was cold. I think one of the guys said it was seventy-four below zero. It doesn't matter when it gets that cold anyway. Machines break in the cold. Pieces sheer off from the cold. Wires break. It was a frustrating night. We finally decided to call it a night and meet up eight hours later. I sent the others home while I put away the equipment. I had my own transportation and my vehicle was running. I was not worried about getting stranded or expecting anything eventful to happen to me."

"So you were alone when the first encounter took place, correct?"

"Yes. I was headed for my vehicle. I had turned off all the work lights, and just as the last one went dark, the whole surroundings lit up like the fourth of July. Red lights, blue lights, white lights shined down on the snow making the place look like a Christmas scene. I looked up to find out the origin of the lights, but they were blinding, particularly the one in the center. At the same time, I heard the recognizable cry of a polar bear. Running for my vehicle, I was suddenly thrown to the ground. I managed to turn onto my back just in time to see something that is almost indescribable."

He dropped his head into his hands and rubbed his eyes.

"Are you okay?"

"Yes, I'm just trying to think of the best way to describe what

I saw. A polar bear was suspended in mid-air like a limp stuffed animal. Its head rolled from side to side, and occasionally I would see it move all four feet like it was trying to run and then it would go limp again as if it had given up the fight. Then it was gone into the white light."

"Are you telling me the polar bear was abducted?" I asked.

"At first I wasn't thinking that way. Then another polar bear came into view and the white light focused on it. The same thing again. This bear was bigger and resisted more, but it was useless. It was gone, sucked up into the white light like the first. I lay there thinking I must be delirious, but then I knew, if I were delirious, I would not be questioning myself. After the white light disappeared, feeling returned to my body and I sat up, but not before seeing the outline of the circular craft that moved upward. Within seconds it disappeared into the night sky. I immediately climbed into my vehicle and headed back to base camp."

"Did you tell anyone?"

"I never told anyone except your uncle and now you. But that is not the end of my story."

"Is that when you had your second encounter?"

"I haven't finished with the first one yet. There is more. Two days later, we were sent to another location to work, but this one was about fifty miles from the original site. When we arrived the Alaskan Natives were extremely agitated. They felt the place was evil and wanted to leave."

"Evil?"

"People are superstitious the world over, but this time, I understood their fears. Directly in front of an electrical shack was a dead polar bear, but it was not an ordinary death. The polar bear is at the top of the food chain in the animal world in Alaska. If one dies, it is the result of a territorial battle over a female with a stronger polar bear. However, this bear had not been brought down by its fellow species. It appeared as though it had suffered death at the hands of a surgeon, or at least it seemed that way. Its eyes had been removed, and the ears. It was slit open and the heart had been removed along with the kidneys. The sexual organ had been removed and the tongue was gone. There was no blood on the snow. If the polar bear had died in battle, there would have been blood everywhere. It was clearly not a death at the hands of human hunters. They would have wanted the meat."

"What about the other bear?" I asked.

"We found it about one hundred yards away. Same thing. No blood and the body parts had been removed."

"And you believe that the aliens did it."

"What else could have happened?" he asked, throwing his hands in the air. "I saw the polar bears taken on board a spacecraft. Two days later, the bodies of two bears showed up mutilated. Their frozen carcasses were enough evidence for me. Have you ever heard of animal mutilations, and are there reports of animal abduction beyond cattle and horses?"

"Yes to both questions. I met a young man in Mexico who told me the story of witnessing the abduction of a crocodile. He said that the next night the alien craft returned and dumped the carcass of the crocodile and took another. I met a Shoshone Indian man who told me about seeing the body of a buffalo thrown out of a spacecraft. The carcass, like yours, showed signs of surgical removal of organs and body parts."

"I knew it," he said. "Cattle and horses belong to someone, so it is natural that those incidents would be reported. Polar bears, crocodiles, buffalo belong to no one. These aliens are just not experimenting on cattle and horses; they are experimenting on all sorts of animal species. We just don't know about it, or they are bound up in secret or superstition and never reported."

"Was your next encounter involving polar bears?"

"No."

"Did you have an encounter with aliens?"

"I was abducted by them, along with my two workers."

"Please start at the beginning."

"We had gone out one morning to secure a site where we had been working. While I checked the electrical connections, the workers set about installing a series of cameras, which are monitored minute by minute by some computer watchdog sitting in an office somewhere. We set up multiple cameras because if sabotage occurs, it is not likely that every camera can be disabled at the same time."

"Sabotage? What were you doing out there?"

"I already told you, it was top secret. Perhaps the nature of what we were doing was what drew the alien spaceship to the site. Who knows why they appeared at that site instead of ten miles away where several polar bears with their cubs had been seen earlier that week."

"Please go on."

"I finished checking the connections and was on the phone with the monitoring center checking the cameras as they were installed. Suddenly there was nothing but static on the line. I looked in the direction of the workers, who were no more than forty feet from me and they were gone. I called for them, but no response. Within the next instant, I was on board a spaceship. At first, I didn't understand. I saw no craft, no lights, and no aliens. I was simply transported onto their craft. I was standing beside the two workers, who appeared disoriented. One of them began to scream in terror as four creatures approach us."

"Were they humanoid?"

"Human forms in that they had two legs and two arms and a head, but they were like midgets. They were small, bowlegged and strong. The Inupiat are small themselves, but they towered over the creatures by at least a foot or more."

"Can you describe their faces?"

"Their heads were large for their bodies. Like they had a disease. I remember a kid back in my village in North Carolina who had a big head. My mother said he was born with water on the brain. He died when he was about eight. Their heads were like his. The medical term is hydrocephalus. Fluids cause an enlargement of the brain. That is what they looked like; big brains encompassed in hairless skin the color of powder. They wore huge black goggles that wrapped around their heads hiding their eyes. I suspected the goggles were some type of computerized equipment."

"Did the creatures take you to another area?"

"Yes, they took us to another level."

"How did they do that?"

"There was an elevator of sorts. A round tube that took us from one level to another."

"Were all three of you together?"

"Yes. When we arrived on the upper level, we were in a dome-like room. There were others there, too. From the looks of them, we were all Native, but not Native like Alaska Natives. I think they had tribal people from many nations. I worked with a Lakota and a Blackfeet Indian in Vietnam. I would swear that there were Blackfeet Indians, Lakota Sioux, Cherokee, Choctaw, and other tribes as well."

"Were there any non-indigenous?"

"None that I saw."

"Why do you think they were interested in Native people?"

"I asked them that question."

"They said because we were different. Clearly there is something in our DNA, which has escaped our scientists, that makes us unique."

"Were these the small men or were you talking with others?"

"No. The small men were the guardians, the captors, and the police force. The scientists who were conducting the experiments were similar in appearance to humans. They ranged in height from about five foot seven to six feet. Their skin was the color of mine, like a constant suntan, I guess."

"Did they have any other distinguishing characteristics?"

"Broad foreheads."

"What do you mean broad foreheads?"

"I should have said their heads were bigger at the top and smaller at the chin."

"Anything else?"

"Not that I recall."

"You are now in the dome-like room. Tell me how you came to talk to the scientists, as you call them?"

"I started counting the men in the room. They were all men. I thought if I kept my mind busy, they could not control me. The others seemed to be in a trance. Disoriented. Almost lifeless. They walked around and around. So as not to appear different, I walked with them, all the time counting."

"How many did you count?"

"Seventy-one before they removed me."

"Where did they take you?"

"To another level, but this time, it was down one level. I was led into a room filled with strange equipment. Their technology was nothing like I had ever seen. They led me to a tube that had a light than ran up and down my body. It made the hairs on my body stand up and the sensation was not as uncomfortable as it was ticklish. They did this several times. I demanded to know what they were doing."

"What was their reaction?"

"I saw none, but the strangest thing happened is that I was able to communicate with them. All I had to do was think about something, and I would immediately know the answer."

"How did you do that?"

"I'm not sure. When I asked a question, they answered it. They could read my mind."

"Did they speak?"

"No, I knew the answer in my head. Telepathy. I know I sound like some quack job, but that's exactly what happened. I assure you I am sane."

"You are not the only person who has told me about communicating telepathically with aliens."

"They told me they were surprised that I had not been affected by their drugs."

"What drugs?"

"As I understand, they have a compound—I called it a drug—in their atmosphere that induces lethargy in humans. When humans are put into their atmosphere, they become like zombies. They said only one human in 20,000 are immune. I must have been one of them because I was aware of everything that was going on."

"Do you remember anything about the atmosphere in the room that was unusual?" I asked.

"There was a mist that emanated from the walls."

"Did they answer your questions freely?"

"They answered my questions, but I always had the feeling they were guarded in their answers. In other words, I do not think they told me the whole truth."

"Do you have any basis for that belief?"

"A gut feeling."

"Did they tell you why you were placed in the tube?"

"They were checking for diseases, abnormalities. They said that too many humans suffer from unchecked diseases. They did not want the blood of those who were contaminated. They had to protect their samples and specimens."

"Specimens? What kind of specimens?" I asked.

"I asked them that question, but they told me it had nothing to do with my visit."

"Visit?"

"Yes, they called their abductions a visit from humans."

"What other experiments did they perform?" I asked.

"They took blood and sperm. They placed a helmet apparatus on my head. They said it allowed them to transfer all my knowledge to their data banks. I told them they had no right to do that, and they responded that I had no right to refuse."

"What other questions did you ask them?"

"The obvious. Where do you live? They told me in a galaxy far beyond our telescopes or probes. I asked them if they believed in God. They said that God was in all living things. They were aware of Jesus and said his teachings were appropriate for universal truths. I asked them if they lived in family units. They said only breeders lived in family units."

"Breeders?"

"Yes, those selected to have children. They control population growth on their planet very carefully. It seems as if they have been able to extend life to nearly a thousand years, but in doing so they can only allow so many children to be born a year. It is equal to the number who dies."

"So they do die."

"Not as you and I will die. They choose death when they no longer feel they can be contributing members of society," Emory said.

"What else did you ask them?"

"I asked them how long they had been traveling the universe. They said for over forty thousand Earth years. When I asked them how they propelled their machines, they said the forces of the universe. There was no fuel, as we know it. The universe contained the propulsion energy, but it would be centuries before our scientists learned those secrets."

"What about diseases. Did you ask about that?"

"I did. They said all living creatures in the universe have the ability to heal themselves. They said in the early days of humans, they had the power but the power was taken away."

"How was it taken away?"

"I asked, but they said, that was one of the secrets of the universe and a question I should ask myself."

"Did you come away with any overall impression of how they felt about humans?"

"I asked them about their impression of the human race and if they believed we would survive. They said we were the strongest of the species that lived on our planet in that we had learned to dominate the animal and plant kingdoms, but in terms of the universe, we were weak creatures."

"Did you ask them what gave them the right to abduct humans?"

"They said they had the right because in the universe, they were a dominant species. When I responded by accusing them as treating us like animals, their response was that our evolutionary status was that of an animal. This made me angry and I demanded to know why they wanted the sperm of an animal. One of them stepped forward and said, 'Because you were once one of us. You had the same opportunity to choose a different path, but your path was one of destruction. Your idea of progress took a different evolutionary path than us. We chose to value life and knowledge. You did not.'"

"Do you believe them?"

"I believe they treasure life only when it comes to them. They don't care about life on other planets. That makes me fearful. The Earth appears to be a compatible environment for them. If they could eliminate us, they could save Earth from the destructive human race. I worry that this is their plan."

"Did you ask them any other questions?"

"I didn't get a chance. They told me that my time with them had ended. They said if I remembered my visit, they suggested I keep it to myself. The final straw was when they told me that if I told it, no one would believe me, and at best, I would look like someone who was psychologically unstable."

"How did you feel about that?"

"I considered it a threat, but I knew there was truth in what they said. I didn't want to go public. Your uncle told me about you and your work. I read your book about American Indians and UFO encounters. I knew you would listen without judgment, and if you considered my story worthy, I would have a way of alerting people anonymously. That is why I am so happy to meet you and so glad you came to Mobile."

"What happened to the two workers who were with you?" I asked.

"Just as we were taken, we were returned. Suddenly I found myself standing with the phone filled with static. I disconnected it and looked in the direction where I last saw the workers. They were struggling with the placement of the camera. When I approached, they apologized for taking so long. I asked them if something had happened. They had no memory. I walked away and dialed the computer center again. There was no static, but the agent on the other end was a different person. They said that Elton, the person I was originally talking to, had finished his shift three hours earlier. We completed the job and returned to base camp. I never saw the workers again."

"I have another question. Do you think the aliens who abducted you were the same aliens who abducted the polar bears?"

"I forgot to tell you. I saw a room with animals on tables with men hovering over them. It appeared like a hospital. I saw tubes that looked like blood being removed. So yes, I do think they are one and the same, but I never got a chance to ask them."

"Where did you see the room?"

"When they took me to the elevator for their individual experiments. An alien came out of the room and left the door ajar. I had only a brief view. But I saw animals."

"A polar bear?"

"No, I saw a whale."

"A whale! Oh my God. Anything else?"

"I got only a brief glimpse, but I definitely saw a whale."

"And what about you? How do you feel about the encounter?"

"I have mixed emotions, and by the way, the aliens had no emotions. No expression at all. Nothing. Blank, nondescript faces. They have no track marks of experience, age, grief, loss, or happiness on their faces. They were more machine than human. If they had not had thinning hair, I might have considered them machines."

"You said you had mixed emotions. Can you elaborate?"

"I feel anger because I can't stop them from abducting humans and experimenting on them. I'm repulsed by their inhumane mutilation of animals. I'm angry at my fellow man. If we were given the same knowledge as our distant cousins, why did we choose the path of war and destruction? I'm fearful for the human race."

"How do you know there are more species in the universe?"

"That's another thing I forgot to tell you. They said there were over three hundred species on other worlds that were more advanced than humans, and not all of them were humanoid in nature."

"Did they elaborate?"

"No. When I asked them to tell me about those species, they said they were not at liberty to discuss them, but that we would see them if we were only watchful."

I have talked with Emory several times since our meeting. While he continues to talk about his encounters, his story has never changed. He told me he was considering retiring when he was seventy and planned a visit to Montana in the summer. He plans to buy a summer home in the state. I will welcome him as a neighbor.

CHAPTER 9
EARTH WAS ONCE THEIR HOME

In 2006, Stephen Hawking addressed the need to find a new home for humankind. According to him, our only chance of long-term survival is to live on other planets. Sergei Krichevsky, a cosmonaut and professor at the Academy of National Economy, agrees with Stephen Hawking. He believes that if humans are to survive, they must go beyond Earth.

In this chapter, you will meet a man who believes that the visitors to his ranch once lived on Earth and return occasionally to enjoy their old home.

He told me his name was Jefferson Tom. He claimed that his mother named him for President Thomas Jefferson. He said he had been a cowboy for sixty years. "I got my first job when I was twelve," he said. "I was paid fifty cents an hour and thought I was rich. I been cowboying ever since."

I looked at the man who sat before me. I met him at a small reservation spring powwow. I was sitting with a group of his relatives at the time. During one of the dance exhibitions, he leaned over and quietly told me that he had a story to tell. Later, he gave me his address and invited me to visit.

Two months later, I found myself sitting at his kitchen table with a cup of black cowboy coffee and a box of Twinkies in front of me. His loyal dog, Mato, sat at his feet and growled at my slightest move. "He is protective," Jefferson said.

Jefferson had a powerful presence. He stood well over six feet tall with broad shoulders that would have been the envy of any rodeo cowboy. If I had not calculated his approximate age in my head, I would have suspected he was no more than fifty. When he joined me at the table, he placed a sweat-stained cowboy hat on the table, revealing well-cropped white hair. A large turquoise ring covered most of his ring finger, and a silver cross with a matching turquoise stone hung around his neck.

"I brought you some tobacco," I said as a slipped the pouch across the table.

"It is good," he said. "I will pray for our journey."

"Journey?"

"Do you like to ride?" he asked, as he opened the tobacco pouch.

"Do you mean horseback ride?" I asked.

"Yes, I want to take you into the hills. I have something to show you but the only way to get there is on horseback."

"Yes, I can ride," I said.

"Good." He did not speak again until after he conducted the prayer ceremony.

When we arrived at the barn, he pointed to two mounts. "Those two mares are June and July. You have your pick. June was born in June and well, you know when July was born. Both are gentle and love to get out of the corral."

I did not comment, but chose June as my horse and led her outside to saddle her. Once mounted and I had a good idea of June's temperament and her feel under my body, we headed toward the hills. It was a beautiful spring morning.

"How long of a ride is ahead of us?" I asked.

"Two hours, give or take a half hour," he replied, as he increased the gait of his horse, Billy Jack, and rode out ahead of me. June was content to match Billy Jack's gait and so for the next two hours, we climbed over rocks, embankments, and road up and down hills. The last half hour of the ride was uphill.

At the top of the hill, we dismounted and allowed the horses to graze. Jefferson led me to a solitary tree and pointed out a small pool of water that bubbled up from under the ground. "I wouldn't drink it," he said, "but it is mighty refreshing." He untied the kerchief from his neck, dipped it in the cool water, and offered it to me. "Come with me," he said, before I had a chance to relax. "I have something to show you." He led me to an adjacent hill. "I don't bring the horses here. I want this place to stay undisturbed."

"What are we going to see?" I asked.

"Just a few more steps and you will see."

He was right. I stopped at the huge lifeless circle the moment I saw it.

"You're the first person to see this besides me, as far as I know."

"This is amazing. Tell me about it."

"There's not much to tell. This is the place where the Star People land. As you can see, it is a perfect circle like their spacecraft. There must be something in the fumes that kills the grass and everything living. I have watched ants come to the edge of the circle and turn around. Same with spiders. Nothing crosses the circle. So do not get too close. I think it might be poison."

"Do you mean radioactive?"

"Not sure, but animals, even insects are smarter than humans and they don't go into the circle. I've seen coyotes and rabbits walk around it."

"Have you seen the creatures that fly these craft?"

"Oh, yes. This is where they come to rest."

"Rest?"

"Well, it seems to me that is what they are doing. At least this is the place they stop on their way to another place."

"What time do you see them?"

"They only come at night. The first time I saw them, I had set up camp under the tree where the horses are grazing. I had a small fire, a pot of coffee brewing, and chili in a pot. I saw them come in from the east. They hovered over the spot and slowly, as though they had practiced this maneuver thousands of times, they descended and came to rest in this very spot. It was a strange landing. They rustled up a lot of wind, but no sound."

"Then what happened?" I asked.

"Once the craft landed, the lights dimmed, and a door slid

open. I quickly doused my fire with the coffeepot, sat in the shelter of the tree, and watched. I saw six human-shaped beings descend from the craft, walk around as though stretching and sit down looking over the valley below. I never heard them speak. It was interesting and frightening at the same time. I wondered about the power and knowledge of such men. I felt small and unimportant in their presence."

"Can you describe them?"

"I only saw them in shadows so I can't describe the details of their faces or bodies, but in silhouette, they looked like humans. They had a human form."

"How long did they stay?"

"Perhaps a half hour. No more."

"Have you seen them since that first night?" I asked.

"I have seen them three times over four years. I make this trip in the spring and summer. We move the cattle to these grazing grounds in the spring. In the fall, we take them back to the fields near the house. I come out about once a month, do a head count, look for strays. Just a part of cowboy life."

"Do you see them the same time of the year?"

"I never really thought about that, but no. I have seen them in the spring and fall."

"Have you ever communicated with them?"

"Never."

"Have you ever revealed yourself to them?"

"Never."

"Do they vary in their visit?"

"It is always the same. They land. They get out and walk around. Then they sit on the edge of the hill that overlooks the valley. After thirty minutes or so, they return to their craft and leave."

"Have you ever noticed anything unusual about them?"

"I have noticed one thing about them: their breathing is heavy. I can hear them breathe. I think the atmosphere on this planet must be different from theirs. They never stay more than thirty minutes. That is probably the reason."

"Do they wear breathing devices?"

"Not that I could see."

"How tall were they?" I asked.

"Smaller than me. Maybe five feet eight or so. They were all the same height like they came out of a mold. Their size was the same. No variation in weight or height. I thought it was because of space travel."

"What do you mean?"

"I think there are limits on size for pilots. Right? Maybe they have weight and height requirements so they just look like they are the same."

"Why did you never make yourself known to them?" I asked.

"I thought it best to keep my distance. If they could come here, they know more than we know. I don't try to interfere with things I don't understand. Whatever they are doing is their business, not mine."

"How do you feel about them encroaching on your ranch?"

"I never thought about it in this way. I grew up here. My mother—she was a white lady—she inherited this place from her parents when I was two. We left the reservation and moved here. My dad made a good living off this place. I have too. But when I think of the Star Men, I think, perhaps it was theirs before it was mine."

"Can you explain what you mean?"

"I saw them two weeks ago. It was a strange sighting. For some reason I felt they knew I was watching them. In fact, for a moment, I thought they spoke to me." He paused and led me back to the horses.

"What do you mean, you thought they spoke to you?" I asked.

"I don't want you to think I'm crazy, but I thought I heard them say, this place was once their home."

"Their home? Did they say anything else?"

"I had a sense that they once lived where you and I stand and that they simply come back to visit, but they have moved on, but come back because they loved it here."

"Anything else?"

"Nothing."

I often think about Jefferson. His reaction to his encounters was unique, and yet, I cannot help but think that perhaps he is right: "Whatever they are doing is their business." However, if they once lived on this planet I could not help but wonder, are there humans who have already escaped the bonds of earth and live among the stars?

CHAPTER 10
A UFO ON BEAR BUTTE

Bear Butte is a geological butte located near Sturgis, South Dakota. Many American Indian tribes including the Lakota and the Northern Cheyenne regard the butte as a place where the creator communicates with them through visions and prayers.

Each year, thousands of American Indians, reportedly from approximately sixty tribal groups, make pilgrimages to Bear Butte and leave prayer cloths (red, black, white, and yellow) symbolic of the four directions, and small tobacco bundles tied to the trees. Many religious ceremonies are held at the site, which is considered a place of prayer, meditation, and peace.

On many occasions, young men go to Bear Butte for their "hambleycia," or vision quest, an ancient ceremony that consists of a person spending one to four days and nights secluded in nature without food, water, or shelter. It is a time for intense spiritual communication where a person typically receives a dream or vision related directly to his destiny in life.

Over the years, I have talked with many young Lakota men who have undergone the "hambleycia." On more than one occasion, they have reported sightings of UFOs and encounters with alien beings. In this chapter, Duane tells his story.

I drove to Bear Butte during the summer of 2013. The last time I climbed Bear Butte was in 1980 when I accompanied a group of Lakota children from the Rapid City Schools to the top of the mountain. It was a school field trip, and several Lakota elders and parents accompanied us. The purpose of the trip was to teach the children about the importance of Bear Butte to their people.

Thirty-three years later, I was making this trip alone. As I made my way along the path, I was aware of footsteps coming up behind me. I turned and glanced over my shoulder and saw the smiling face of a young man no more than ten feet behind me.

"*Hau*, Auntie," he called, as I stopped and waited for him to catch up. His greeting did not surprise me, although the approaching young man was no blood relation to me. In the Native culture, all women are addressed as "Auntie" when they reach an age of respect.

"Hello," I replied.

"I see you like to get up early," he said.

"I wanted to beat the crowds and the hot sun."

"Me, too," he replied.

"Have you climbed Bear Butte before?" he asked.

"Thirty-three years ago, I made this trip with a group of Lakota students. We were on an all day field trip."

"I did my *hambleycia* on Bear Butte last year, marking my 18th birthday."

"That's wonderful."

"It changed my life," he responded thoughtfully.

For the next few moments we followed the path silently. Occasionally we stopped as he pointed out the wild turnips and medicinal herbs that grew alongside the path. As the trail became rough and winding on our ascent to the top, he often offered his hand to steady my footsteps. Everywhere there were reminders that this was holy ground. Almost every tree and bush was strung with tiny bundles of tobacco and pieces of cloth. Some were faded, others bright and recent additions. We watched two baby buffalo romp in the knee-high grass under the watchful eye of the herd. Nearby a sweat lodge stood abandoned. As we reached the top, it was obvious that countless individuals seeking spirituality had visited the site. There were hundreds of tobacco ties in the small trees surrounding the back of the site. My eyes were drawn to a Reese's candy bar that sat untouched near the base of a bush. There were other things, too. Photos, a mirror, beaded earrings, and a baby rattle had been left as offerings.

"By the way, I'm Duane," he said.

When I introduced myself, a wide smiled crossed his face. "Did you work in the Rapid City Schools several years ago?" Duane asked as I stood looking over the valley below.

"Many years ago."

"I think my father was in a dance club you sponsored. Did you help organize a traditional dance club for the Indian kids in the Rapid City Schools?"

"Yes, along with several young Lakota men who volunteered as a drum group and dance instructors, and parents who committed to making dance regalia for the children. It was a community effort. I was just the facilitator."

"My dad was sorry to see you leave Rapid City. He always remembered you. He said he once climbed Bear Butte with you."

"Wow! What a small world. What was his name?"

Duane smiled and nodded. "Ray."

"I remember him."

"He will be happy to know you remembered him."

"I remember that when we took the field trip, Ray walked beside me. Sometimes, he reached out and held my hand. He once told me that he wished I was his mother. That's when I found out that his mother had passed. It was very emotional for me."

"I know he missed you when you left Rapid City. When he married and my mother left us, he told me that I should be careful when I chose a wife. He told me to find someone like you."

"Please give him my regards. I've lived in Montana for more than thirty years now. It was a good move for me. I've been happy in Montana."

"My dad also told me that he came across a book a few months back that you wrote about UFOs and Indians."

"That's true, too."

"I have a UFO story. It happened here during my *hambleycia*. Well, not exactly at this location where we stand, but on the site set aside for us. On the second night into my vision quest, a UFO appeared. It changed my life."

I looked at the young man standing beside me. He towered over me by several inches. An arrowhead carved from obsidian hung around his neck on a rawhide cord. His Levis were worn and a t-shirt announcing, "The Black Hills are not For Sale" with a small hole near the collar revealed that it was a favorite shirt. His long, black hair hung down his back. When he smiled, his whole face smiled, revealing two dimples cut deep into his bronze face.

"I want to hear your story. Where are you headed when you leave here?" I asked.

"Back to Rapid City. Dad still lives there."

"I'm going to Rapid, too. I plan to spend the night there. Maybe we could talk there."

"That sounds like a plan," he said, smiling and offering his hand, as we descended Bear Butte.

Two hours later, we were sitting at a corner table at the Ixtapa Mexican Restaurant on Omaha Street in Rapid City. After ordering the chicken enchiladas and ice tea, Duane filled me in on his life and his father. When the chips and bean dip arrived, Duane began his story.

"Since I was a boy, I've seen strange things in the night sky. Wherever we lived, New Mexico, South Dakota, North Dakota, I'd see strange lights and UFOs. For some reason, I always felt I was chosen by our space brothers to know they existed. Have you ever heard of such a thing from others?"

"I have met others who have told me stories about UFO encounters throughout their life beginning in childhood."

"I've seen them for as long as I remember, but I have no recollection of interacting with them until that night on Bear Butte."

"Can you tell me about that night?" I asked.

"I had committed to staying on the mountain for three days and nights. The first night it was warm. There was no wind and the night passed uneventfully. But on the second night, the rain began about midnight. The wind blew unrelentingly. The rain pelted my skin. It smarted like hundreds of bee stings. Shortly after midnight, the rain turned to snow. I was freezing. I prayed and asked the Great Spirit to give me a sign for my future. I questioned myself. Had I taken on too much?" He paused and looked out the window. He tapped the table nervously with his fingers.

"Is there something that happened that night that you don't want to talk about?" I asked.

He shook his head.

"That night, through the snow, a beam, a bright white light that lit up the whole place suddenly appeared. A man descended on the beam of light and walked toward me. He told me not to be afraid. Even though it was snowing and the wind was howling around me, I suddenly felt warm. He told me that they had been watching me for a long time, and that they wanted to show me something. He took me on board their ship and the next thing I know, we are observing another world…a dying world. He said this planet was like Earth at one time. But now it is dying. The inhabitants forgot to take care of their world and now they struggle daily to survive. This will be the earth of the future."

"Where was this planet?" I asked.

"I have no idea. All I know is that it was a barren, dying world."

"Was there anything that could be done to change what had happened?"

"He said if things did not change on Earth, it would be too late for humans, too. He said I would someday be a leader and would be in a position to make decisions that could change the Earth. He said that all major changes are brought about by one individual or a small group, and that I am destined to be a part of that."

"What do you think of that prediction?"

"I'm not sure. I'm a simple man. I don't know how I fit into this."

"Did you talk to the elders about it?"

"I did. They said my dream was powerful. I explained that it was not a dream and that I was taken on board a craft. I remember Grandpa Luther became very serious at that point and said he believed me, but there was no escaping it. My destiny had been planned. I was destined to be a leader among the stars," Duane said.

"Did he explain what he meant by that?"

"No. I have visited with him several times. I still do not know."

"When the spaceman returned you to Earth, did he tell you anything else?" I asked.

He shook his head.

"Shortly after I was taken to another world, I was back on Bear Butte. The snow had not let up. I was alone and I prayed for direction from *Tunkansila*. When I left the mountain, I knew I did not know enough to lead anyone. I enrolled in college the next semester. I have three more years until I get my degree, but I feel I must learn more if I am to make a difference."

"What is your major?"

"Physics," he said. He paused and laughed after finishing off the bean dip. "I can't explain that either. I never cared for science in high school. In fact, I avoided it, but when I was asked to declare a major, I wrote down Physics." He shook his head as if in disbelief. "Do you think the spaceman influenced this decision?"

"I think you chose it for a reason. How are you doing in your major?" I asked.

"I've only had one physics course, but I aced it. It was like I knew everything in the book without opening it. I am doing well in my core classes, too. I tested out of math, which was another surprise. I'm on a fast track and may graduate earlier than the four years expected."

"I'm impressed."

Suddenly Duane's cellphone rang and I could tell it was his father on the other end. When Duane explained that he was sitting in Ixtapa with me, I heard the voice on the other end of the phone. Duane hung up the phone smiling. "Dad is coming to join us. He wants to see you."

Ray arrived within minutes. I remembered the little boy who once shared his most private wish with me. He was now a man in his early forties. As we reminisced over coffee and desert, the resemblance between father and son became more obvious. We ended the day with a barbecue at Ray's home. Around eight that evening, some of Duane's friends arrived and they spent the evening drumming and singing traditional songs while Ray and I watched the night sky.

I've kept in touch with Duane and followed his college career with interest. He graduated with a Bachelors degree in three years. During those years, he served on the Student Council and as President of the Indian Club. He is now in a Master's program in Physics and has been offered an officer's commission in the Air Force when he graduates. He hopes to become a pilot and eventually an astronaut. I cannot help but wonder if Duane is fulfilling his destiny or the destiny described to him by the Star Man during his hambleycia. Whatever the reason, I believe he will be a leader who will make a difference.

CHAPTER 11
THEY ARE MY OBSESSION

According to a recent Huffington Post *poll, forty-eight percent of Americans believe that UFOs have visited and observed our planet. Ten percent of Americans say they have seen spacecraft and many claim to have been abducted. Most recall their abductions under hypnosis, but it has been suggested that twenty percent of that group have total recall without hypnosis.*

In this chapter, you will meet a woman who witnessed the landing of a spacecraft and is in contact with its occupants.

I met Joni when she was a nursing student at Montana State University (MSU). I was having lunch in the Student Union Building, when she approached my table and asked if she could join me. Throughout the half hour she kept up a constant dialogue about how much she loved MSU and how moving to Bozeman had been a major adjustment from living on her reservation.

Over the next four years, Joni and I visited on many occasions and frequently had lunch on her day with the afternoon labs. After she left Montana State, she accepted a nursing position at an Indian Health Hospital in the state. Two years later, she married Emil Roberts, a young doctor from Boston, who was paying off his student loans by working in a disadvantaged area, namely an Indian reservation. After his college loans were paid, he set up practice in a small community outside of Salt Lake City. Every year at Christmas, I got a card and photo of Joni's growing family. An occasional email showed up filled with the joys of parenthood and news of their growing practice.

In December 2014, I received an email from Joni asking me if

I had any plans to travel to Salt Lake City in the near future. She said she had recently purchased my book *Encounters* and that she wanted to visit with me.

In June, I took a road trip to the Southwest. Joni and I met for breakfast at Denny's across the street from the Best Western Mountain View Inn off I-15. As I started to follow the hostess to a back booth, the door opened, and I saw the same independent woman I had come to admire even though more than a decade had passed since she had graduated. Her long black ponytail had disappeared and in its place was a soft, layered cut. Her flawless skin, high cheekbones, and engaging smile made her look as though she belonged in a celebrity magazine.

"I can't thank you enough for making arrangements to see me," Joni said. "It has been a long time, too long." She reached out and embraced me.

I noticed the urgent tone in her voice, and said, "I didn't realize it was urgent."

"More than you could ever know. I didn't want to write it in an email." She paused as we placed our orders.

"Tell me, what is going on?"

"Lately, I've taken an interest in UFOs. You might say I'm obsessed with the topic." She paused when the waitress appeared and poured coffee.

"You never told me you were interested in UFOs."

"Probably because the subject never came up. I've been interested in UFOs since I was a child."

"I was wondering if you might listen to my story."

"Your story? Have you had an encounter?"

She nodded and began nervously fiddling with the silverware setting.

"Yes. My husband doesn't believe me. When I showed him your book, he refused to read it. He thinks UFOs are the made-up fantasies of psychotic people. He's upset with me because I've bought so many UFO books. He doesn't want the kids exposed to them."

"Have you told anyone else about your encounter?"

"My mom and dad. My dad remembers the stories of the elders about Star People, and he has had two encounters in his lifetime." She paused and pulled a tissue out of her purse. "I've told no one else. I'm not upset about the encounter. It has developed a hunger in me for knowledge, and I need an objective opinion about what happened to me. My parents have encouraged me to let it go, because of the gulf it has created between Emil and me. My husband is incapable of an objective opinion. You are my only hope."

"I will do all I can, but first you have to tell me what happened." I reached in my bag and asked permission to tape her story. She nodded.

"It happened on Tuesday. Tuesdays are my 'me' day."

"So you were alone when the encounter occurred."

"Yes. It was a shopping day for me. I was running a little late. I picked up a pizza for the kids on my way home. I glanced at my watch as I got in the car. It was 5:10. I expected to be home by 5:35 at the latest. As I approached the turnoff to our road, the car started vibrating. I held on tight to the steering wheel to keep it under control. I slowed, but continued driving, thinking I have to get home and tomorrow I would worry about getting it to a garage. But just as soon as it started shaking, it stopped."

"When you say vibrating, can you tell me exactly what that means?" I asked.

"The steering wheel was shaking. It was making a strange whining noise like metal scraping metal. But it stopped and just as I came around a sharp turn, I saw the woods ahead were illuminated. The lights were brilliant. At first, I thought it was lights from a helicopter searching for something. Then the thought occurred to me that perhaps someone was injured, and I slowed down to a crawl trying to assess the situation."

She paused and poured cream and sugar in her coffee before continuing. "I stopped the car, and thought that perhaps if I could pinpoint the area of their search, I could help. After all, if someone was in need of medical help, I could at least be the first responder until a medical team arrived. I got out of the car to look around, and an unexpected wind blasted me. That's when I saw a huge object setting down in a gravel pit across the road from where I was parked."

"Can you describe it?"

"It was huge tubular craft. It appeared several stories high like a big blimp, but it was long, very long. Perhaps the length of a football field, maybe longer. I watched as it slung gravel all around it. It was like a tornado."

"Were you hurt by flying gravel?"

"No, I was on the opposite side of the car so the passenger's side received the damage. I ducked down behind the car, and I could hear the gravel bouncing off the car." She pulled out a photograph. "The car was dinged in several places and my windshield was cracked. When I showed it to Emil he said I'd probably passed a gravel truck and didn't realize I'd been hit by flying gravel." She handed me the photo. "It's not a very good photo, but you can see the damage."

"I see it," I said, returning the photo to her.

"After the craft settled down into the pit, the wind stopped. Since the pit was only about fifty feet deep, the top of the craft was visible. I ran across the road and climbed the fence that circled the pit. At this point, I wasn't afraid. I was excited, and if you can believe this, I felt happy. I felt I was privileged to see it."

"How long did it stay in the pit?"

"Twenty or thirty minutes, maybe."

"Did you get close enough to see anything else?" I asked.

"When I reached the edge of the gravel pit, I lay down on my stomach and strained to see what was going on below. The bottom of the craft was lighted and I could see about ten human shapes walking around. They were oblivious to my presence. They were all dressed the same in light suits. They were all about the same size. I think somewhere around six feet. They wore no head gear, but I couldn't make out anything about their faces."

"What can you tell me about the craft?"

"As I said, it was huge. It was metallic. There were no windows but there were lights. Many lights. It looked like a multistory submarine."

"Was there anything else you remember about the scene? Could you tell what they were doing?"

"Nothing. I couldn't make out anything in particular. After about thirty minutes, they entered the craft and shortly after that, the wind began to stir again, and I watched it lift off and move straight upwards. When it was above the pit, it turned toward me. For a moment, the lights focused on me. Suddenly peace and happiness settled over me. I raised my arms and called to those on board, but they moved on. As it left, it lit up the earth below including the area where I stood. At first, it moved slowly. I counted thirty white lights mingled with ten blue ones on each side of the craft. Blue lights were across the back and front of the craft, but I didn't get a chance to count them. Then it turned southerly and within seconds, it was gone."

"Did you see any lights from inside the craft?"

"None."

"You spoke about an event that probably took no more than thirty minutes, and yet you said you were gone for more than six hours. How do you account for that?"

"After the craft was gone, I sat in my car and waited for it to come back. They told me they would be back for me. I waited and waited. I fell asleep."

"What do you mean they said they would be back? You said you did not meet them."

"I didn't physically, but they told me they would be back."

"How did they communicate that message to you?"

"When they were above me, and I was waving and calling to them, they told me, they would be back. I heard a voice." She paused and took a bite of her pancakes.

"Are you sure they didn't come back for you? After all, six hours is a long time to sleep by the side of the road with no one stopping to check on you? Don't you have neighbors along that road?"

"I don't think they came back for me. Surely, I would know that. I remember after they were gone, I waited because I thought they would return immediately. Then I remember feeling drowsy and I decided to take a little nap."

"Joni, I want you to think about that. You wanted to get home to your children, but instead you took a nap. Do you think that sounds reasonable?"

"I don't know. I never thought about it."

"What about your husband? Does he follow the same route home?"

"No. He takes a service road, a short cut."

"Have you seen them since that night?"

"Not yet, but I know I will. I can't talk about this with Emil. He is upset with my obsession with UFOs, but not angry. He said as long as I didn't discuss it with him, and I kept my books hidden from the children, he would just chalk it up to a temporary obsession."

"How do you feel about that?"

"Angry. Frustrated. But you have to understand. I want to save my marriage. I have three kids. I want them to have a mom and dad, but I feel so frustrated. I feel like I'm being pulled in two different directions. My loyalty to my family and this inconceivable longing to be with the Star People. I know they will come for me."

"How do you know?"

"They send me messages. I know it sounds crazy, but I hear a voice that says they will return for me."

"So you are telling me that you were receiving long distance telepathic communication from star travelers."

"That's exactly what is happening."

"Have you told your husband any of this?"

"No. Not because I don't want to tell him, but for the sake of my marriage, I will never talk about the Star People again. I promised him that; I did not promise to forget about my interest in them."

"Did you tell your husband you were coming to see me?"

"No. As my mother told me many times, wives are allowed to keep secrets from their husbands as long as it doesn't hurt them or their marriage. Emil is a good man and a loving husband and father. I asked the Great Spirit for a man like him. Truthfully, I never expected it to be a man from Boston, but I wouldn't trade him for anyone else. There are cultural differences, which I hadn't expected."

"Can you explain?"

"Well, as I said, my father told me of tribal stories of Star People. It is as if my people know of their existence. My dad had his own experiences. It is different with non-Indians. They have to have scientific proof. Do you think my secret makes me a bad person?" She paused, took a sip of her coffee, and looked anxiously around the room.

"I think you do what you have to do," I replied. "I make no judgments. That is a decision you have to make for yourself. At some point, you may have to choose and if you do, you will have to accept the consequences. As your mother cautioned, will your obsession hurt your marriage? Only you can answer that."

After lunch, I followed Joni to the gravel pit where she had her sighting. Our visit was cut short by a man in a hard hat and fluorescent vest who demanded we leave immediately. When we parted, Joni told me she would keep in touch.

A few months later, I received a Christmas card and newsletter along with the usual family photo, and a personal note thanking me for my visit and the hope I would "return" soon. I recognized the word "return" and the quotation around it. It was a code we had agreed upon should the Star Men return. I looked at the photo again. Joni is holding hands with her husband. Her three children are kneeling in front of them. They appear to be a happy, well-adjusted American family. My prayer for her is that it stays that way.

CHAPTER 12
A DEPUTY SHERIFF'S ENCOUNTER

Some researchers have noticed a strong connection between the appearance of UFOs and power failures. Entire streets have lost electrical service in the presence of a UFO, while others have reported car engine failure and car radios ceasing to play. TV reception can also be affected.

In this chapter, you will meet a deputy sheriff who reported engine failure in his pickup and his grandfather who lost a satellite TV signal when a UFO was spotted nearby.

I met Jimmy when he stopped me in the middle of nowhere on a two-lane county road in South Dakota. I was startled when I heard the siren and quickly looked at my speedometer. I was going the speed limit. I pulled to the side of the road and waited.

"Where are you headed?" the officer asked as he leaned down and looked at me. I recognized his uniform. He was a deputy sheriff for the county. I was a little surprised, as the county was not known for hiring Indian officers.

"I'm on my way to see a friend. I promised to bring him some groceries and cook dinner. I haven't seen him in three months and I don't want to be late."

"Who's the friend?"

"Percy Good Man."

"So you know crazy old Percy, do you?"

"Look Deputy, crazy old Percy, as you call him, is my friend. You should have more respect for your elders."

He stood, readjusted his cowboy hat and laughed. "I know who you are. You're that crazy woman who writes about UFOs. You and crazy old Percy make good companions."

I nodded, keeping my hands on the steering wheel while avoiding eye contact with him. Suddenly he burst into laughter. He took off his hat and leaned his elbows on the edges of the window.

"I've been joshing," he said. "I'm glad I caught up with you, I heard my grandfather say you were coming for a visit, and I have a story to tell. I didn't want to talk to you where others might see us."

"So you knew who I was before you stopped me?"

"Something like that."

"You could have chosen a more subtle approach."

"Sorry about that," he said, tipping his official cowboy hat and smiling.

"Is Percy Good Man really your grandfather? Crazy old Percy."

"He's my pap. I'll see you at the ranch."

He laughed and hit the top of my Subaru with his hand.

I pulled onto the road and adjusted my rear view mirror to keep an eye on him. True to his word, he kept pace with me as I negotiated the isolated road that had suddenly turned to gravel, announcing that we had crossed the reservation border. When I parked on the cement slab by Percy's small house, the lawman parked behind me. He appeared by my side as I opened the hatch, took the bags of groceries, and headed for the front door.

"Come on," he called. "I'm sure Percy has the coffee on."

I followed obediently behind him, and as I stepped across the threshold, my old friend greeted me.

"Thank you for coming," Percy said, taking me by the hand and leading me to the kitchen. "Your visits are too few. I see you've met my grandson, Jimmy. His mother was Marlene. You remember her, don't you? She married that Northern Cheyenne from Birney."

"I think I met her when she visited you a few years ago."

"Jimmy is my only grandson. He grew up in New Mexico. His dad worked for the BIA. Jimmy went to college down there, joined the Marines, and came back. There was a vacancy in the county sheriff's office and he got the job."

I listened to Percy but watched Jimmy as he unpacked the groceries. There was no question he was a man who commanded attention. His uniform fit perfectly on his six-foot frame. He wore it with ease and confidence as if he was born to wear a uniform, whether Marine or a deputy sheriff. And despite the circumstances of our introduction, I had to admit, Jimmy was a charmer.

"Jimmy, where do you live?" I asked, as I stuffed the chicken I brought for dinner. I motioned to the bowl of potatoes, and he picked up the knife and began peeling.

"When I'm not working, I stay with Percy. During my shifts, I have a small apartment in town. I'm a city Indian and just getting adjusted to reservation life." He paused, smiled that charming grin, and took a sip of coffee. "I worry about Grandpa Percy being out here alone. There's a lot of drug-trafficking going on in this area. There is drug manufacturing both on and off the reservation. I spend a lot of my time working with the FBI and DEA, following up on leads and checking out abandoned houses both on and off the reservation. I don't have time to come out here and stay at night as much as I would like to, but I try to make it once or twice a week. I'm here every weekend."

"I'm glad to hear that," I said.

"I'm happy to be here. Pap is a special man, but you should be worried about yourself. Life on the reservation and nearby counties has changed dramatically in the last five years and even much more in the last six months. We have evidence that a Mexican cartel is operating in this area in connection with an Indian gang, and that's nothing to take lightly."

"I never travel the roads at night if I can avoid it."

"So when you come out here to cook for Pap, do you go back to the motel in town?" Jimmy asked.

"I spend the weekend with Percy. He has a spare bedroom, but I guess not anymore. It's probably your bedroom now."

"You can still use it," Jimmy replied. "We have some spare sheets, and the sofa is comfortable. I prefer it."

I put the chicken in the oven, made a salad, and joined Jimmy and Percy at the table. I pulled a tape recorder out of my bag and notebook.

"You said you have a story to tell. Are you ready?" I asked Jimmy.

Jimmy pushed away from the table, leaned the chair against the wall, and began his story. "It was on the road you traveled today, down by the group of willows on the river. There is an old abandoned Model-T there. It's about five miles inside the reservation border."

"I know the place. That car has been there forever."

"It happened about three months ago. It was late when I left headquarters. We spent most of the night dismantling a meth lab. I checked the time. It was 1:57 a.m. when I left the sheriff's office. I had the next day off, so I decided to make the drive to the ranch and spend the following day helping Pap brand some cattle. On some nights when I work until midnight or all night, for that matter, I stay in town, but it was Thursday night and the Sheriff told me to take Friday off, so I decided to come out here."

"Tell me what happened."

"I saw a spacecraft in the middle of the road. Do you remember how you come up over those rolling hills and drop down on the other side of the river valley?"

I nodded.

"That's where I saw it. It was straddling both sides of the road. If I'd been driving any faster, I wouldn't have been able to stop."

"What was your first reaction?" I asked.

"At first I didn't know what was going on. I just knew there was something massive blocking the road. My first thought was to get out of the pickup and walk up there to find out what was going on. Then I considered slipping over the side of the barrow pit and driving around it. Then, I thought better of it. I could have upended my vehicle. The drop-off is about nine or ten feet and takes a skillful drive during daylight. But just as I made the decision to get out of the pickup, the lights went out, the engine sputtered and died. I tried to start the engine again, but it was dead. I sat there for a moment, staring at this object. A blue light came from underneath it lighting the landscape. I hate to admit it, but I was scared. But don't tell anyone that. I have to keep my warrior image."

I looked at him, and he winked and smiled self-consciously. "Don't worry your secret is safe with me."

He stood and refilled his coffee cup and offered to refill mine.

"I pride myself on not being afraid of anything. Not even the Taliban could scare this Indian," he said, referring to himself. "I spent twenty-four months in Afghanistan and was never afraid; cautious, but never afraid. But this thing, this object, this spacecraft, scared me."

"Can you tell me what happened after you decided against driving around the craft?"

"When I couldn't restart the vehicle, I removed my shotgun from the rack and quietly slipped outside. I inched around the back of the vehicle and literally dived into the barrow pit headfirst, rolling my body to avoid getting hurt. Once I was hidden, I listened and heard nothing. I crawled up the bank to get a better look, hiding myself in the buffalo grass."

"Can you describe the craft?" I asked.

"It was about forty feet high and the width of the road, which would make it about thirty feet wide and about sixty feet long. It was shaped almost like a football. Oval. Very strange shape. There was a blue light, like a fluorescent light, that lit up the bottom of the craft. It cast an unnatural glow in the darkness, like something out of a science fiction movie. There was complete silence, which seemed strange to me. In the summers, there are always cricket sounds, mosquitoes buzzing, always some sound. But it was as if the world had stopped all sound."

"Did you see anyone?" I asked.

"Not at first. I waited and waited for what seemed like an hour, but it was probably only ten minutes at most. I decided I was going to move closer and get a better look. Just as I was about to make my move, I heard a swishing sound and three beings came into view. I thought it strange. I heard no footsteps, only swishing, like there was air between them and the hardtop. Stranger too, they just appeared out of nowhere."

"What did they look like?" I asked.

"I couldn't see them very well, but I swear to God, they looked like big, tall bugs. Maybe half human, half bug. One look and I knew I was outmatched. They were huge. Maybe seven feet tall. Even though they were similar to a human shape, their large heads seemed to set on their shoulders. I saw no neck so they moved stiffly, moving their whole body when they wanted to look in a different direction. Their legs were enormous, and I swear, I didn't see any clothes. I don't think they wore any. I loaded a shell into the chamber of my rifle and slid backward into the barrow pit. I figured I would be the first person to shoot an alien if they came after me. I heard strange sounds like grunts and hisses. I think they were communicating."

"Did it sound like language?"

"Just sounds. No syllables. When they appeared, my first reaction was to run. I looked behind me. There was a barbed wire fence a few feet away, and I ran the danger of exposing myself if I climbed over it. I saw about three dozen cattle in the field, most were clustered around a water tank."

"Do you think they were aware of your presence?"

"They had to see my vehicle. It stopped no more than twenty feet from their craft."

"Did they search for you?"

"At first, I thought they were looking for me, but then I heard the cattle. They were frightened. I can always tell when there is a predator among cattle. They make a distinctive cry and begin to run, trying to escape their enemy."

"Were they after the cattle?"

"The moon was full, and it lit the pasture quite well. That's when I saw the three of them. They were in the field. It was a strange sight. They had singled out one of the cattle. It was so terrified that it could not move, or maybe they did something to it, but I saw them drop the six-hundred-pound steer to the ground like it was a stuffed animal. They hovered over it for a couple of minutes, and then they stood and disappeared. The next thing I know, they are back in front of their craft and within a minute or so, the craft began to move upward and within seconds it disappeared. It was gone."

"What did you do after that?"

"Once I saw the craft lift off the ground, I figured I was safe. I ran back to my vehicle and retrieved a flashlight. In the field, I found the dead carcass of the steer. The eyes had been removed and most of its innards. The tongue was missing and the two front hooves. There was a strange smell. It hit me before I reached the steer. I expected to smell blood or death. You know the smell of animal death."

I nodded.

"But this smell was chemical. It burned my nose. I coughed until my lungs felt like they were on fire. It must have been something they used to control the steer. Perhaps a chemical that made it docile. It was a horrendous odor. I covered my nose with my jacket and did a cursory examination. Then, I felt the strangest urge to get to Pap. I ran back to the pickup and just as I got to the door, I heard a familiar noise."

"What do you mean?"

"I heard helicopters. I couldn't believe it at first, but the moon was full, and I saw the outline of two helicopters headed in my direction."

"What did you do?"

"I jumped in the pickup, and the engine started immediately. I quickly turned out the lights and drove down the highway by the light of the moon."

"Why?"

"I didn't want them to see me. I had no intention of getting involved. I think they were military. In my rearview mirror, I saw their strobe lights searching the ground. I think they were searching for the UFO."

"Did you tell anyone what you had seen?

"I told Pap. He was watching TV when I got home."

"At three o'clock in the morning?" I asked.

Percy shrugged his shoulders and smiled. "Sometimes I wake up in the middle of the night and can't go back to sleep," he said.

"When I arrived home," Jimmy said, "Pap was complaining that the TV had gone off—we have Dish Network—he said the screen went pink and there was nothing on for a half hour, and he missed his program."

Jimmy got up and prepared another pot of coffee. "When I told him about what I had seen, he figured that the spacecraft had something to do with his TV reception."

"That's right," Percy said. "When the TV went off, I walked outside to examine the dish on the side of the house. I saw the UFO streak across the sky. I'm sure it's the same one Jimmy saw on the road. I saw the helicopters, too. They flew over the house. If they were military, that meant they knew what was going on."

"When Pap told me he saw the helicopters, we turned out all the lights. We sat up for a while and sure enough, we heard the helicopters fly over the house again."

"How long was it before you heard them again?" I asked.

"About an hour."

Jimmy looked at his grandfather, who nodded in agreement.

"Did you ever find out what happened to the steer?" I asked.

"No. I decided the best thing to do was to mind my own business. After all, I'm an Indian. If I went around telling stories about aliens butchering cattle, people would probably say I was drunk. It doesn't matter that I don't drink, around this part of the country, people think all Indians are drunks."

Later that evening as Jimmy, Percy, and I ate dinner, Percy told me that he was sure that his television was tied in directly to the aliens.

"For about a month," Percy said, "my television would go off for no reason whatsoever. I called Dish, but they had no explanation for my loss of service. How could they know? I was always talking to some guy in the Philippines. I stood in my back door and watched the spacecraft zipping back and forth. They couldn't see that in the Philippines. I never did talk to an American about my TV problems. After about a month, things went back to normal, and I haven't had any problem since, so it had to be the aliens."

"Jimmy, do you think the two were related?" I asked.

"I know the craft interfered with my pickup's lights and engine. The pickup inexplicably stalled when I came upon them. When they were gone, the engine turned over immediately and the lights came on. Yes, I think there was a connection."

Percy and Jimmy still share the ranch house on the weekends. A few weeks ago, I spent a couple of days with them as they prepared their cattle for market. Jimmy is still a deputy sheriff, although lately, with the increase in the price of beef, he is talking about becoming a full-time cattle rancher. He has never seen another UFO, but he assures me he keeps his eyes open. As for Percy, he heads outside each time his television reception is interrupted. He is worried the aliens have designs on his cattle, and he plans to stay alert. He keeps a loaded shotgun and a .30-06 by the door, just in case.

CHAPTER 13
A UFO AT HEBGEN LAKE

There are old-timers in Montana who still talk about a morning in August 1949 when nine UFOs reportedly flew across Hebgen Lake in formation, two of them crashing in or near the lake. They tell of angler in his boat at the end of the lake who saw one disc crash into the lake, sending up a geyser several hundred feet in the air. They talk about the military men who came to investigate. Supposedly, according to the angler, another disc crashed in the woods. The others disappeared in the sky. Even though there were other witnesses, they all refused to talk to the authorities for fear the news would bring curiosity seekers to their small village. While no UFOs were ever found in the surrounding woods, according to the locals, something was retrieved from the lake, but the FBI concealed it.

A decade later, in 1959, a 7.3 earthquake hit this area of Montana. This earthquake caused twenty-eight deaths and eleven million dollars in damage. As a result, the fear expressed by the old-timers about visitors changing their village, occurred anyway. Today, Hebgen Lake is one of the most visited tourist attractions in the state, not because of UFOs, but because of the earthquake.

In this chapter, you will read the story of a young man who claims to have had an encounter one night while fishing on Hebgen Lake.

In June 2013, I decided to take an extended camping trip through Yellowstone National Park. My tour itinerary included a stopover at Hebgen Lake and various campgrounds in the park with my final destination being Jackson, Wyoming, and the Jackson Hole Writer's Conference.

Hebgen Lake is located in southwestern Montana about twenty

minutes from West Yellowstone and the entrance to Yellowstone National Park. The lake itself is about fifteen miles long and four miles wide. It is known as the premier still water fishing lake in Montana. I arrived at the Lonesomehurst campground, which is located on the lake, in the late afternoon. It was a perfect afternoon, and because of my early arrival I rented one of the few available sites with an electrical hook-up, a fire pit, and picnic table. As I busied myself readying my campsite, I noticed that I was the only traveler except for a small, orange tent pitched at the far end of the campground.

Within two hours, however, the campground was bustling, and all sites were occupied. As darkness fell, voices and laughter filled the night air along with the smell of wood smoke and hamburgers. As I made my way toward the shore of the lake, a group that had formed across from my campsite called out and invited me to join them. They were telling ghost stories and making s'mores.

"There's always room for one more and you seem to be alone, Ma'am," a middle-aged man dressed in Bermuda shorts and a tank top announced.

I hesitated, but after an invitation from his companion, I agreed to join the group. When I entered the circle, everyone stood and introduced himself or herself. As stories were told round robin, I heard about a prostitute dressed in a red bustier and not much else, who haunted a casino in Deadwood, South Dakota, which was once the location of her place of employment. I learned about a woman dressed in a flowing, white gown who would sit on top of a tombstone in a cemetery in Des Moines, Iowa, and call to passersby to join her. I listened to a story about a small child who walked a lonely road in Fargo, North Dakota, looking for his parents who had gone off in a blizzard to get help when their car broke down; the little boy had frozen to death while his parents were gone in search of help, and his ghost spent every night wandering the road looking for them. I listened to stories of a Bigfoot who attacked two loggers in Maine when they were clear-cutting his habitat, and a story of little people who lived on the Crow Indian Reservation.

When it came my turn, I told them about the night a young girl, on her way to an outhouse, encountered an alien spaceship and was invited onboard by an elderly woman who called her "grandchild." After I completed my story, a silence fell upon the group for a moment, until the next person announced she also had a UFO story to tell.

As I listened to the paranormal experiences described by a circle of strangers, I couldn't help but be reminded that these individuals were Middle America. They were the heart and soul of the country, the blue-collar workers who had experienced the paranormal, and even though they had little explanation of what had happened to them, they were willing to share their experiences and to voice their fears, questions, and wonder. They were white, red, black, and brown Americans who came together around a campfire to share their stories, and despite their ethnic differences and the color of their skin, they displayed one common denominator: they all had an interest in the unknown.

After everyone in the group had told a story, I stood and said goodnight, and continued my planned walk toward the shoreline. Suddenly I became aware of footsteps behind me. I looked cautiously over my shoulder. I saw a towering silhouette jogging toward me. When he got closer, I recognized him as a young man who had been the focus of three teenage, attention-seeking girls in the group. While he graciously responded to their questions, he politely kept his distance. I secretly admired his behavior, which was uncharacteristic of youthful males when dealing with uninhibited females.

"It's me, Kevin," the interloper said. "I told the story about the little people on the Crow reservation."

"Of course. You just startled me for a moment."

"Sorry about that. I wanted to talk to you privately. One of the women at the campground said she recognized you—that you're a writer and you wrote a book about UFO encounters. Are you a writer?"

"Yes," I said.

"And you write about UFOs?"

"Yes, that's true too."

"Awesome. This is awesome. I never met an author before. I'm impressed."

He paused for a moment as though embarrassed by his admission.

"God, I sound like a teenage girl! You must think I'm a weirdo, but I'm really not."

I watched as he paced in fronting of me slowing my walk toward the shore.

"I had an encounter one night," he blurted out. "On this very lake. I never talk about much, but since you write about UFOs and are Indian, I think you might understand. All my friends laughed when I told them I saw a UFO. I expected them to take me seriously; instead they asked me if I was drunk and yet, everyone knows I don't drink."

"Really?"

"No. I never drink, honest to God. When you grow up in a home with two alcoholics and drug pushers, you learn that alcohol and drugs lead to destruction. I know, you're probably thinking you've never met a college guy who didn't drink, well, now you have. As God as my witness, I have never had a drink and never will." He paused and made the sign of the cross.

"I believe you and I applaud you for your convictions."

"When you're a child raising yourself, you learn to walk a different path. That's what I did. I found my own way. The best way, even if it is not the road most traveled."

I looked at the young man who had just paraphrased Robert Frost's poem and must admit I took a renewed interest in him.

"Were you alone on the lake the night you saw the UFO?" I asked.

"I was alone. I like to fish alone on the lake at night. It's the time I can connect with the Creator and fish at the same time. I go to the university in the fall and winter, but I spend my summers on the lake."

"Do you live in Bozeman?"

"You could say that. I live out of my car most of the time. I couldn't afford to go to the university otherwise. During the summer I do odd jobs for the Forest Service, work for different fishing guides, and with my salary, tips, and the Pell Grant, I pay my tuition. During the winter, I work at various places in Bozeman for food and incidentals."

"What tribe are you?" I asked

"Blackfeet on my mother's side. My Daddy was a Chippewa-Cree."

"Do your parents live in Browning?"

"No, I grew up in Great Falls. My parents are in prison now. I haven't talked to them since they were sent away. My best friend's mother took me in and helped me until I graduated from high school. I have relatives on the reservation, but I don't plan on going there. I like it out here, away from all the problems."

"I'm sorry to hear that, but you're motivated to get an education. I suspect your tribe would be happy to have you return to the reservation and work for them."

"I don't want to be like my parents. There are no opportunities on the reservation. I don't want to wake up someday an old man and think I could have done this, or I could have done that. No, I don't belong on the reservation. I want more from life."

He paused and picked up a stone, and I heard it skip across the lake.

"I can't live on a reservation where I will always be the son of the two drug dealers. That's not a life for me."

"I understand. But you caught up with me to tell a story. I would love to hear about your UFO encounter, but I always tape the stories people tell me. My tape recorder is in my RV. Would you mind going back to the campground?"

"Lead the way," he said, as we turned and walked toward my campsite.

When we reached the RV, I invited Kevin to sit at the picnic table while I retrieved my tape recorder and made hot chocolate. I set a Coleman lantern on the end of the table and placed the tape recorder between us. I offered him a cup of hot chocolate, a ham sandwich, and fruit, which he graciously accepted.

"I haven't eaten anything since breakfast except for the S'mores," Kevin admitted.

I watched the young man who sat across the table from me. He was tall, well over six feet. He had the shoulders of a college football player, and yet the voice and mannerisms of a poet, a gentleman, a man of culture. A single dimple appeared on his left cheek every time he smiled, which was often. While it was obvious that he hadn't had a haircut in a long time, from the way his black hair curled around his collar making him look like a bed-head, it added an innocence to his appearance.

"Are you ready?" I asked, after he finished the last orange wedge.

"Ready as I'll ever be," he said. "Thanks for the food. It was delicious."

"You're welcome."

"That's a good thing about Indians. They always feed you. You're like my auntie. Every time I went to her house, she fed me."

I watched him nervously rub his hands on his Levis, as I pushed the record button on the tape recorder.

"Please, ready when you are," I said.

"I don't know where to start, so I will start at the beginning. It happened about this time last year. I worked for one of the fishing tour groups, putting in long hours. I'd had little time for fishing. The owner of the tour company gave me three days off, and allowed me to use one of the smaller fishing boats he had stored in his garage, but hadn't used for the current season. I was excited. I decided to spend the night on the lake. I packed two peanut butter sandwiches and a large thermos of coffee. I had my fishing tackle, my lucky rod and reel, and set off on my adventure."

"Was it from this campground where you launched the boat?"

"Yes. I set out about 9 p.m. Right before dark. I went out to the middle of the lake, shut off the engine, and cast my line.

Along toward midnight, I saw a light in the distance. Earlier in the day, there were helicopters getting water from the lake to put out a small forest fire to the south, so I thought it was a helicopter retrieving water. I gave little thought to it, since I felt a tug on my fishing line, the first one of the night."

"So even though you saw the light, you paid it little attention."

"Correct. I was too busy fishing."

"When did you realize it was not a helicopter?" I asked.

"When I looked up and saw it, maybe a couple hundred feet from me, hovering over the lake. There were lights pulsating from blue to white, but there was no sound, no wind, which you would expect from a craft of that size. There were no waves or motion on the water. It simply hovered there."

"Could you make out the outline of the craft?"

"Not a first. I have to admit that seeing these lights and the lack of sound and wind was unnerving. I sat down in the boat, put my fishing pole aside and watched it. I couldn't believe what I was seeing."

"How long did you watch it?"

"A few minutes, no more than five, if even that. The lights were mesmerizing. As they throbbed and changed color, they would fade from bright to a dim light. I watched it move up and down the shore of the lake from one side to the other, as though it were searching for something. As it came nearer, I lay down in the boat. Partly to hide myself, partly so I could get a good look if it flew over me."

"And as you were lying in the boat, did anything significant happen?"

"At one point, the craft flew above the trees and disappeared. I didn't expect it to return, so I sat up and cast my line again. But within minutes it was back, searching among the trees and shoreline. There was a search beam that went back and forth among the trees and along the shore."

"Why do you think they were searching for something?"

"I don't know. I've seen helicopters search at night. They are very methodical. They search every spot where a victim might be. It reminded me of that, but there was no sound and no wind. It was not a helicopter."

"When it returned, did you get a good look at it?"

"When it returned, I laid down in the boat again. From my vantage point, I kept track of it. I figured that if it headed in my direction, they would not notice me. Frankly, I was taking no chances. I've heard about abductions, and I didn't want to be one of those statistics."

I watched him nervously rub his hands on his jeans again. "So by this time, you have decided that you are watching a UFO. Is that right?"

"Without a doubt. It had to be. It's maneuverability along the trees and shoreline alone was masterful. We don't have, or at least I don't think we have, any aircraft capable of such aerobatics."

"Did you ever get a good look at the shape of the craft?"

"It was a long, canoe-like craft."

"What do you mean, canoe-like?"

"If you look at a canoe upside down, you will notice the curvature of the bottom of it. The spacecraft had a similar curvature. It was a long craft, but wider and higher at one end."

"What else do you remember about the craft?"

"It had blue lights along the underside of the craft that changed from blue to white. When it was overhead, I saw three red lights in the front and the rear of the craft. They were stationary. The craft was larger toward the rear—wider I mean. I was very surprised at its size. It was at least a hundred feet long. I could not tell how tall it was, but as for width, it cast a shadow that almost covered the lake from one shore to the next. I wondered how such a large craft could stay airborne. It had no wings. It made no sound. Certainly not one of ours."

"At this point, were they still searching?"

"No. At this point, they had decided to give up, I guess. They moved north and I watched them as they disappeared in the sky. I never saw them again even though the next two nights, I came to the same spot and waited."

"Did anyone else see the craft?" I asked.

"I stayed on the lake for a couple of hours. I did not get one single bite, which is strange for this lake. When I docked, a man and woman raced toward me. They asked me if I had seen the UFO. When I told them that it hovered over me, they touched me and suggested I take a shower. They worried about radiation. They had observed the craft search along the bank from the shore. They said they went through the campground yelling the word, 'UFO,' but no one woke up or came outside. Finally, they gave up and watched it as it made its final sweep along the shore and then vanish in the night sky. They were the only other witnesses to my knowledge."

"Did you get their names?"

"No, I never even thought about it. They told me they were from Georgia and had just retired and were making a cross-country trip across America, a dream journey of a lifetime. We parted, with them encouraging me to take a shower. I never saw them again."

"What are your impressions of what you saw?"

"I've thought about that encounter a lot. There isn't a day that goes by that I don't think about it. On one hand, I'm glad I saw it. I learned that night that we are not alone and that we are not the only intelligence in this vast universe. On the other hand, it baffles me. Why would they come here? What do they want? Does our government know about them? If so, why do they not share the truth with the American public? Is it because they are hostile and want to take over the earth, or is it because we want to be the only country on the planet to have access to their great knowledge?"

"And how does that make you feel?"

"In one sense, helpless. In another, empowered. At least I know the truth now."

"Do you think your encounter impacted your life?"

"Yes, it changed me as a person. Knowing there is life beyond this planet makes me feel hopeful that someday humans will use their intelligence to travel among the stars. I hope to see that happen. So I have more hope about the future. I had lost all hope, now it's back."

"By the way, did you take that shower?"

"I did. Just to be safe, of course."

"Did you have any skin problems or anything you related to the craft?"

"Nothing. I guess that ice cold Montana water saved me," he said, laughing.

I left the next morning for Yellowstone, but not before giving Kevin my phone number. Over the next year, I often hired him to do odd jobs. Last May, he graduated with a degree in engineering. A contractor in the Bakken oil fields in North Dakota hired him immediately. He likes his new job and calls occasionally to update me. As for UFOs, he tells me that he sees many strange things in the skies over North Dakota, but he has to see me in person to tell me. I have invited him to spend the holidays with my family and he has accepted.

CHAPTER 14
A WATCHER IN DEATH VALLEY

In 1933, Death Valley National Monument was declared a U.S. National Monument, placing the area under federal protection. Fifteen years later, two prospectors reported seeing a UFO crash in Death Valley. They estimated it was flying at three hundred miles an hour at the time of the crash. Reportedly, the disk hit a sand dune, and two small creatures hopped out and ran off into the desert. According to the prospectors, they gave pursuit but the creatures were too fast for them, and the weather was too hot for a prolonged chase. They gave up and returned to the site of the crash, only to discover the saucer-shaped disk was gone. The story was reported in the Bakersfield newspaper on August 31, 1949. It also appeared in Grolier's Book of Knowledge, *as a legitimate UFO event. Most people discount it as a hoax today.*

However, there are other stories from Death Valley, untold stories that have never made the headlines. In this chapter you will read about a man who watches the desert sky and records all UFO activities.

In August, I traveled to the Star Trek Convention in Las Vegas. While I am a Star Trek fan, attending a convention had never been a part of my plan, however fate has a way of intervening in life. Shortly after my book *Encounters with Star People* was published, a number of my readers suggested that they would like to meet me and tell me their stories. All prefaced their request by telling me that they were not Indian, but that they needed to tell their story to someone. I agreed to meet them at the Star Trek Convention.

Instead of flying, I decided to drive to Las Vegas and take a camping vacation. I outlined an RV trip that would take me through the Navajo Reservation to see former colleagues and to visit some national parks. Death Valley was at the top of my list.

I arrived at the park shortly before dark. My reserved camping space was waiting for me, and once I completed all the connections, I ate a microwave dinner while watching the evening news. After taking a shower, I put on my sweats and took a walk away from the campground to get a better look at the night sky. On my way out of the door, I grabbed a flashlight and miniature tape recorder. Outside the campground, there were no glaring lights so I did not need to venture far to view the heavens. As I settled myself on a large rock warmed by the hot sun, a voice came out of the darkness.

"Looking for UFOs, Missy?"

"Where are you?" I asked.

"Here," the male voice replied. I shined the flashlight in the direction of the voice. A small man with thin white braids in worn, disheveled jeans and a faded plaid shirt stood on the fringes of the campground. He covered his eyes to escape the glare of my flashlight. I lowered the light, pushed the button on my tape recorder in my pocket, and stood making sure the boulder was between us.

"No need to fear me, Missy. I mean you no harm," he said in a gentle soothing tone.

I heard the shuffling of his feet on the hardened desert earth. "I'm just an old Indian who watches the night sky. This is a perfect place for doing it."

"What tribe?" I asked.

"Many tribes. A hybrid I guess. Osage, Oklahoma Cherokee, Choctaw, German and a Vietnam vet."

When he came closer, I turned off the flashlight. He smelled of wood smoke and ketchup.

"Are you a camper?" I asked.

"Every day."

"I don't understand."

"I'm homeless, Missy. I camp out every day of the year. I'm here fourteen days, and then I have to go away fourteen days, and then

I come back. Park rules. They have a fourteen-day limit."

"Where do you go when you're not here?"

"There are other parks, but this is the best place. Few lights make for a perfect view of the sky. At night I watch for those little grey bastards. They're mean, you know. They take people. I seen 'em do it, too. They don't think anyone is watching, but I watch. I keep a tally too."

He reached in his pocket and pulled out a small notebook.

"It's all in here. Dates and people, males or females, and how long they were gone. I write down their descriptions, too."

"Are you telling me that you have observed people being abducted?"

"That's what I'm saying. It happens one or two times a month."

"Do all of them return?"

"Only five times they did not return. They're always alone. Some are backpackers who travel with all their belongings on their back. Others are young women traveling alone. No one ever comes looking for them, but there has to be someone out there missing a son or a daughter. At least I remember. I keep a record."

"Did you know their names?"

"Hell no, Missy. I'm just a watcher. A watcher watches. That's all. Most of the people who camp here are family people; they have no use for the likes of me. They consider me the lowest of low. Sometimes I hear them talk about me. They wonder if I'm an Indian, probably because of my skin and my braids. They say I'm a crazy man, but I'm not."

"I'm sorry people are so cruel."

"I'm pert near seventy, and I've gave up on society a long time ago. I stick to myself or others like me."

"So why are you talking to me?"

"Because there's not a day that goes by that I don't fear they'll return and someone like you would be an easy target. You're alone, right?"

"Yes."

"That's when you're at your most vulnerableness. I watched you from the darkness. I feared for you. You have that vulnerableness about you. You're trusting."

"I'm not so sure about that," I said.

"Oh really? Do you see anyone around who could tell the world what happened to you if they took you? Nope, it's just me. And I'm telling you, never wander in the desert at night, not even this close to the campground. When they take you, you'll not have any chance to run away. Hell, when they lock onto you, you'll not want to run away. They have such power they will make you think they're your friends."

"Well, I really appreciate your concern. I travel alone most of the time."

"Don't underestimate the power of the greys, Missy. They're dangerous."

"Have you been abducted? You sound like a voice of experience."

"When I was a teenager, no more than seventeen, me and some of my friends came out to the desert to party. It was not too far from here. We graduated from high school on Friday night and came out to the desert on Saturday morning. We were drinking and cooking hot dogs. I got up and went away from the fire to relieve myself, if you know what I mean."

"Are you telling me that you were abducted that weekend?"

He didn't answer right away. He fished in his pocket and pulled out a pack of cigarettes. I saw a lighter flame and the heard the cigarette sizzle when the flame touched it. He took a long drag and let the smoke out slowly as he walked away from me to smoke.

"It happened that weekend. When I walked out of view of the group, I saw a small person standing about ten yards away looking in the direction of our campsite. My first reaction was that it was a kid, but then I thought it was a pervert. As I called out for him to get the hell away, my friends, or at least what I thought were my friends, joined him. All of them looked at me and began laughing. I thought they were playing a joke."

"But they were not your friends?"

"No. The little grey bastards played a trick on me."

"When did you realize they were not your friends but aliens?"

"The next thing I know I'm strapped onto a cold metal slab with three of these bug-eyed monsters examining me. That's when I discovered they can take any form. They can look like you or me or anything else they want to imitate. They had disguised themselves as my friends to trick me."

"How did you discover they could shape shift?"

"I saw them do it while I was strapped down. I'm telling you, Missy, they're dangerous. Besides me—I'm Jim Gray Dog, by the way—was my best friend, Roger Benally. He's become a watcher, too. He's based outside Phoenix. I go down to Phoenix and join him in the winter when it's too cold to stay here. Sometimes he comes up here for a few months in the spring."

"So you're telling me that your friend was also abducted?"

"Right, but not just Roger. All of them. We were all abducted and examined. They stuck suction tubes over our privates. They took blood from each of us. They punched holes in us. They put machines on us and stretched our bodies until it hurt. They nearly squeeze the brains right out of my head with a helmet-like contraption."

He paused and hesitated as though reliving that night. He stopped pacing back and forth, dropped his cigarette on the desert floor, and stamped it out with his boot.

"We all became watchers of sorts, but Roger and me are the only full-timers now. Heidi, Roger's sister, died two years ago, childless and alone. She married three times; every husband left when they discovered she could not have kids. Them bastards ruined her. Rachel has Alzheimer's. She doesn't know me anymore, but she drives the nurses crazy talking about UFOs. She didn't have kids either although she lost a child once, but she could never find it. The hospital told her it was a false pregnancy, but she knew the aliens took her baby."

"How many of you were abducted that night?"

"There were the five of us. There was Roger and his sister, Heidi, Ted, and his girlfriend, Rachael, and me. Shortly after I got back from Nam, we got together about once a year and talked about that weekend, but after a while, we just stopped."

"Did you ever think about warning people about the abductions?"

"At first, I did. But the park people told me if I scared one more person with my crazy stories, they'd ban me from the park forever. So I kept my trap shut, and I watched. Someday my records might count for something."

We sat in semi-silence on the boulder for nearly an hour. Four eyes peering into the darkness of the unknown. Occasionally, the stranger pointed out a satellite or called a star or constellation by name. By midnight, I decided to go to bed.

"I have a confession, Jim. I taped your story. I collect stories about UFOs and write books about them. I'll give you the tape if you wish. I'm sorry. I should have told you."

"Good, write about me, Missy. Tell my story and Roger's story and tell about Ted, Rachel, and Heidi, too. People need to know the truth about these little grey bastards. They're not peaceful space travelers. They're sadistic. If they catch you, you'll never be the same."

I found Jim the next morning. He was camped near the rock where we sat the night before. "I have coffee and eggs and bacon, or if you prefer, I make some pretty good pancakes. Would you like to join me?"

"I'm in no shape to be entertained by a lady," he said. I looked at the man who stood before me. His face was that of a troubled man, his slouched shoulders made him appear like a man who carried the weight of the world on his shoulders. Although he wasn't the cleanest man I had ever met, his mission in life made him stand head and shoulders above many.

"You look fine to me. Besides, I like the rugged type," I said smiling.

He laughed uproariously. I waited as he packed up his gear into a backpack and led him to my parked RV.

For the next two hours we sat at the picnic table and ate

breakfast and talked. He shared with me the details of his notebook and the abductions he had observed. After each entry, he had a short description of the individuals. The women appeared to be younger than the men who were abducted. In all cases, they were lone travelers.

"What happened to their belongings?"

"Most of them were abducted with their belongings. I can't recall an exception. Mostly they had few possessions. I saw a young woman, real small-like and frail walk to the very spot where you sat last night. She wore a red print dress that dragged the ground. It was the strangest thing. She raised her arms toward the sky, and they took her. It was as though she was expecting them to come for her."

"Did she return?"

"Never saw her again."

"When I saw you last night walk to that boulder and sit down, I was fearful. I was afraid for you. I was sure they were going to take you. That's why I called out to you."

"I'm glad you did. Otherwise, I would have never met such an interesting gentleman."

He smiled but seemed uncomfortable at my compliment, making me think he probably never heard too many kind words. At that moment, I felt extremely sad for him, but I wondered what it would be like to live such a life. Knowing I could not dwell on my feelings, I continued my questioning.

"Did you ever talk to any of the abductees once they returned?"

"A few times, but none of them appeared to remember their encounter. I never really asked. Several were disoriented. I remember one young man. Told me he was from Akron, Ohio, and had been hitchhiking around the country. He said he fell asleep and when he woke up he didn't know where he was. Later that night, he became quite delirious with a high fever."

"Do you think it was the result of his abduction?"

"Hell, heck yes. There was no question, but I didn't want to tell him that. He was suffering enough."

"So what did you do?"

"I gave him some Indian medicine I learned from my grandmother. I kept him in my camp for two days. On the third morning, his fever broke and he was fine. He took me out to breakfast, and after that, he left. Mostly the abductees are faceless and don't seem to remember anything."

"What do you think happens to those who do not return?"

"I try not to think about it. I know what they are capable of from experience."

"Of the five abducted, how many women never returned?"

"Four men and the young woman in the red dress."

"Does your friend, Roger keep a notebook, too?"

"Oh, yes. In fact, he told me at last count there were fourteen near Phoenix who have not returned. Phoenix is a hotbed for abductions. Young kids partying, wandering around. Fourteen that did not return."

He shook his head as if in disbelief.

"Do you think that only the Greys visit earth?"

"I'm not sure about that. All I know are the Greys, and I want nothing to do with them."

"Why do you call them the Greys?"

"Because they have grey skin. Ugly bastards, but the strength of ten men. After I got back from Vietnam, Roger showed me some things he found out about them. He showed me pictures at the library. He said these were the guys who took us, and he was right. Buggy-eyed monsters."

Shortly before noon, Jimmy and I said our goodbyes. He asked me to stay another night, and since I had the time, I tried to get another parking permit, but they were all reserved, so it was time for me to move on.

I hated leaving Jimmy that day. Of all the people I had met during my travels, Jimmy touched my heart. Before I left Death Valley, I gave him an envelope with my phone number and a prepaid phone card I always carried with me. Inside the envelope, I placed some money and a note, which read: "Thanks for being a watcher." Although I haven't seen him since that night, I have a post office box number where I send him messages. I know he gets them because he has called me twice. He still keeps his vigil as a watcher. He tells me that Roger recently got an apartment and has invited him to move to Phoenix. He is seriously considering it. He has promised to keep in touch. On my next trip to Arizona, I hope to meet Roger, too.

CHAPTER 15
WE ARE THE PROTECTORS

There have been many cases where several credible individuals, including business owners, police officers, retired academics, and others, have witnessed an unknown object taking up water from a lake, a river, or the ocean. Some witnesses describe a column of fog, mist, haze, or water ascending from the surface of the water up to the craft. The terminology used in the description of the observation is "sucking up water." Researcher Bob Pratt wrote about a sailing ship that was forced to slow because of another boat in their path. When they got closer, they realized that it was a UFO sucking up a column of water about as wide as the UFO. Several shipboard witnesses reported a UFO about six meters off the surface of the ocean that was sucking water. Bruce Maccabee and Ed Walters reported similar events in their 1997 book, UFOs are Real: Here's the Proof.*

In this chapter you will meet an elderly father and son who report a history of visitations to their ranch by UFOs that collect water.

I had known Scott for over ten years when one afternoon he told me about a UFO that frequented his brother's ranch and the Star People who stopped there. Both Scott and his older brother, Walter, grew up on the reservation, but only Scott, who was too young for Vietnam, had chosen to marry a local girl and remain there. Walter, on the other hand, who had been drafted right out of high school, took nearly twenty years to return to the land of his birth.

"My brother Walter owns a place that juts up next to the reservation. After our Dad took sick, I moved my family into the home place, and Walter took Dad to live with him on his ranch."

"How old is your father?"

"He will be ninety-two in June."

"And Walter?"

"Sixty-eight."

"Any children?"

"None."

"Do you think Walter would talk to me about his experiences?"

"I'll see if I can get in touch with him. Sometimes I catch him in town in the afternoons."

He reached for his cellphone and walked outside. Within minutes he was back. "He's at the cafe. If we hurry, we can catch up with him."

As we entered the cafe, Scott pointed to a man sitting in a back booth with a black cowboy hat. "That's him."

When we approached the booth, Walter stood, took off his hat, and shook my hand. He placed his hat on the bench beside him. I was impressed that he felt it appropriate to take his hat off, a gesture most men had forgotten.

"It's a good thing you caught me," he said looking at me. "I planned on heading home as soon as I finished lunch. I don't come to the reservation often."

"I'm glad we caught up with you, bro," Scott said. "The doctor here wants to talk to you about the Star People."

Walter looked up from his plate of French fries. A small frown crossed his forehead.

"Scott and I have been talking about UFOs and Star People," I explained. "He says the Star People visit you at your place. Could you tell me more about it?"

Walter looked around the restaurant. After he was sure there was no one within range of our voices, he spoke.

"I don't like talking about the Star People. Dad and I protect them, but seeing Scott thinks it okay, I will consider it." He paused and drained his coffee cup. The waitress appeared immediately and refilled it.

"Who are you anyway?" he asked. "An anthropologist or a

busy-body?" A sly grin crossed his face.

"She's a writer, Walter," Scott said. She writes books about UFOs and Indians. I've known her a long time. She's okay."

"That's even worst. I don't want to be in a book. First thing I know, people will come around looking for aliens and taking photos. I don't live on reservation land so I can't count on the tribal police escorting them off my place."

"I will never reveal where you live or your name," I said. "Your story is safe with me."

"I'm a private person, and I don't like talking to people," Walter explained.

"I promise I'll never reveal your identity."

"Are you staying over the weekend?"

"Yes."

"Then be ready by 6. If I show, then that means I will talk to you. If not, just go back to wherever you came from."

He picked up his hat and placed it squarely on his head.

"In the morning?" I asked.

"Yes. Six a.m. sharp and be ready. I might change my mind if you're late."

"I won't be late," I said.

"Good, I don't take to women who are always late. My wife was never late."

The next morning, I was up at 5 a.m. Walter pulled into the parking lot moments before 6 a.m. I didn't give him a chance to get out of the pickup before I was out the door. I wasn't sure whether I should talk or stay quiet as we sped down the highway and off the reservation. Walter broke the silence.

"The first time I ever left the reservation was when the Army drafted me. I ended up in Vietnam, and it changed my life forever. I didn't come home when I got out of the service."

"How long did you stay away?"

"Twenty years. The war changed me. I was barely twenty-one when I got out. Hell, I didn't even know who I was. For years I roamed around, visiting other vets trying to make sense of what happened over there. Then one day, I wanted to see my brother and dad. I was in New Orleans and I started hitchhiking." He slowed the pickup and reached for a pack of cigarettes. He popped the cigarette lighter on the dash and waited for it to get hot.

"About three hours from the reservation, a woman stopped in a battered old pickup. She asked if I needed a job. I nodded and the rest is history."

"So you never made it home?"

"She hired me to work for her. She owned a seven hundred acre spread and was trying to run it alone. She gave me a home. It was the first time in years that I felt like I belonged again. Eventually we married. She died of cancer a few years back, but I never married again. Don't plan to. I married for life."

Although in his late sixties, Walter was still a handsome man. He stood a little shy of six feet tall, but his cowboy boots added a couple of inches to his height. His black hair was parted in the middle and rested on his shoulders. He wore a bear tooth around his neck, which he claimed was a trophy from the first bear he killed when he was twelve years old. A silver belt bucket revealed a champion bronco rider in his high school days. On his left hand, which was calloused from working on the ranch, he still wore a wedding ring although his wife had died seven years earlier.

"It keeps the women at bay," he said, chuckling as he referred to the gold band. "But then again, they're not standing in line for the likes of me."

"So when does your ranch begin?" I asked.

"Right over this hill and as far as you can see. It is a beautiful place. Many people would like to get their hands on it, but it will be over my dead body."

"And this is the place where the Star People come?" I asked.

"I don't know how much Scott told you, but my family has had a longtime relationship with the Star People. It goes back generations to my great-grandfather, my grandfather, my father, and now me."

"And will it continue when you are gone?"

"I hope so. I hope Brandon will take over."

"Brandon?"

"My nephew. Scott's son."

"Is the ranch where you had your first encounter?" I asked.

"No. They used to come to my dad's place on the reservation. Scott lives there now. But now that Dad is with me, they stop at my place. It's better on my land. It's far from the prying eyes of neighbors or the highway."

"I'm looking forward to seeing your ranch," I said, as he slowed and made a left hand turn off the main highway.

"By the way, my dad might think you're my wife. He's suffering from Alzheimer's. His long-term memory is great, but he forgets people, their names, and can't remember what he did yesterday. I'm sure he'll like you. And don't be surprised if he wants to keep close to you. He keeps asking me about my wife, Lily."

"I can handle it," I said. "Don't worry."

As promised, we pulled into the driveway at 9 a.m., exactly two hours after leaving the reservation town. When we pulled into the front yard of the ranch house, a black snake was sunning itself on the concrete slab designed as a carport. I watched as it slithered away into the tall grass. The ranch land was mostly rolling hills as far as the eye could see with several meadows of good pastureland. A band of trees that served as a windbreak on the west side of the house stood at attention. A small vegetable garden near the rear of the house brimmed with red tomatoes and zucchini. Pumpkins vines with pumpkins of all sizes had taken over the chicken fence, which surrounded a dilapidated chicken coop. A dozen or more hens ran to the fence as I approached. Clearly they were more like pets than stock animals.

"Come, I want you to meet my father, Sam. He's the reason the UFOs come. When he passes, it will be my turn."

We walked into the small living room. A couch, coffee table, a lamp table, and a TV completed the décor. The kitchen was an eat-in kitchen. His father sat at the table drinking coffee.

"There you are," his father said as he stood up. "I've been looking for you."

I walked toward him and accepted his embrace.

"I wish you would quit traveling for that job," he said, "and stay out here with us. We sure miss a woman's touch."

I looked at Walter knowingly. I was glad he had warned me.

"It's good to be home," I said as he released his embrace.

"Dad, we're going outside to look at the spot where the Star Men come," Walter said.

"I want to go, too," Sam said.

Walter looked at me and shrugged his shoulders. Sam steadied himself and with the energy of a man half his age, brushed by us, and we followed him out the door.

"We'll take the pickup," Walter said as we walked outside. I climbed inside the cab and straddled the gearshift, while Walter boosted his father into the seat beside me.

"The place they come is over those hills," Walter said, pointing toward the north.

We drove no more that fifteen minutes when Walter brought the pickup to a stop.

"This is where they come," he said as we came to a butte overlooking several stock ponds that dotted the landscape below. "We catch the run-off from the snow in the ponds. They provide water for the livestock during the summer. In the winter, we use our wells."

Walter opened the door and ran around to the passenger door to help his father. I slid under the steering wheel and walked to the edge of the butte.

"That's one of the reasons they come here," Sam said, as he came to my side. "There is water here. They need water just like humans."

"When did you first encounter the Star People?" I asked.

"The first time I saw them was when I was about four or five," Walter explained. "Dad took me there. He said he wanted me to meet his friends. When we arrived, they were at the stock pond taking water onto their ship. I asked them what they were doing, and they took me and Dad on their spaceship and showed me how they stored the water."

"How do they store water?" I asked

"In the walls," Sam said. "The walls of the ship are hollow, and they fill the walls with water. The water serves as an insulator, a cooling agent when combined with certain chemicals, and drinking water after the chemicals are filtered out."

"They told you this?" I asked.

"That and much more," Sam said.

"Can you explain?"

"They say humans don't use knowledge for the good of the species," Walter interjected. "They are bound by selfishness. They told me solutions to the universe's greatest problems have already been solved, but the cures are not made public because they're not profitable for those in power. In the world of the Star People, everything is for the good of all, not the few."

"It used to be that way with the Indian," Sam said, "before the white man came."

"Did they tell you what kinds of problems had been solved?"

"Diseases," Sam replied. "Old age. The use of water as fuel instead of oil. Many things."

"Let's talk about the water. Isn't the water too heavy for them to lift off the ground?" I asked.

"That's another thing. On liftoff, the water acts as a propulsion system to help them, and once they are in space, the water is converted for other uses," Sam said, smiling. "Isn't that genius?"

"As you can see," Walter said, "Dad has had a long term relationship with the Star People. The Star People tell him many things."

"It runs in the family," Sam said. "My grandfather, too."

"Sam, how old were you when you first saw the Star People?"

"I think it would be better to ask me how old I was when I first met them. It is one of my first memories. My grandfather, who would be Walter's great-grandfather, introduced me to them. They called him Four Stars, by the way. The night he was born, four spacecraft appeared over the camp. They looked like stars from the distance and he was named for them. Four Stars held my hand and took me on board the spaceship. I was four or five years old. I am ninety-two, so it was back in the early 1900s."

"So you have had a long history of encounters," I said, looking at Walter, who smiled and did not interrupt his father.

"We are the protectors," Sam said. "There are people like us all over the world, generations of families who protect the Star Visitors. They can come and go on Earth and are protected from the authorities. They need places to land, collect water, check and repair their ships. We protect them while they carry out their business. My grandfather and my father was a protector. I am a protector. Walter is a protector."

"Does the military not see them on radar?" I asked.

"That's another way they use water. They do something with the water to make their ships invisible to radar."

"Our military could certainly use that secret," Walter interjected.

"What can you tell me about the Star People?" I asked.

"They look human," Sam replied. "Some are fair and some are dark like me. Some have dark brown hair like yours and some have white hair. They have no freckles. Their skin is perfect. They don't talk much. They make conversation by thinking. At first I didn't understand, but they taught me to think my responses and then they think their responses. It is easy once you get a hang of it."

"Is there anything different about their physical body?"

"None that I can think of," Sam said, as he reached for my hand and held it.

"Yes, there is," Walter said. "They have long arms, longer than humans and long fingers that allow them much more flexibility with their hands. I watched them work with their hands and I could not duplicate what they do. Their skulls seem longer than humans, too. Their faces are about two or three inches longer than a human face."

"Anything else?"

"Probably the thing that stands out the most," Walter said, "is that they all resemble one another. Like they are all from the same mother and father. It's hard to distinguish one from another."

"For me," Sam said, "the strangest thing is that they can disappear. Humans can't disappear. Except for you. Tell me daughter, where do you go when you disappear?"

"It's okay, Dad," Walter said. "She's home now. So don't worry."

I ignored Sam's question. "What else can you tell me about the Star Men?"

"They carry no weapons. They have no formal religion. I offered to teach them about the Great Spirit. They like Bible stories. I tell them Bible stories and old Indian legends. They like those stories."

When we returned to the house, Walter led his father to a chair on the patio. Sam insisted that I move my chair to his side. Walter moved the chair and I sat down.

"You will have to excuse Dad. I can vouch for him about everything except the Bible stories. I'm not sure about them," Walter said, looking at his father.

"Did they ever tell you anything about their food?"

"Plant based foods," Sam said. "They grow plants and make their food on board their ship. It's like baby food and is tasteless to me."

"I think food for them is just to nourish their body," Walter added, "not to enjoy food. I don't think I could live on their planet. They eat the stuff they grow. They don't eat or drink for pleasure, only for nourishment."

"In their world," Sam said, "water is not as plentiful as on earth, so they've learned to use and reuse it in their society. That's the reason as I understand there are multiple uses for the same water."

"Do they visit regularly?"

"There's no schedule," Walter said. "We never know when they will come. I have been away a longtime, and I am relearning all the things I had forgotten about Star People. Dad is a good teacher when he is not in one of his Alzheimer's fogs. He believes they will come for him before he dies and take him away where he will complete his life in their world. He will not have Alzheimer's there. If he is right, I will be happy for him."

After a lunch of grilled hamburgers and corn from the garden, Walter took his father inside to rest. On the way back to town, Walter talked about his childhood.

"It wasn't an ordinary life," he said. "I grew up thinking it was ordinary, but before I left for boarding school, my grandfather and father sat me down and told me the importance of being a protector. I was told never to reveal anything about the Star Men."

"Did your wife know about the Star People?"

"No, it's something I kept to myself. She wasn't an open-minded person. She was a good person, a good Catholic. I think the Star People would have made her lose all faith, and I didn't want that for her. If there is a white person's heaven, I'm sure she's there."

"I'm curious about something." I said. "If your great grandfather was a protector, and then your grandfather and your father, and now you—what will you do if Brandon does not choose to be a protector?"

"That's a good question. Would you like the job?" he asked, smiling.

I laughed at the question, not knowing how to respond.

"I hope it will be Brandon, but if not, Scott has an eleven-year-old. Chase loves horses and ranching. He's a great little bull rider. He's already won several trophies and has a bank account larger than me." He laughed softly. "He loves this ranch. He spends most of his summer's here. I've talked to Scott. He's open to his son taking over this place and becoming the next protector. This summer, Dad and I will introduce him to the Star People. If his reaction is what we expect, I will have that heir. He will be a good one. He's a responsible boy, even at eleven years old."

"So why do you think the Star Men left the home place where Scott lives?"

"Once Dad moved to my place, the Star Men moved here. The connection is with the elder of the family. My dad is like a young man when he is with them. He has great long-term memory. It's the short-term memory that is the problem. He will forget tomorrow that you visited and will be wondering where Lily is. He says the Star Men will take him before he passes. They call him, old friend."

I see Walter about once a year. His father is ninety-four and still functioning. He has his days when he is mentally in another world, but when the Star Men arrive, he is like a young man. He has never wavered in his belief the Star Men will come for him before he passes over, and lately he has been looking forward to it. Chase, Walter's young nephew, is now living full time with him and is being home-schooled. He loves the ranch and has taken his responsibility as a protector in stride. Walter told me that when they last visited, they took him on a tour of their spacecraft. Brandon has moved to Albuquerque and enrolled in art school. Meanwhile, the Star People have begun calling Walter an old friend, too.

CHAPTER 16
MY DAUGHTER IS NOT MINE

In 1987 abduction researcher Budd Hopkins suggested that not only were genetic materials being removed from abductees, but also that females were being impregnated and the fetus removed around the third or fourth month of gestation. Hopkins further speculated that even "normal" human babies born to abductee mothers might have undergone genetic modification by the aliens.

In this chapter, you will meet a woman who, unable to get pregnant, found herself expecting a child after she encountered a UFO.

Mary grew up on a reservation in the Southwest. She graduated from a state college at the age of twenty-two and decided to take an administrative job with an Indian social program in Phoenix. She worked in that position for twenty years before I met her. She and I were seated together at a luncheon honoring Indian women leaders. I was invited to speak to the group about my book, *Sisters in the Blood*. As we waited for dessert, an elder across the table asked me if I was still collecting UFO stories. I nodded. "Meet me after your talk. I want you to meet someone."

I nodded again.

Mary leaned toward me and whispered, "When you have some time, I have a UFO story that you will probably not believe."

While I hadn't expected such revelations to come my way at the luncheon, I was more than happy to follow up on them.

The next day, I went to Mary's office a few minutes before noon. She had invited me to hear her story over lunch. I was ushered into a small conference room and an inside door opened. "I took the liberty of ordering lunch. I'm so happy you came."

I sat down at the table. She asked her secretary to hold all calls for the next two hours as she walked to the door and locked it. Mary was an attractive woman in her mid-forties. Her black, curly hair had been dyed to give her reddish-brown highlights. Before she sat down, she took off her blazer and carefully hung it on the back of a chair. While slightly overweight, she appeared comfortable with her curvy figure. She was the mother of a fourteen-year-old daughter and a widow. Her husband died in a car crash six months before Cherie was born. Since then, Mary had been devoted to her job and her daughter.

"I've heard about you," she said as she reached for a can of Pepsi. "I've wanted to tell you my story, but the opportunity never came. I want to find out if you have heard similar stories to mine. I warn you that if someone told me the story I am going to tell you, I would not believe it myself, but I swear to you, it is true. It has consumed me since my daughter, Cherie, was an infant."

"Don't worry. I've heard some strange stories."

Mary nodded and indicated I should choose a sandwich.

"My first encounter happened about twelve years ago. My daughter and I live on the outskirts of the city. My husband built a house in a small rural development outside Phoenix. Nothing pretentious. Just a small house for the three of us. My husband wanted us to have our own home before the baby was born. After he was killed by a drunk driver, my friends and family wanted me to move to the city, or at least into an apartment in Phoenix, but I liked my house. My husband built that house for me and Cherie, and I was not about to give it up. I convinced my mother, Pearl, to come live with us. She was alone; no need for all of us to live alone."

"Your husband sounds amazing. But please, tell me why you invited me here."

"One evening I was driving home. It was winter, so it was dark. I had stopped off to pick up dinner and Cherie from the Montessori School. She was only two, but they allowed two year olds in the program three days a week. On other days, my mother took care of her. I was on the road headed home, when I saw a stationary light up ahead near the highway. Although it appeared low to the ground, I thought it as a plane from the airbase. Then as I got closer, I realized it was not a plane. This light was motionless."

"What did you do?"

"I knew there had to be some rational explanation so I drove toward the light. It never occurred to me that I was dealing with a UFO."

"When did you realize it was a UFO?" I asked.

"I was driving along and suddenly the blinding light disappeared, but at the same time my headlights went out. Then the dashboard lights faded, and the car stopped. Fortunately, I guided the car to the side of the road when the headlights went out. I got out of the car, unstrapped Cherie from her car seat, and decided to walk. We were no more than a mile from the house. The night was clear and the moon was bright. I told myself I could make it."

"But at this point, do you know there is a UFO?"

"No, I just think I'm having a streak of bad luck. I was long overdue for a new car and I'd had similar problems with it."

"So what did you do?"

"I decided that instead of walking down the highway, I would cut through the neighbors' field. I thought I could cut a quarter mile off the walk, and Cherie was a little heavy to carry a mile. I was about halfway across the field when the light returned. This time I realized it was no plane or helicopter. A light searched the ground all around us. When it fell on us, it stopped."

She paused and took a bite of her sandwich.

"The next thing I know I'm on board a spacecraft, and I don't know how I got there."

"And Cherie?"

"She's with me, but they are telling me she doesn't belong to me."

"Who is telling you?"

"I don't know. They are saying she belongs to them. I remember screaming at the top of my lungs at the voices in my head."

"Did you see them?" I asked.

"Fleeting glimpses, nothing more."

"Then what happened?"

"They returned me to Earth. In fact, they placed me in front of my door with Cherie in my arms."

She paused again and sipped her Pepsi. She pushed back her chair from the table. I saw her eyes water.

"And you aren't going to believe this. My car was parked in the driveway."

She got up, looked at me, and held her hands up to stop me from speaking. "I know it sounds impossible. But it is true. At that moment, I was overcome with pain. I sat on the doorstep and cried. Cherie was trying to comfort me, but at that moment, seeing my car in the driveway, I knew how powerful they were."

She walked to her desk, got a tissue, and wiped her eyes.

"Sorry," she said. "I get a little emotional when I think about that night."

"Is there anything I can do?" I asked.

She shook her head. "I'm okay. It's just that I'm emotional. When you hear the rest of the story, you will understand."

"Have you seen them since that first incident?"

"Many times. The next time was when Cherie was four. It was the same. But this time, instead of walking through the fields, I stayed on the highway, and they took us onboard their ship. They took Cherie from me, and the same, chilling voice filled my head and told me that Cherie was not mine. Afterwards, the two of us would be in the car with the engine running. I began to think I was losing my mind."

"Did they ever say anything else to you?"

"Yes. When Cherie was six they took us—it was like clockwork, every two years at the beginning—then they came every year."

"Was their communication different after she was six?"

"Yes, that year, it was different. They took us into a room, and there they repeated what they had been telling me: that Cherie was not my daughter. They explained that I only provided a means for her birth on Earth. They reminded me how I had been told by doctors that I could not have children."

"Was that true?"

"Yes, my husband, Dean, and I had been trying to have children for seven years and nothing happened. A few months before he was killed, I got pregnant. These aliens, these star people or whatever you call them, said that they knew how much I wanted a child, so they gave me one. But only to keep while she was a child. When she became a woman, she was to go with them."

"Did they tell you when she would become a woman?"

"When she is seventeen. She is fourteen now. I only have her for three more years, and then she will be gone. I don't know what I am going to do. Do you think if I move away from here that they will not find me? I have been thinking about New Mexico or Oklahoma. There are many Indians there. Maybe I can lose myself in the desert."

She paused, her body shook, and she broke down in tears.

"I don't know what I will do without my baby."

She melted into sobs at the thought of life without Cherie. After a few moments, she wiped her tears. "I'm sorry," Mary said. "I needed to talk with you. Has anyone else every told you a similar story in Indian country?"

"Never. I have never heard anything even slightly related."

"I'm so frightened of losing my baby," she said.

"Mary, I think you need to talk to a psychologist. Perhaps it would help you get through these events."

"So you don't believe me!"

"No, Mary. I didn't say that. I . . ."

"I knew I shouldn't say anything. They warned me."

"What do you mean, they warned you."

"They said if I told anyone, they wouldn't believe me."

"Mary, it is not that I don't believe you, but I think someone could help you deal with this. You need a friend. . ."

"I wanted you to be my friend."

"I am your friend, and I will help you in any way I can."

For the next four months, I talked with Mary weekly on the phone. Although her main story stayed the same, occasionally she elaborated. On my next visit to the Southwest, I stayed at Mary's house outside Phoenix. I had no sooner walked inside her home than she began to share additional information about the UFO travelers.

"They told me they were collecting young women from all over the world. They are the same age as Cherie," she said as she handed me a Diet Pepsi.

"Why?"

"They haven't told me yet. All I know is that single mothers have raised all the girls. They have no other relatives except a grandmother. No siblings, no cousins, no fathers."

"But there must be a reason."

"They have not told me yet."

"But you seemed to be calmer. Are you accepting the situation?"

"Cherie tells me I have nothing to worry about. She said they told her that I would always be with her. Cherie believes them. She thinks it is an adventure."

"Do you believe them?"

"I don't know, so I don't think about it."

Six months later, I was in Phoenix. I stayed at Mary's over the weekend. Mary's mother was visiting a friend on the reservation, and Cherie had a sleepover with a friend in the city.

"I have something to tell you," Mary said. "My mother talks about meeting them."

"Are you telling me that your mother, Pearl, is being abducted by the aliens?"

"Yes."

"Why?"

"I'm not sure. They haven't told me, and if Mother knows she doesn't tell me. I do know that she appears younger and healthier."

"Tell me about that."

"It's hard to explain, but I know she gets around better. She can out walk me at Walmart and Costco. The doctor has taken her off her high blood pressure and diabetes medicine."

"Has she changed her diet?"

"She has become a vegetarian. So has Cherie. I can't get into it. I still like my roast beef and hamburgers."

"Perhaps that explains it."

"Perhaps," Mary said.

I didn't see Mary for eight months. Cherie was now sixteen. When I told her I was coming to Phoenix the following week, I could have sworn she thought my visit would be an inconvenience, but I said nothing. When I showed up on her doorstep, she welcomed me with a smile. In my absence, she has lost about fifty pounds. While I marveled at her transformation, she bounced around the kitchen like a teenager. I watched as she poured a glass of white wine and offered me one. "I will miss wine," she said.

"What do you mean?" I asked as I sat down at the kitchen bar.

"They said I can go, too."

I saw the excitement on her face.

"When did they tell you?"

"Four months ago. They told me I had to prepare myself. Thus the weight loss."

She stood and twirled around the kitchen floor showing off her new body.

"I had to give up all meat. Only vegetables and fruit. You should try it," she said.

"Why?"

"Where we are going, there will be no meat. We will live on fruits and vegetables."

"Tell me exactly what they told you."

"They told me to get my things in order, because if I wanted to go with Cherie, I was welcome to go. Even my mother is being invited."

"Mary, do you know what you are doing? What have they told you?"

"Not much. But it is for good reason."

"I don't understand."

"They don't want us talking about it, but I'm taking a chance with you. Don't write about this until I'm gone. Promise."

"I promise."

"This is what they explained to me. They call themselves 'Seeders.' They travel the universe looking for livable planets. Once they find one, if it is devoid of life, they populate it. They have tried populating planets with adults from Earth, but their experiments never worked out. They have discovered that adult males often take violence, vengeance, and greed and take them to another planet."

"So they have decided to select women with no relatives, other than a grandmother, help them become pregnant with a hybrid baby, and take them to another planet. Is that what you are telling me, Mary?"

"Not exactly. Cherie is one-hundred-percent human. She is Dean's daughter and my daughter, but she also has implanted within her some of their DNA. They just made her birth possible to a childless couple who wanted a daughter, but at the same time wanted to see if they could influence human behavior. They decided the female was more acceptable for this test than the male."

"What would have happened if Dean had lived? Would they have taken him, too?"

"I don't think so. Women will only populate this planet. They will take care of procreation without men. We will develop a society, a world, free of war and hatred."

"What will happen in this world when baby boys are born?"

"I asked them the same question. They said they would make sure no boys were born. This is an experiment."

"Do you think you will be happy in such a world?" I asked

"I do. I look around and I see that men cause ninety percent of the pain, heartache, and violence. I see women working every day to support men. I see men taking their money and spending it on alcohol and drugs. Oh, yes, it is definitely a world I would like to join. My mother, too."

"Mary, I'm worried about this. Are you sure, you know what you are doing? And what about Cherie? Don't you want her to grow up here among her friends and go to college and marry?"

"Cherie wants to go. She has already made friends with some of the girls who will go on the trip with us. She's excited."

"But you're her mother."

"Yes, and that's why I'm going. I can't lose my baby. I have no choice."

For a moment, I thought I noted sadness in her voice, but then in an instance she changed into the exuberant person who met me at the front door.

"I wanted to wait to tell you all this, but I will be leaving soon."

"What about your house?"

"I've already taken care of that. I've given it to a charity that helps young Indian girls. They will take possession in two months."

"Two months. Are you leaving in two months?"

"Not sure. I only know that we are supposed to be ready in two months and, no, you cannot come to see me off. I know what you're thinking."

Mary and I spent the weekend together. She looked forward to the next stage in her life, and there was nothing I could say or do to change her eagerness to embark on this new venture. At the end of the weekend, I was not sure I wanted to try. I continued to stay in contact with Mary over the next two months. After that, her phone was no longer in service.

I have not seen Mary since that weekend. When I returned to Phoenix six months later, another woman sat at her desk. When I inquired about Mary, I was told that she had moved away. She did not leave a forwarding address. For months, I could not get Mary out of my mind. Every time the phone rang, I expected to hear her voice on the other end; the call never came. I have repeatedly asked people who knew her if they have ever heard from her. I even went to Pearl's ancestral village, but no one had seen her. When I look at the stars at night, I think of Mary, Cherie, and Pearl and a world inhabited by women. That is when I try to imagine a world without men. The truth is, I like and respect the men in my world and could not imagine being happy without them in my life.

CHAPTER 17
MASTERS OF DECEIT

The term "alien abduction" describes claims of humans being kidnapped by extraterrestrials. The first alien abduction narrative to be widely publicized was the Betty and Barney Hill case in 1961. Since then, the credibility and mental health of abductees have been questioned.

Skeptics argue that the phenomenon is nothing more than vivid dreams occurring in a state of sleep paralysis. UFOlogists maintain the commonalities of the experiences serve to reinforce the claims of the abductees. Many abductees report repeated abductions that begin as early as two years old and continue into middle age.

In this chapter, a teacher in a rural Montana town sheds light on the encounters between aliens and humans.

I knew there was something extraordinary about Drew the first time I met her. She stood about five feet ten, but it was her outgoing personality and natural wit that made her stand out. She moved to the small Montana town shortly after graduating from college accepting a job as the high school English teacher. Arapaho and Lakota by birth, a white family adopted Drew when she was two weeks old. When she was twenty-four, she found her birth mother, who lived on a reservation in South Dakota. While they attempted to make amends, the fact that her mother refused to acknowledge her publicly, or introduce her to four siblings as her daughter, dashed all hope for reconciliation.

"Living in a rural town carries many responsibilities. Sometimes too many, but I can't leave," Drew said as we shared a table in the school cafeteria. "I'm bound to this place. I'm not sure I will ever be able to leave."

From my records, I knew that Drew had been living and teaching for seven years in this small community. "I'm not sure I understand. The same road that brought you here is the one that will take you away," I said, not realizing the gravity of her statement. She did not respond to my comment.

"Are you free tonight?" she asked. "I made a pie last night. Would you like to stop by around seven? I have something I want to share with you."

I arrived at Drew's house at seven. She welcomed me inside and led me to a kitchen table, which had already been prepared with two place settings, a pot of tea, and her promised apple pie.

"What brought you to this town in the first place?" I asked, as Drew served the pie.

"It was both my birth mother and a spirit of adventure. I grew up in Chicago. I was the only Indian in the private schools I attended; a square peg trying to fit into a round hole." She paused and smiled. "I always had this romanticized idea about the west and when I found my birth mother, I'd hoped things would work out. It was difficult. I wanted a family; she wanted to forget about the part of her life that included me. She had a stroke two years after I moved here so our relationship was never resolved."

"I'm sorry to hear that."

"I took this job, hoping that in time she would change her mind, but it didn't happen."

"I'm sure that was difficult for you. Do you have a support group? A social life?"

"There's no man in my life, if that's what you're asking. All the bachelors in the area are either eighteen or over sixty. My work is my life."

"You mentioned that you can't leave. If you have no social life and you aren't married, why would you stay? What keeps you here?"

"It's complicated. As you know, I've become good friends with my principal, Barry, and his wife. One night after a barbecue, we were outside enjoying the night and talking. The conversation turned to you. Barry told me that you were one of his professors at Montana State." She paused again and then looked at me intently. "He also told me that you collect stories about UFO encounters."

"That's true. I've been collecting stories ever since I moved to Montana."

"Barry told me about your books. I found them on Amazon. I read them and fell in love with them. I have bought about fifty books over the past seven years about UFO encounters, but I connected with yours the most. You told the stories with such sensitivity. I was impressed. It made me want to tell you my story."

"Do you have a story about UFOs?" I asked.

"I do, but it is different from the stories in your books."

"Do you mind if I tape it?" I asked.

"I don't object, but if you put me in a book, please don't use my name or the name of the school."

"You have my word," I promised.

"First of all, I want to make it clear, I'm not crazy. I'm not given to hallucinations. I don't sleep walk, and I rarely dream. My encounters never happen in a bedroom or in my house. I'm definitely not interested in publicity or notoriety. That's the last thing I need. I would probably never be able to teach again. The kids would never stop teasing me, and my life would become unbearable. But what I am about to tell you is true. I swear on a stack of Bibles it is true, and I take that oath seriously."

"When did you have your experience?" I asked.

"Seven years ago. They have been regular ever since."

"Would that be from the time you arrived here until the present time?"

"Yes. It always occurs when I'm alone, always at night. It happens when I'm driving on a deserted highway mostly. I've encountered them three or four times a year."

"Have you read books on alien abduction?"

"Budd Hopkins, John Mack, and Whitley Strieber."

"So you know that people will say your story is influenced by what you have read."

"Yes, I know, but that doesn't mean it isn't true. I think the aliens choose people like me because they don't want witnesses. They find a woman or a man, or even a couple driving at night on some rural highway, and abduct them. No one will ever know and if you do remember, who's going to believe you? It's the way they operate."

"So are you saying that you do not believe their abductions are random?"

"No. I believe they are random to the point that it is easier to abduct someone in Podunk, Montana, than to take someone off the streets of Chicago when there are so many possible witnesses."

"When was the first time you were abducted?" I asked.

"The first time I encountered them was the weekend before school started."

"Were you abducted near here?"

"One of the biggest events of the year is a Fiddler's Fest that is hosted by the chairman of the school board."

She paused when the teakettle on the stove whistled and scurried to the stove. Seconds later, she returned carrying the teapot.

"The Fiddler's Fest begins around noon and ends about midnight or until the last guest has left. The chairman's ranch is only about five miles from here, so I was not concerned about driving late at night. After all, what could happen in a small isolated town in Montana, right?"

"Right."

"When I pulled out of their long driveway, I turned left instead of right. About two miles into the trip, I realized what I had done. I slowed trying to find a place to turn around. Suddenly I saw a light, a bright sphere hovering over the highway in the distance. Initially I dismissed it as the moon, but then reality set in and I knew it was no moon."

She poured a cup of tea and offered sugar and cream.

"As I drove further, the sphere moved from side to side but stayed in front of me. Then it set down on the highway blocking my way. At this point, I became frightened. It was no longer a huge ball of light but a circular object much like spacecraft seen in old science fiction movies. It had a small, domelike rise on the top. It spanned both lanes of the highway. Standing beside the craft were two humanoid creatures."

"Can you describe them?"

"They looked like humans, but they were not. They were about eight feet tall and were dressed in one-piece coveralls. I remember being told to come with them. I pulled the car to the side of the road and got out. I followed them willingly, but I was fully aware of what I was doing. Over time, I realized their appearance was an illusion. They have the ability to control the human mind so that we think they look human, but it is only a false impression."

"Can you explain?"

"This is going to sound outrageous, but it is the truth. Over the past seven years, while they were studying me, I have been studying them. First of all, they do not speak like you and me. They are incapable of speech. They communicate through thoughts. Their ability to control the human mind is incomprehensible. They can make you believe almost anything."

"Can you give me an example?"

"One of the things that struck me over the years is that they are not benevolent creatures. But they are able to convince abductees that they are compassionate and benign through mind control. That allows them to carry out their bizarre experiments and leave their victims feeling they are privileged or chosen. They often implant the idea that they are helpful aliens who bring messages of peace and warnings about the environment. These are all planted ideas to make the abductees appear special."

"How did you come to this conclusion?"

"Beginning with my first encounter, I was fascinated with the fact that they spoke through thoughts. After all, I'm an English teacher and words are my world. I always tell my students, I have never met a word I didn't like."

"So did you ask them about their manner of communication?"

"Oh, yes. They said I was the first human to ask this question, and they were more than willing to respond to my questions. They told me that in their world, the inhabitants never used speech. It was not an evolutionary thing as some scientists suggest, but they have never used oral speech. They considered oral language babble and very annoying."

"So our messages sent into outer space fall on deaf ears, so to speak. Is that what you are saying?"

"Actually, they can hear, but oral language, as humans use it, is not common in the universe. To them, it illustrates the primitive development of the human."

"So they communicate only through thoughts."

"Yes."

"Did you have difficulty communicating with them?"

"At first, but when they discovered my interest in language and communication, they taught me to think what I wanted to say before speaking. When I did that, I realized it was unnecessary to speak. After that, there was no problem."

"Did they perform any tests on you?"

"They took samples of my hair. They used a machine to scan my body. I could see the images on the wall of my insides. It was not like an x-ray, but an actual image of the inside of my body. They were interested in the functions of each organ or at least, as I perceived them. Of course, I didn't have all the answers, but told them I would find out."

"How did they respond to your offer?"

"They showed no emotion, so they simply said it would be valuable information."

"What other characteristics did you notice?"

"They are weak physically, but mentally they are powerful. They control abductees through their mind control. They expect humans to submit to them somewhat like a puppy submits to his master."

"You said they appear as humans…"

"Yes. But they are not human. They just control our minds to make us think they are human."

"Did you see them in their true form?"

"Several times. There are two groups who work cooperatively. One group is the typical Greys that we hear about and are popularized in contemporary movies. They are gray in color with large heads and eyes with long arms. The common descriptions are quite accurate." She paused and picked up the empty plates and walked to the sink. "The other group is more terrifying. They are giant insect-like creatures. They are not humanoid at all." She paused again, and I saw her shiver. She hugged herself and shook off her chill.

"Drew, are you sure you want to continue?"

"Oh, yes. Just thinking about them makes me uneasy. They are the enforcers for the Greys. When a resistor is abducted, they take over and force the human into compliance. They are powerful physically. They only have three digits on their claw-like hands. They have no neck. Their heads set on top of their bodies and I've seen them swivel their heads three hundred and sixty degrees. They stand about eight feet tall, and they give off a pungent odor. I avoided them as much as possible, but I watched them carefully."

She paused and asked if I would step out onto her back deck. I followed her outside. I saw a match flame and made out the red glow of a cigarette.

"I smoke to settle my nerves. Thinking about the Grasshoppers makes me nervous."

"Are you sure you want to continue?"

"Oh, yes. I don't suffer from PTSD or anything psychologically. Thinking about them just makes my skin crawl."

"Which species abducted you?"

"The Greys."

"But you said your abductors looked like eight-foot-tall humans."

"True, but that was mind control. I learned to keep them out of my mind. Instead of thinking, I talked. They did not like this, but if I talked, it confused them, and they were not able to control me. Sometimes I would sing, 'America the Beautiful' or repeat a poem aloud or just talk about anything. Sometimes I would just think about things to confuse them."

"Did you see any experiments being conducted on humans?"

"Yes. And the stories about harvesting sperm and impregnating human females are true. Not because they are a dying race but because they create a hybrid species for seeding other planets. They also create clones. The hybrids and the clones are used for seeding. Some of the clones are placed on Earth to interact with the human population. They also use adrenal glands from humans, but I've yet to discover their use. I am working on that."

"Someone else mentioned adrenal functioning to me. He said it was for longevity experiments. But what about the seeding?"

"They colonize other worlds with hybrids and clones."

"Why have they allowed you to learn these things about them?"

"First of all, they think they are in control. Secondly, even if I do remember, what am I going to do with this knowledge? I am a teacher in a rural town in Montana. People will say that I've gone crazy living here. Can you imagine what the skeptics would do if I told this story? I think they don't view me as a threat to their presence or the activities they are conducting. I have led them to believe I am under their control. While the majority of Americans believe in UFOs, the majority are still skeptical about hybrid babies and harvesting of eggs and sperm. So they are not threatened that anyone will take me seriously. In fact, they seem to enjoy allowing me to know these things."

"Can you tell me, what is the most amazing thing you've learned about your abductors?"

"They can take any form they wish. If you are a white American, they will plant in your mind the image of a white American. If you are Chinese, they will be Chinese."

"Anything else?"

"There are so many people who hold out the belief that aliens will someday make themselves known to the people of the Earth. The aliens I've met, and admittedly, they are not the only species in the universe visiting Earth, have no intention of making themselves known. The earth is their laboratory. They have no respect for human life. Humans are only a means to an end. They are specimens to use to meet an objective. The aliens I know are inhuman and behave in very inhuman ways."

"What stands out most in your mind about them?"

"I've had more than one occasion to observe them with other abductees. Although they show no emotion, they have little tolerance for resistors. They expect humans to be compliant, and I have watched them be very cruel to those who are not. Some humans have an ability to resist them, others are extremely docile. The resistors get the worst treatment and the most pain. Therefore, I see them as malevolent. On the other hand, I have seen them perform surgeries and heal those who are compliant, but I always get the idea that they do it just to see if they can, like you and I might fix a broken toy. In my opinion, they are vindictive despite the fact that they show no emotion."

"Is there anything else you want to share tonight?"

"Yes. They plant images in the minds of humans. For example, they can make men think they have met the woman of their dreams or vice versa for women when there is no passionate alien female or male. They are objects of the human imagination. They can make an abductees feel their healing is from God's hands when it is no more than advanced medical science. They are masters of deceit."

"So tell me, are these encounters the reason you believe you cannot leave this town?"

"Partly. Each time I have an encounter, I get more insight into their behavior. Perhaps someday this information will be valuable. That is the reason I'm telling you. If you decide to write another book, be sure to include my story. I want the world to know what's really going on. Things are not always what they seem."

"Over the seven years you've been abducted, have you noticed any change in your abductors?"

"There was one difference. I told you about the aliens planting images in the minds of the abductees."

I nodded.

"I discovered how they do it, and the fascinating thing about it is that the younger you are taken, the more effective the conditioning is."

"I don't understand."

"The brain of a seven-year-old is easier to condition than that of a seventeen-year-old or a twenty-seven-year-old or a thirty-seven-year- old. I discovered they rarely abduct anyone beyond the age of forty and that is the reason."

"Please explain."

"They have a machine that they connect to the brain. I think they know more about the human brain than our scientists know. They have discovered a way of planting images into the brain that makes the victim believe that he or she had certain experiences. When an abductee is young, their brains are easier for implants. As we grow, apparently that part of the brain grows smaller and weaker. After forty, it is more difficult to fool the brain. Once they make a connection with a suitable candidate, they continue to abduct him or her over the years. They now have a compliant specimen. Sometimes they abduct entire families because they have discovered that the physical trait of brain compliance is an inherited trait. Therefore, if it is present in one family member, it is likely to be present in all."

"So that is the reason for the ongoing lifetime abduction of the same individuals and the reported family abductions," I said.

"Correct. Children are often planted with the idea of imaginary playmates to throw the parents off from suspecting anything."

"Of course. That makes sense."

"The older a person is, the more likely they will remember the abduction or have flashbacks of the experience."

"How did you discover this?"

"Like I told you, while they were studying me, I was studying them. I've been able to disguise that I am not under their control. Therefore they do not see me as a threat."

"How are you able to do that?"

"I fake compliance. I know they are going to abduct me, so I've led them to believe it works, while at the same time staying alert to what is going on. I have watched other abductees and am able to fake submission."

"There is one question I need to ask you. One of the common themes around abductions often includes sexual activities. Have you witnessed any sexual exploitation of abductees?"

"Yes. One of the things they use is to convince a man that an alien female is sexually arousing him. There is no alien female. It is another implant using the victim's own fantasies. I have seen this technique used as well as machine manipulation."

"Machine manipulation?"

"Yes. They attach a suction-like device to the male private parts and bring about an ejaculation. Both achieve the same purpose."

"What about women and phantom pregnancies and removal of eggs. Is there any truth to those stories?"

"I have seen two things. I have witnessed women abducted and never returned. They become an incubator for hybrid babies, giving birth to several. I have also seen women who are mechanically impregnated and returned to Earth only to be captured again and the fetus removed. I'm not sure how they decide whether they are going to keep the female on board or release her, but I know both practices are common."

"Are men ever kept on board to father children?"

"I have not seen that, but I have seen what appeared to be human captives who are on the ship permanently. I never learned how they achieved this status or role, but I have seen human males cooperating and working with the alien visitors."

"Do you think that those males are willing collaborators?"

"It would seem so, although I never had a chance to talk with them. During my abductions, I was very guarded. I wanted to be fully aware of what was going on and I did not want to give myself away. If they were collaborators, I feared they would expose me."

"Were you ever a victim of sexual abuse?"

"No, I was too skinny, I think." She paused and laughed out loud. "They liked voluptuous women. I think that was their idea of human motherhood. They favor women with broad hips. I didn't have that. I'm built more like a boy." She giggled.

"It sounds like it worked to your advantage."

"In my case, it did."

"Do you have any idea why you were continually abducted?"

"At first, I think they were smitten with my interest in communication and language. Then I became a specimen for aging. They were very interested in how the human body aged, so their experiments on me included taking body samples, hair, swabs, and their infernal machine that examined my internal organs."

"Were you ever in pain?"

"Discomfort, but no pain. The machine was oppressive. Very heavy and emotionally quite frightening. There are times you feel like you are buried alive inside it."

"Another question: How did you conceal that you were not under their control?"

"I simply acted like a zombie. That's how the others appear as though they are devoid of human life. I acted the same way while observing what they were doing."

"Did you see more than one abductee at a time?"

"There were dozens and dozens and dozens. There was a holding area where individuals were taken into separate rooms. There was a huge laboratory where several tests were conducted simultaneously. Each abductee had his or her own set of attendants who were performing tests. I never discovered the purpose of many of their tests. Human reproduction was certainly one. Removal of body fluids was another. Aging process was another. Another was intelligence."

"Intelligence?"

"I think so. Once when they communicated with me, they asked me about brain deterioration in humans. I assumed they were talking about Alzheimer's. They said they had ways of increasing intelligence. They told me such aging diseases did not affect their population."

"Did you see anyone cured of Alzheimer's?"

"No. As I said, I rarely saw older abductees. When I did, they were a part of a family. They appeared uninterested in old people."

"Did they ever tell you anything about their world?"

"No, I was not considered their equal or someone they would want to share information. These aliens were not interested in friendship or cooperation with Earth people. Although I understand why some abductees come forth with stories of benevolent aliens who love Earth and Earth people. Again these stories come from their ability to control the mind of the abductee."

"Do you think they plant these ideas so that the individual is better able to handle what has happened to him if he suddenly becomes aware of the abduction or has some memories of aliens?"

"At first I gave them the benefit of the doubt, but I see it as a way to cast doubt on the individual experience as well as promote a false agenda should the abductee remember the encounter. Why would humans fear benevolent aliens? They want to create a false sense of safety in those who remember."

"And those like you?"

'I think I'm in danger of being eliminated if they ever catch on to what I am doing. I practice keeping thoughts of my observation out of my mind so they cannot tell what I am thinking. I believe if they ever discovered me, I would be eliminated. No one would ever know what happened to me."

"Some abductees say that they have seen military officers on board spacecraft cooperating with aliens. Have you seen any such thing that would lead you to believe that the American military or any other military are cooperating with them?"

"None whatsoever. I have seen abducted military men, men and women in uniform, but they were abductees, not collaborators."

"Another myth about abduction is that individuals are chosen to spread a message to the world or that they are being sent back to become ambassadors for their arrival on Earth. Any evidence that this is true?"

"None. Again, this is a part of the false impressions they use to manipulate people. I believe they draw upon the memory and fantasy of individuals. If you fantasize (and I don't think people are always aware of their buried fantasies) that you are more important than you really are—then you may be led to believe you are chosen. If on the other hand, you fantasize about alien sex, I think they accommodate you. I have no proof of any of this, but over the seven years I have observed them, I believe this is what is going on."

"Have you ever seen anyone you know or knew onboard?"

"Never."

"There are a number of myths associated with abduction. I would like to touch on each one of them and ask for your reaction. For example, most abductees report being taken from their beds in the middle of the night and floated onto a spacecraft. Others suggest sleep paralysis, whereupon you wake but cannot move. Have you ever had such an experience?"

"Never. All of my experiences have happened on the open road, generally in rather quiet two lane roads or remote areas. I have been kidnapped on the Interstate between Glendive and Billings. I have been abducted near Roy, Montana. I was abducted from a campsite two years ago on the Madison River and one time at Greek Creek in the Gallatin Canyon. I was abducted once at Sleeping Buffalo. Are you familiar with those areas?"

I nodded.

"Well then, you know how isolated those areas are. My abductions vary but always seem to be in areas where there are no witnesses. That is the reason I believe that they want no witnesses. They do not want to be known."

"Some researchers maintain that abductees tend to exhibit fantasy proneness, which often begins in childhood. When you were a child, did you have an invisible playmate or do you daydream?"

"There were no invisible or make-believe playmates. My father was a mathematician. My mother was an engineer. Both were PhDs. I grew up in a very black and white world in terms of logic and logical explanations for events."

"One researcher has suggested that mystical psychic experiences and paranormal beliefs contribute to the stories about UFO abduction. What do you think of that theory?"

"Before I moved to Montana, I heard of UFO abductions, but only in passing. I had no interest in the subject. I was grounded in science, not science fiction. I have never been involved in the paranormal, psychic experiences, Ouija boards, or fortune tellers. I was not interested. I don't take drugs and I only drink an occasional glass of wine. I'm a very conservative person who loves life. I don't need to explore unexplained phenomena to be happy. I don't want to know the future. I want to live life."

"But you admit to reading several abduction books."

"After repeated encounters, I bought every book I could find on the subject and read them. That does not make me a weirdo; only a searcher of knowledge."

"Other abductees have claimed that aliens have implanted various objects in their bodies and come to realize they had been abducted. Have you found an implant?"

"No implants," she said laughing. "I have never seen anyone given a physical implant. The only implants I have witnessed are the implants of false memories or experiences."

"Other abductees claim that the aliens have only one purpose. They want to raise human consciousness. Any reaction?"

"I think that is probably the furthest from their plan. They want submissive human specimens, not resistors. They have no interest in improving the mental abilities of humans, although I do believe they have the ability to do so. Keep in mind, I'm speaking only for those extraterrestrials I have encountered, and I believe there are other entities from space visiting Earth with different agenda."

"Many of abduction experiences are only recovered years later, during psychological treatment for other issues. Research has proven that careless psychologists can create false memories in the course of therapy. People can actually come to believe they were abducted or abused when they were not. What is your reaction to that research?"

"I have never seen a psychologist, and I have never been hypnotized. I have never told anyone except you about my encounters. I do not intend to talk about them to a psychologist, and I do not plan to be hypnotized. I have total recall of what happened to me."

Drew and I continue to keep in touch. Two years after our first conversation, she married a former student who was six years her junior. He had returned to take over his father's ranch after graduating from college with a degree in agricultural management. As I write her story, she and her husband, Kent, recently became parents of twin boys. While she now has another reason to stay in the Montana town, her encounters are no longer the focus of her life, despite the fact that they have continued. She hopes when she is forty, her abductions will cease.

CHAPTER 18
I'M NO LONGER A SKEPTIC

Skeptics insist that anecdotal evidence and personal testimonies do not qualify as scientific evidence. Thus, the skeptic generally regards the existence of UFOs and Star People as folklore.

In this chapter, you will meet an individual who described himself as a skeptic, until an unusual encounter made him a believer.

Jonathan moved to Alaska in November 2010 to assume a teaching position in a small community about two hundred miles from Anchorage. I had served as the Chair of Jon's Master's degree program at Montana State.

He was the oldest of my advisees that year, but having spent the last twenty years as a rodeo cowboy he was fitter than the younger men in the program. Coming to the university had been a major change for him and during his first few weeks on campus, he struggled with adjusting. A handsome man who wore a black cowboy hat and expensive western boots, Jonathan was attractive to women of all ages. While familiar to female groupies on the rodeo circuit, he had not expected such a distraction in academia and would often end up in my office to discuss what he called his "female problems."

After two years in Alaska, Jon returned to Bozeman on the first day of summer classes, called my office, and invited me to lunch. We met for lunch at Ted's, a local restaurant in the city. While I was expecting to hear about his "female problems" with Alaska Native women, he surprised me with a story of a different nature.

"When I moved to the village, I took only my clothes, a few

paperback novels, and my computer. Even growing up on a reservation never prepared me for the isolation of an Alaskan native village. During my first year, I lived in a small, school-owned efficiency apartment. There was room for a single bed, a hot plate, and a TV. I had one chair and a TV tray for a table. I spent most of my evenings at school. My entertainment was DVDs that were swapped and traded throughout the village. I kept my mom and sisters busy mailing me DVDs and paperback books. On the weekends we played basketball."

Jon continued with details of his life in the Native village, including a lengthy description of a field trip to Russia with twelve Native students. As I watched him pour salt on his buffalo burger, I decided to steer the conversation back to the story he had to tell.

"You said you made a special stop in Bozeman to tell me a story, so I am ready to hear it," I said.

"I've been setting the stage for the story," he said smiling. "All stories must have a backstory."

He paused and motioned for the waiter to bring more coffee. When the waiter appeared, Jon asked him to leave the pot. At that moment, I knew, I would have to be patient and allow Jon to tell his story in his own time.

"After spending several months in the small apartment, I knew I had to escape the village for the summer. I planned to go home for a few weeks, but I wanted to see more of Alaska before making the eighteen-hundred-mile drive to the reservation. I found a used camper trailer and set out exploring Alaska. I did not expect to be abducted by aliens."

"So you are traveling around Alaska, alone, and you are abducted by aliens, is that what you are telling me?"

"Yes, and don't tell me you're surprised. I know you collect stories about UFOs. So that is one reason I wanted to see you."

"Well, tell me what happened," I said.

He reached over, picked a French fry off my plate, and smiled. I shoved my plate toward him, signaling he should help himself. He finished off the French fries, filled his coffee cup again, reached in his pocket, and pulled out some photos.

"It happened around midnight at this spot," he said. He handed me a photo and pointed. "I parked my trailer there," he said, placing more photos on the table. "Those are shots of the lake, my trailer, and a stray dog I picked up near Fairbanks."

"You said the abduction happened around midnight. Were you awake or asleep at the time?"

"I had just put out my campfire. I had fried some fish I caught during the day, mixed in some freeze-dried potatoes, and feasted. I had a cigarette and a beer to finish off the evening. I poured water on the campfire and went to bed. Seconds later, a brilliant white light engulfed the whole trailer. I opened the door and realized the light was coming from overhead."

"What did you think was happening?"

"My first thought was that it was a helicopter, but there was no sound. I walked beyond the trailer to the edges of the light beam for a better look. I made out the silhouette of a huge, cylinder-shaped object above the tree line. It was just hovering there, no sound, no wind, nothing. A searchlight fell on my trailer and stayed there. By this time, I assumed they knew about me. After all, I had come out of the trailer while the light was centered on the trailer."

"How did you feel?"

"That's the strangest part of the whole event. I wasn't afraid. In fact, I felt peace. I don't believe they chose me. I just happened to be in the wrong place at the wrong time."

"Why do you think that?"

"They came for water. I watched them siphon water out of the lake. So I'm sure my presence there was a surprise."

"Can you tell me what happened next?"

"I ran into a small group of trees and watched them take the water. Once that was completed, the light began searching again. Once they found me, the light didn't move. Within minutes, a man came toward me. He was at least seven and half feet tall. He asked me to come with him."

"He asked you?"

"Yes. He asked. I'm not sure what he would have done if I refused, but I never considered that. I wanted to go with him. I knew this was a UFO and I wanted to explore it."

"Did you go onboard the craft?"

"Yes. I don't remember how that happened. One moment I was on terra firma, and the next moment I'm onboard their ship."

"Did you see others?"

"Yes, all tall men, at least seven feet tall or more. They looked human or I should say, they had a human form, but they were different. Not just in height, but they were different in appearance."

"Can you explain?"

"Their skin was…" he paused for a moment searching for a word, "spongy."

"Spongy. Can you explain?"

"When I touched them, their skin felt like a sponge. My fingers left an imprint, but when I let go, it restored itself like a sponge when you squeeze it and release the pressure. They had no hair on their heads. They had huge round eyes, not slanted eyes like you see in TV movies. They had no ears. Can you believe it? They had no lips, although there was a mouth. I saw no teeth. They had these strange openings on their necks. It reminded me of a fish gill."

"Did they communicate with you?"

"Not much. Somehow, they made me feel at peace, but they never talked. I asked them where they were from. One pointed his finger toward the ceiling. I understood his gesture."

"Did they perform experiments on you?"

"I don't remember. I remember very little of my time onboard."

"Do you have any idea how long you were on their craft?"

"I found myself outside my trailer at 6 a.m. So give or take an hour or so, I was onboard their ship for five hours at least."

"And you have no memory."

"Right. There is one thing. I had a huge red bump on my upper arm. I don't know how I got it, but I noticed it when I brushed up against the trailer door. It hurt like hell. When I took off my shirt,

I saw this red bump, almost like a boil. It went down after a few days, so I never went to the doctor. I don't know if they did something to me, or if I did it to myself. I have no memory of either one."

He paused and unbuttoned his shirt. He took it off and pulled up the sleeve of his t-shirt. "This is the place the bump appeared on my arm," he said. "The bump eventually went down, but the imprint is still there."

The waiter appeared at our table and asked if there was a problem. Jon said something about performing a striptease as he buttoned up his shirt again. The waiter disappeared behind the bar as I thought about the red imprint on Jon's arm.

"I really don't care what happened," Jon said.

"But you felt compelled to tell me you story."

"That's true, but you were more than a professor, you were my therapist and my friend. You are the one who encouraged me and believed in me. You helped me get a job that I love. But there is something else that made me come to see you. I have another reason for telling you this story."

"And what was that?"

"Do you remember the time you took me and three other graduate students to South Dakota to help you with pretesting a group of students at a BIA Day School?"

I nodded. "Yes, I remember."

"On that trip, I met a young boy named Chaske. I told you about him. I have never forgotten him. He impressed me so much."

"I do remember you telling me about him."

"One of the questions we asked the students was to imagine the place they would most like to be. He told me about traveling in a UFO. He said he wanted the aliens to come back for him. That he was at peace there. This little boy talking about space travel, and the peace he felt when he traveled with the aliens blew me away. I told you about his story. Do you remember?"

"I remember," I said.

"I remembered feeling jealous of the little boy for the peace he felt. I wanted that peace in my life, and now I understand what he was talking about. I felt the peace he described when I was with them. I knew I must tell you. If you could find Chaske, maybe he could give you more information about space travel and aliens. If you find him, could you ask him if I could see him again?"

"I will see what I can do."

"You know, Doc. There is something I want to make clear. I was a skeptic when it came to aliens and UFOs. I just thought it was a way of getting attention on the part of the so-called abductees." He paused and drained his coffee cup. "Even Chaske, who impressed me so much, didn't make me a believer. I just thought he was a little boy who watched too much TV. I just saw him as a child with a vivid imagination that I hoped could be nurtured and developed. It never occurred to me that he might be telling me the truth. Now, I think he spoke from experience. Since he is older, I would like to learn more about his encounters."

I never found Chaske. I spoke with the principal of the school about the year that we did some testing on the reservation. She found the records of the third grader named Chaske, but he had moved when the school year ended. The records show he moved to Arizona. There was no other information.

I keep in touch with Jon via email. This past winter, he married an Alaskan Native who returned to her village to teach after five years in the Fairbanks School District. Every time I hear from Jon, I cannot help but think of Chaske, who wanted the aliens to come for him. I wonder if they ever did. Jon said they have not returned for him.

CHAPTER 19
ENCOUNTER ON A WYOMING HIGHWAY

According to the reports, just before midnight on October 27, 1992, two Minuteman missile personnel from the 44th Strategic Missile Wing at the Ellsworth Air Force Base were approaching the squadron's operations hangar when they saw a group of bright, white lights moving rapidly in rigid formation. While no solid object was visible, the fact the lights did not vary in their positions one another led the witnesses to conclude that they were arranged across the surface of a large but unseen craft. They watched the light formation move directly toward the Minuteman missile maintenance hangar, hover over it momentarily, and then move away, disappearing behind a bank of low clouds. Both of the observers estimated that at its closest approach, the object was about a quarter-mile from them.

In this chapter, you will meet Rocky who believes that he encountered the same spacecraft on a desolate Wyoming highway just two hours before the Ellsworth sighting.

On November 1, 1994, I drove to South Dakota to attend the funeral of a friend. When I arrived at her home, her son Rocky greeted me with a warm embrace. "I'm so glad you were able to come," Rocky said, as he guided me down the hallway, suitcase in tow. "You have to stay here in your bedroom. Mama would have wanted it that way."

In the late afternoon, I sat with Rocky through the Catholic ceremony, the traditional Indian ceremony. and the gravesite prayer. Afterwards we drove to his Auntie's house for a reception and a traditional give-away. After gifts of Mary's most precious possessions were handed out, Rocky suggested we go back to his mother's house.

When we entered the living room, we both collapsed on the couch. Rocky turned on the TV. We sat there staring at a show about UFOs.

"I saw a UFO," Rocky said, as he turned down the sound on the TV.

I looked at him, surprised at his revelation, and yet his solemn face revealed that he was serious. Rocky was a precocious little boy. He took his role as the man of the house seriously and was devoted to his mother. As a teenager, he did all within his power to making Mary's life easier. He shopped, cooked the meals, and cleaned the house. This was in addition to making straight A's in school and holding down a part-time job as a box-boy at the local grocery store.

"Would you like to tell me your story?" I asked.

"I like that idea. Let's do something besides sitting on this couch and being sad. Mama wouldn't want that." He stood, turned off the TV, and headed for the kitchen. "There must be something in the refrigerator to eat," he said, bending down and examining its contents. "Let's see, we have beer and Diet Coke and every casserole you can imagine. What would you like?" he asked.

He pulled out a chair and slid the Diet Coke across the table. "I know it must seem strange to you that I'm talking about UFOs on the evening of my mother's funeral, but it's more fitting than you might think. The night I encountered the UFO, I was on my way home to see Mama from the University."

I knew that Rocky had received a full scholarship to the University of Wyoming.

"She was waiting up for me, as usual, when I arrived home," he continued. "She was watching TV, and there was a report about the UFO at Ellsworth. I told her, I'd seen a UFO in Wyoming, which looked exactly like the one being described. She became very excited. After that, every time I was home, she asked me to tell her the UFO story." He paused, took a sip of the Budweiser, and smiled. "Perhaps she is up there listening, so it is right I tell this story one more time."

He held up his beer in salute. "Mama, I know you are in a better place, but I wanted more time with you. This story is for you." He paused and wiped tears from his eyes with a sheet of paper towel. "Every time I told this story, Mama and I would have a Budweiser. She kept beer in the refrigerator for that purpose. Otherwise, neither of us drank alcoholic beverages."

I took out my notebook while watching the young man. The loss of his mother would be difficult for him. Even though he was an adult, he used every opportunity travel from Wyoming to South Dakota to visit her.

"About two hours before the incident at Ellsworth, I was traveling on a two-lane highway headed for South Dakota. My classes at the University had been canceled for a few days due to several professors attending an international conference. I decided to take advantage of the unexpected holiday and return to the reservation for the long weekend to visit Mama. About five miles from the border of South Dakota, I saw a brilliant white light in the distance on the right side of the highway. The lights were stationary and non-moving."

"Could you make out any shape?"

"Not at the time. I saw a straight line of lights. They looked like headlights lined up."

"How many?"

"I counted them. There were twelve. As I continued driving, I couldn't help but wonder about the lights. It was not something I had seen before, and I discounted them as emergency lights, and yet I had this feeling that it was something else."

I knew that Rocky, who was a senior in biological science, had made this trip dozens of time during the past four years and was familiar with the region.

"As I got closer," he said," it became obvious they were not emergency lights. Emergency lights flash. They're red; these lights were white. It was about that time I realized the lights were on an object hovering no more than fifty feet above the ground. I pulled off the highway to get a better view and got out of my car."

"Was anyone else around?" I asked.

"I saw no one else. Suddenly the car radio blasted static through the speakers and startled me. I realized the car was still running. Then the car lights dimmed and went out. At that moment, I was having second thoughts about my decision to stop. That is when I saw the object move. It crossed the road and came directly toward me."

"How did you react?"

"I jumped back in my car and tried to start the engine. It wouldn't start despite repeated attempts. I tried to relax as the craft inched closer."

"Was it moving slowly?"

"Yes, it moved slowly. It had to be controlled by some intelligence. I was frightened. I slid down in my seat and looked through the sunroof."

"Can you describe what you saw?"

"I saw a huge craft move slowly over the top of the car. Once it was out of vision, the radio came alive with a blast of static and then a Rapid City disc jockey came on advertising car polish."

He paused for a moment and shook his head. "It was the most amazing thing I had ever seen. I had heard of UFOs all my life, but I never expected to see one."

"Can you tell me anything else about the craft?"

"When it came overhead, only the front was visible, the rest of the craft was not. I would say, it would set down in the middle of a football field with little room to spare. Red and blue lights outlined the bottom of the craft making a circular shape."

"Did you hear anything?"

"Nothing. The craft was silent."

"Did you see anything after that?"

"I chased it. I was so excited that I turned my car around in the middle of the road and headed back toward Laramie. Suddenly it made a turn and headed toward South Dakota. I pursued it, until it made a zigzag flight pattern and disappeared."

"When you say you chased it, do you think it was aware of your presence?"

"Definitely. It waited for me, or at least it seemed to wait. Every time I got close, it would fly off again. We carried on this cat and mouse game for the next hour. I would arrive at its hovering position and pull off the road. It would remain stationary for a moment or two and then move away. On two occasions, it beamed a searchlight onto my car. I stood my ground. We must have gone through this exercise a half a dozen times. Finally, it made one last move, zipped across the sky toward the East, and vanished. I glanced at my watch. It was 10:17. I had spent over an hour in pursuit of the craft."

"Did you see the craft again?"

"Not that night, but there is an interesting footnote to this story."

"Please go on."

"I arrived at my mother's house late that night, and as usual, she was waiting up for me. I told her what had happened. She did not seem concerned. She believed in the existence of UFOs, and after eating half of a chocolate cake, I went to bed."

"Is that the ending?"

"No. The next morning, I walked into the kitchen and they were reporting a UFO incident at Ellsworth. It was too much of a coincidence. It had to be the same craft."

"I read that report. The news article said that they could not make out a craft."

"The lights in the front of the craft were bright. Blinding, in fact. I am sure it was the same craft. It supported my experience. It was a confirmation. Just a couple of hundred miles away, military personnel had seen the same thing. I was satisfied. I now know that UFOs are real and whatever the government says, I know they're simply giving out false information for whatever reason."

"You said you did not see the craft again that night. Does that mean you saw it again?"

"At Christmas break, I headed home again. It was about the

same time of night, 8:46 p.m. when I spotted the light in the distance. You can't imagine the excitement I felt. How could this happen a second time on the same road just a few miles from the South Dakota line?"

"Did you see the craft?"

"I spotted it, but this time it was hovering over the trees on a small hill. Just as I pulled off the highway, a group of military vehicles came careening around the bend. Overhead, I heard the motors of helicopters. The sound was deafening. The hovering craft began to move upwards. The helicopters were in pursuit. I saw them disappear over the tree line. I decided it was time to get back on the highway. When I crossed the South Dakota line, I pulled off the highway and got out of my car. I searched the night sky for any sign of the UFO. There was none. I got back in my car and pointed my car toward home. The rest of the night was uneventful."

"Did you make out anything about the craft?"

"It was the same one I had seen in October. The moon was bright that night and I could see its silhouette against the sky. The lights were different. They pulsated dim to bright. That was the only thing different."

"Did anyone else report a UFO sighting that night?"

"It did not make the TV news, but there was a story in a small local newspaper I picked up at a gas station in Belle Fourche. A farmer at St. Onge reported a UFO hovering over his barn the same night. When the sheriff's deputy arrived, there was no sign of the UFO."

I have seen Rocky several times since he graduated from college. After his graduation, he took a job in California at a government laboratory. About twice a year, he takes a road trip back to the reservation. On those trips, he stops in Montana and spends a few days with me. He has never seen another UFO, although he admits he keeps his eyes and mind open to the possibility.

CHAPTER 20
TINA AND A HYBRID BABY

In a typical alien abduction, humans are taken out of their normal environment by extraterrestrials. The abductees are rendered passive and cannot resist. They are taken on board a UFO, where a series of physical, mental, and reproductive procedures are administered. The abductees' physical bodies are probed and examined. Sperm is taken; eggs are harvested. Women sometimes report being impregnated by the aliens. After about eleven weeks, abduction occurs again, and the fetus is removed.

In this chapter, you will meet a young woman, who claims she met her alien–human son.

"Do you believe it is possible for aliens to create a hybrid baby?" Tina asked. "You know, half human and half alien?"

I looked at the young woman who stood at the bottom of the steps leading toward the deck where I was sitting. She had arrived at my Auntie Josephine's house unannounced.

"I know there are many women who believe they have been abducted, and some claim they have had alien babies," I replied.

"Your Auntie told me about your UFO book, so I bought it and read it. I thought it was informative and honest. I hoped you might be able to answer some lingering questions about hybrid babies."

She approached the steps, but looked at the opened screen door as though she was concerned that my Auntie might overhear our conversation. I studied her closely. I recognized her as one of the Lone Man girls. She was a tall, slender woman in her late twenties. Her straight black hair fell to the middle of her back. Her long denim skirt, western boots, and a white blouse cinched at the waist with a silver concho belt made her appear as though she had just stepped off the cover of a western magazine.

"Do you know someone who makes such a claim?" I asked.

"Yes, I know someone, but I need your guarantee that you will never tell anyone what I tell you."

"I promise. Your identity is safe with me," I assured her.

"Would you mind if we take a walk?" she asked as my Auntie walked onto the deck. As the two of them engaged in casual conversation, I checked my backpack for my tape recorder and added two bottles of water before joining Tina at the bottom of the steps. After excusing ourselves, we walked toward the river. We sat on a familiar boulder that jutted over my favorite swimming hole when I was a youngster. I removed the tape recorder from my bag. I noted her anxious look as I placed it between us.

"The tape recorder allows me to write the stories in your words," I explained.

She let out a stifled breath and nodded.

"I just want to make sure my identity is safe. My family would freak out if they knew what happened to me."

"I assure you, no one will ever know. I never use names with the tape. I use a code to match the tape with my notes. I destroy them once I write the story, and I always disguise the location."

"Thank you for that extra assurance." She pulled a pack of cigarettes out of her bag. I watched the match flame and hit the start button on the tape recorder. "When I was seventeen, my sisters and I were driving home from a state basketball championship," she began. We planned to spend the night, but there was a mix-up with the room reservations. We had no place to stay. We called our mom and told her we were driving home."

"What year did that happen?"

"Well, I'm twenty-eight now. Eleven years ago."

"Please, continue."

"We got on the road about 10:30, just a few minutes after the championship game ended. I told my sisters I'd drive and they could sleep. I promised to wake them if I took a break."

"Did you stop anywhere on your trip home?"

"Yes. It was only about a three-hour drive, and I promised Mom I would drive straight home. About fifty miles into the trip is when it happened. I was driving below the speed limit. That section of the road was known for deer on the highway. Suddenly a light appeared and the whole landscape was washed in light. I slammed on the brakes and yelled at my sisters. I was scared out of my wits. I kept yelling at the girls, but they didn't even move." She paused and threw her cigarette butt into the river. I watched it as it swirled in a small eddy and got caught up in a wave and disappeared. "I tried to wake my sisters, but I couldn't. I even reached in the backseat and shook them, but they didn't respond. As I sat there trying to figure out what I was going to do, I saw two figures walking toward the car."

"What happened next?"

"I screamed when I saw the two figures. I shook Minnie. She didn't move. I yelled at Rosebud and she didn't wake up. They did something to my sisters."

"Do you think the strangers approaching your car did something to them?"

"Yes, the aliens," she replied, lighting another cigarette. "They were aliens. They didn't belong here."

"What do you think they did to your sisters?"

"Something with their minds. They had a powerful way about them. They controlled minds. They tried to control my mind. It took every bit of power in my body to resist them, so I believe they controlled their minds. I was taken on board a spaceship, and placed in a room that was so hot that I thought I was going to suffocate. My sisters were there too. I was fully awake, but they were still asleep. A few minutes later, four figures entered the room."

"Can you describe them?"

"No. They were shadowy characters. I couldn't make out any features. I think the atmosphere affected by vision. Two of them attached me to a table in the center of the room. I looked at my sisters. They were slumped in the corner like rag dolls. One of the four figures came toward me. I screamed but could not move. I was attached to the table from the neck down. I could only move my head."

"What do you mean when you say you were attached?"

"I can't explain it. There were no shackles, but I was bound to the table. I could not move at all. It was like I was part of the table."

"When the alien approached you, did he communicate with you?"

"No. He placed a metal device over my face. I must have blacked out. I don't know what he did to me. I was a virgin that night, but after the encounter, I was never a virgin again."

"What happened next?"

"The next thing I remember, I was sitting behind the steering wheel of my car."

"And your sisters?"

"I looked in the backseat. They were both there sound asleep."

"Did your sisters remember anything about that night?"

"Nothing. I asked them many questions without revealing what had happened, and they knew nothing."

"Do you think they examined your sisters?"

"I don't think so. I somehow felt they took them to protect them from other motorists. If someone came up on two sleeping girls in a car, they would want to know where the driver was. This way, our car just looked like an abandoned vehicle on the road. My sisters were only eleven and twelve, so I don't think they had a use for them."

"Do you believe they impregnated you?"

"I think they harvested my eggs and used my eggs to create hybrid children."

"Why do you believe that?" I asked.

"They showed me my son."

"Can you explain how you met him?"

"I was taken a few months ago. I was walking home from

visiting my cousin. She lived down the road from me. Less than a half mile. It was about 9:30 at night. I saw a bright light in the woods across from my house. I thought somebody was in trouble, and I walked over there to check it out. Suddenly I saw a strange craft hovering about twenty feet off the ground. Immediately, I started to run. But these creatures came out of the trees and stopped me."

"What did they look like?"

"Very scary. They were short. They had big heads and big eyes and the color of their skin was a grayish-white. I struggled with them. Their skin felt like they were made out of non-human, synthetic material. They took me onto the spaceship and led me down a corridor to a room and showed me a little boy. They said he was my son."

"How did that make you feel?" I asked.

"It made me feel confused. Angry. Sad. Many different emotions. I did not know how it could be. I told them they were lying, but they said no, he is your son. We just wanted you to see him. It didn't make sense to me. Why would they show me a child, tell me that he was mine, and not let me take him?"

She stood up on the boulder and looked up at the sky. She shielded her eyes from the sun and scanned the eastern sky. She lowered her arm and sat back down. "I have to be realistic. I don't think a child like that could survive on earth, but why were they so cruel? It would have been better not to know of his existence."

"What did the child look like?" I asked.

"He did not look like me. His hair was dark but thinner than Indian babies. You know what I mean."

I shook my head in agreement.

"He was small. They said he was two in earth years. My sister has a two-year-old, and he was much smaller than my nephew. He was almost dainty like a little girl. He had the biggest, roundest eyes I have ever seen."

"Did he look like a human child?" I asked.

"He had a human form, but dainty. His skin was the color of

mine, but when he held out his arm, he looked like he needed to get out in the sun and play."

"Did you see other children?"

"No. He was alone in the room, but they said there were others."

"Others?"

"They said they had used my eggs to create other children."

"How many?"

"They said there were seven boys. All different ages. This child was the youngest."

"I asked them their names, but I can't remember them. They had not named the boy-child in front of me. They said I could name him. I called him Silver Man. Silver Man was my mother's maiden name."

"As you watched your child, what was he doing?"

"He was just sitting there. Just sitting. Only once he looked my way and we looked at each other. I smiled, but he did not return my smile. My two-year-old nephew is all over the place, running, crawling, playing, but not this baby. He sat there and hardly moved."

"I asked them if I could go in the room and talk to him, but they refused. To tell you the truth, I felt very connected to him."

"Did they tell you why you couldn't touch him?" I asked.

"They said it was too dangerous. I might give him a virus or disease. When they led me away, I fought them. I had an overwhelming need to mother this child. I wanted to stay and take care of him. He was so alone. So dainty looking. I was afraid he would die."

"Have you seen him since that night?" I asked.

"No. But they said I would see him again. That one day, when the time was right, he would come to me." She paused and wiped tears from her eyes with the palms of her hands. "They have not returned. I cannot help but think of that child. What if he is my baby? I should take care of him. I am just so upset."

As we walked back toward the house, I suggested that Tina should see a counselor. "If you like, I would like to help you find a good one."

"I don't need a counselor. I just needed to tell someone who might understand my feelings."

"And I do understand," I said, "but a counselor can help you through this."

"I just wanted to talk with you. You're a counselor and you've studied this phenomenon. I don't want anyone else to know. A counselor might think I am hallucinating or fantasizing. I want nothing to do with them. I need to talk with someone who knows about these things, and you fit the bill."

Over the next year, Tina and I remained in regular contact. I visited her four times during that year. Gradually, Tina seemed to accept the fact there was little she could do. If she were the mother to a hybrid baby, she accepted the fact the child would have a difficult time surviving on earth. She did hold out the hope that someday when he was grown, he would find her.

CHAPTER 21
THERE ARE MANY ALIEN SPECIES

*In 1967 astronomers in Cambridge, who were monitoring deep
space with their radio telescope, heard signals pulsing at regular in-
tervals. Some considered it a message sent by intelligent beings from
another galaxy; later the signals were found to have a natural explanation—they had discovered pulsars. But Martin Ryle, the future As-
tronomer Royal, had taken the possibility seriously: if the signal came
from extraterrestrials, they should dismantle the telescope and keep the
signals a secret. He felt if they responded, they might be alerting hostile
aliens to our location. Stephen Hawking agreed. In fact, he suggested
that an alien visit might resemble the time when Columbus landed
in America, which eventually resulted in the destruction of American
Indian tribal groups.*

*In this chapter, you will meet a spiritual leader who issues a similar
warning.*

"Since I was a small child, I have been aware of the Star People.
I discovered that just as there are different races on this planet, there are many species in the universe. Some we know about;
others we do not. There are some who come as scientists, others
come to discover our weaknesses, and others come to take from us
what they want."

I was sitting with Jimmy, a well-known healer among his people. He was celebrating his seventieth birthday as a guest of honor
at the Annual Rodeo and Powwow Days. I had known Jimmy for
nearly thirty years. A veteran and the first college graduate of his
tribe, he held many respected positions both on the reservation
and nationally. A spiritual advisor to presidents, he was known for

his frankness and openness about the Star People, although lately I heard that Jimmy had issued warnings about a new kind of extraterrestrial visiting Earth.

"Do you think their visits are harmless?" I asked.

"Some are harmless, but there are those who have no regard for us as a species. They consider us no better than someone might regard a bug."

"What do you think is their purpose?"

"I believe that, depending on the species, they have many agendas."

"Why do you think they have their sights set on Earth?"

"Although they aren't human, we have many things in common. They breathe air like we do. They react to heat and cold like we do. They appreciate the beauty of the environment like we do."

"Why do you think they are already here?" I asked.

"I have seen them."

"Do you believe that aliens abduct humans?"

"I know they do, but they're careful. They don't mind if their victims know. Who is going to believe them anyway? They just don't want someone to see them do it. They go to extraordinary lengths to keep their devious actions secret. I've been watching them for decades. I know what they do."

Jimmy paused and lapsed into a coughing episode. I offered him a bottle of water from my backpack, which he gracefully accepted. After taking a few sips, his cough subsided.

"Do you think our government knows about the aliens?" I asked.

"All of the government experts know what's going on, but they don't know what to do about it. They continue to approach the problem based on human social rules. They expect the aliens to behave according to human laws. But many of these species are invaders. They don't tell the truth unless it serves their purpose. You would think they would recognize that since our own government lies. Indians have known that for centuries."

"So are you telling me that the Star People are devious and

dishonest?"

"No, not the Star People. The Star People are those who came before us. They are the ancestors. I am talking about some of the other species that inhabit this great universe. They make their victims believe they are special or chosen. They play on their fears using nuclear war, pollution, or greed as warnings for Earth and its people. They are using the people so they remove any fears about their shameful deeds. And humans accept their lies and say they are peaceful and loving. There is nothing loving about them."

"What about the women and men who report sexual abuse by aliens?" I asked.

"They speak the truth. These aliens are advanced scientifically and medically. They are capable of all kinds of manipulation. Hybrid babies and clones are within reach of our scientists if the truth were known, so I'm sure the aliens have perfected hybrid humans."

As we talked, I realized that Jimmy, who had never been shy about speaking of his encounters with Star People, had suddenly become much more pessimistic. "Can you tell me what is going on? I feel like there is something you are not telling me."

"Stop by my place tomorrow. I have something I want to show you."

The next morning, I got up early, stopped at the gas station and filled up my Subaru, made a quick stop at the grocery store and headed out of town. Jimmy lived roughly twenty miles from the tribal city center on a ranch he had inherited from his father. When I arrived at his place, he greeted me with a cup of black coffee.

"I brought the sweet rolls, your favorite, chocolate covered éclairs," I said, as I grabbed a box from the backseat. We stood for a moment looking over the rolling hills. From this vantage point, I could see a neighboring ranch house and a barn, which was about five miles away as the crow flies. "That ranch looks abandoned," I said as we walked up to the steps to the house.

"It is abandoned," Jimmy said as he led me to the kitchen. He offered me a place at the table as he busied himself filling our coffee cups. I opened the box of éclairs as Jimmy placed a plate in front of me and one at his place. "It was about a year ago when it all began. I had seen the lights in the sky on several occasions, but none ever came near the ranch. It was different for the neighbors. Over the next year, they were harassed by aliens."

"You are talking about extraterrestrials, correct?"

"Yes, ETs, if that's what you want to call them. The first sign was when Samantha came up missing. She was their sixteen-year-old daughter. Alfred stopped by my place one morning and told me she was gone. They had gone to bed around ten and when they got up the next morning, she was missing. He wanted to know if I'd seen her. I told him I hadn't seen her, but I would be happy to help him look for her. Since she had no form of transportation other than walking, we decided to saddle up a couple of horses and look for her."

"Maybe someone picked her up."

"We thought about that and Rachael, her mother, had called all of her friends and had ruled out that possibility. Even her boyfriend had not seen her or talked to her. In fact, he was on his way to help Alfred look for her."

"Did you find her?"

"We searched for hours. There was no sign of her. We gave up when darkness set in, and I told Alfred to call me if he heard anything. Around midnight a call came. Samantha simply reappeared, wearing her night clothes, with no knowledge of what had happened to her or where she had been. The doctor at the Indian hospital diagnosed her as a sleepwalker, and we thought that was the end of it, until it happened again two nights later. Her disappearance and reappearance occurred several times over the next few weeks. Alfred even stayed up at night to watch, and she still disappeared. He enlisted my help to keep a vigil, and she still disappeared."

"What do you think was going on?"

"At first, I had no idea, but about a month into the disappearances, I arrived at the ranch and found no one home. I spoke with

Alfred on the phone only moments before. He told me he was waiting for me, and yet when I arrived the house was abandoned. I went to the barn, and except for some very unhappy and agitated livestock, there was no one or nothing around. I returned to the house and sat down on the porch, but not before retrieving my shotgun from my pickup. At this point, I had no idea what was going on, but I decided it was better to be armed than vulnerable."

"How long did you wait or did they even return?"

"They returned all right, but not the way I expected." He paused and finished off the sweet roll and reached for another and continued. "As I sat there in the dark, waiting for any sign of the missing family, I suddenly became aware of a bright light coming from behind the house. I crept around the house searching for the source of the light. That's when I saw it. Hovering between the house and the barn was a circular spacecraft. I saw a bright light come down from the bottom of the craft and floating on the light was the family. There was Alfred, Rachael, Samantha, and Tony, their eight-year-old son. I watched them stand there, as though confused about their surroundings, and waited until the craft moved upward and out of sight. They turned and walked into the house. I knocked on the door. Alfred greeted me and welcomed into the house."

"Was he unaware that he had been abducted?"

"Right, he didn't know. When I told him what I saw, he walked with me out to the backyard. There was a glowing circle on the ground where the craft hovered. The grass within the circle was brown. Outside the circle, it was green and lush. Inside it was dead, brittle and brown."

"Is the circle still there?"

"It has faded, but you can still see it at night. I invited you here so I could take you there tonight."

"Have you encountered any aliens personally?"

"Several times. I took it on myself to keep an eye on Alfred's ranch. At night, I stood in the shadows and watched. Several times I saw the craft appear and aliens descend from the craft. They were monsters. Like walking bugs. They often shifted into a human appearance. That is how I know that they are shape shifters. I saw them with my own eyes."

"Is that the only time you saw them at the ranch?"

"I saw them three or four times. Two nights after the first incident, Alfred called for me to come to his house. I drove up and immediately noticed that both of their pickups were packed with suitcases and household goods. Alfred pulled me aside and told me that his daughter, Samatha, was pregnant. He was taking his family to New Mexico, where his mother-in-law lived. He asked me if I would buy their livestock. I had very little money, only a couple of hundred dollars. Alfred said that was enough. They gave me the keys to their house, and I agreed to keep an eye on it while they were gone. Rachael gave me a telephone number on a sheet of paper, and I stood in the driveway and watched them disappear down the road."

"Have they come back?"

"No. That was eighteen months ago. The next day, I drove up to the ranch with my horse trailer. I loaded up the horses, three mares and a colt, and took them back to my pasture. Along the way, I picked up Blackie."

I looked at the dog that rested at his feet. "But you said you saw them three or four times."

"Yes. The next day, Blackie and I went out to their pasture to drive the cattle back to my place. He had a small herd. About twenty. Two of the steers were dead, but not from natural causes. It looked like someone had carved them up. Strangest sight I'd ever seen. I wanted to salvage the meat for Blackie, but he refused to go near them and whined all the time. I left them there for the crows. Never went back. We drove the other cattle to my pasture. In fact, they're still there."

"Are you talking about cattle mutilation?"

"I wouldn't have believed it if I hadn't seen it with my own eyes, but I do think it would fall into that category. I think the aliens did that to the cattle and Blackie knew it. It scared him and not much scares Blackie."

"Did you see the aliens again?"

"The next day. I made one final trip to their place to gather their chickens. I was in the henhouse when I heard a racket outside. I saw the craft hover over the same spot as before. Five aliens drifted down from the craft. Once on the ground, they transformed into humans. They shape shifted before my eyes. They walked into the barn and the next thing I know, they were driving an old, '55 Chevy that had been stored in the barn for twenty years. I couldn't believe that it even worked. I stayed in the hen house until they were gone. I put the chickens in the cages I brought and drove back to my place. I don't think they saw me or my pickup. It was parked on the far side of the house in the shade. I hate to think of what they might have done to me if they had discovered me."

"That's an incredible story."

"Incredible, but true. I have no reason to make up stories at my age. We humans are in danger. We just don't know it. You could warn people. These aliens have an agenda. I think they are slowly substituting the humans of earth with aliens, and the day will come when a real human will not exist. People need to know, this is a real threat."

"Have you ever talked to Alfred since he moved to New Mexico?" I asked.

"Twice. He told me that Samantha was not pregnant. She suddenly didn't have any symptoms of pregnancy. He did admit that they had seen similar lights in the New Mexico sky, but Samantha no longer disappeared. The next time I heard from him, he told me he was not coming back to the ranch. He has put it up for sale."

I spent the night at Jimmy's place. When darkness fell, we drove to Alfred's ranch. With flashlights, we walked to the place where the spacecraft had hovered. Although diminished with time, a faintly glowing circle could still be seen. Before we left, we checked the barn. The '55 Chevy was back in its place.

CHAPTER 22
NIGHT FISHING IN WYOMING

American abductee Carl Higdon believed that he was rejected as a guinea pig for a hybrid-breeding program because his captors discovered that he had had a vasectomy. Luis Oswald, an elderly Brazilian abducted in 1979 by beings who claimed to be from "a small galaxy near Neptune," reported that he had endured a lengthy examination. Later he was told, he was of no use to them.

In this chapter, you will meet Emory, who claims that he, too, apparently failed an alien medical test.

There is a lake in Wyoming between Moran Junction, the southern-most exit to Yellowstone National Park, and Dubois, Wyoming, that is surrounded by one of the most awe-inspiring mountain ranges in the country. On numerous occasions, I have visited this lake, walked its perimeter, photographed it, and even stopped for a picnic lunch. I have never spent the night there, although many locals and travelers have parked at the site for the night. On one such night, Emory, a sixty-nine-year-old Shoshone Indian, who often went night fishing at the lake, had an encounter.

I met Emory through an acquaintance who lived in Dubois and ran a seasonal tourist shop. As a favor to me, she carried my books in her shop, which often led to discussions of UFOs from both travelers and locals who told her about personal encounters. Emory was one of those individuals who had confided in her. When she told him she knew me personally, he expressed an interest in meeting me. She explained to me that she considered Emory a reliable witness. She had known him for years and described him as eccentric, but an honest, down-to-earth individualist who was not prone to tall tales or fantasy. She arranged for me to meet him at her shop one Sunday afternoon while I was on my way to the Wind River Indian Reservation.

Emory was a small man who walked with a slight limp, the result of being kicked by a horse when he was nine. A cowboy hat, which seemed too large for his small frame, covered a full head of white hair. The white stubble on his chin and one gold tooth, which he obtained when he lost the original one in a barroom brawl, highlighted his tanned face. An expensive pair of Ostrich skin cowboy boots set off his faded Wrangler jeans. We sat on a bench in front of Dylan's shop and drank ice tea as he told me of his encounters.

"I like to go night fishing," he began. "It was late August last year when Badger, my dog, and me decided to do an all-nighter. We settled at my favorite spot, when I saw a bright light descend over the mountains, hover over the lake, and then disappear. About an hour later, I had caught my limit and Badger began growling. Feeling a little uneasy, we decided we best call it a night, so I packed up my things and headed for my camper, which was about a hundred yards away at the entrance to the lake. As we were walking along the path around the lake two figures appeared in front of us. Badger began barking furiously."

"Was it unusual to see someone on the lake at night?"

"It was unusual to see someone on the lake at this time of night. Most everyone goes home around ten or so. Badger and me have a routine. We fish most of the night or until we catch our limit. Then we sleep in the camper, and the next morning we make our way down the mountain and have breakfast before going home and feeding the chickens. Badger and me like the peacefulness of the night. That place allows me to be close to the Great Mystery."

"So did you greet the strangers?"

"I stopped dead in my tracks. Badger was barking. These were no ordinary men, not anyone from Wyoming. I knew that right away. They were only about four feet high. They were dressed in these shiny outfits that stood out in the moonlight; something kids might wear on Halloween. Their heads were covered with motor-cycle helmets. I thought for a second they must be some kids on vacation with their parents, but that didn't explain why Badger was so upset."

"Did you try to quiet Badger?"

"I did, but nothing would calm him down. Then, all of a sudden, one of these little guys pointed a rod at Badger, and he fell to the ground whimpering. Well, that didn't set too well with me. I told the little bastards to get the hell back to their parents, or I was going to kick some butt."

"What did they do?"

"Nothing. Just stood there as if they were mocking me. So I reached in my fishing creel, pulled out my .38, and fired a shot into the sky. I thought maybe a gunshot would scare them or alert their parents, but they still didn't move."

"Did it alert anyone?"

"If it did, I didn't see anyone. The next thing I know, they tell me I have to go with them, and that I have to leave Badger alone. I tell them that I go nowhere without Badger."

"They approached me and I pointed the gun at them, but suddenly, I am overcome with a feeling of helplessness. The gun drops from my hand and I can't pick it up. They reach for me and drag me toward the woods. I don't want to go with them, but I have no will to fight them. Then, I see it. A round, saucer shaped craft. I give up. I know there is no use to resist."

"When you get to the craft, do you remember what happened?"

"Heck yes. They dragged me up a set of steps into the saucer. By this time, I have decided I have nothing to lose. I might as well find out what they want."

"Can you describe the inside of the craft?" I asked.

"I remember it wasn't very big. The ceiling was low. I barely could stand upright. I'm five foot four and my head nearly touched the ceiling. There was a funny smell like rotten eggs. Everything was smooth. No seams. No screws or bolts holding it together. It reminded me of something that was built from a mold. It was hot and humid inside. Almost stifling."

"What did the strangers look like?"

"You mean the aliens. I never got a look at their faces. They kept their helmets on all the time. I was surprised, but later I realized the atmosphere was for my benefit and not theirs. They can't breathe our air, at least I think so."

"Can you describe them?"

"They were scrawny. Their heads were too big for their skinny little bodies, but that might have been because of the helmets. Their arms were thin and too long, making them appear as though they didn't belong to them."

"What do you mean?"

"Not sure, but it seemed like they were too long. Maybe it was because they were so thin."

"Anything else you remember?"

"They led me to a cone-like apparatus and told me to enter it. I climbed inside and a blue light ran up and down my body."

"Did it cause you pain?"

"I felt nothing. I kept my eyes closed. I remember they told me to do that."

"Was there anything else in the craft that you recall?"

"There was nothing else. Only a barren room with the cone."

"Did they tell you the purpose of the cone?"

"They said that it could tell them about my body."

"What happened next?"

"They asked me how many earth years I had lived."

"When I told them I was sixty-nine; they said I was too old."

"Did you ask them why you were too old?"

"No. They just said I was too old and I could go. They had no use for me."

"What happened next?"

"The next thing I remember, I was back at my fishing place. Badger was beside me, my .38 pistol was beside him, and I had a trout on my line. The biggest one I ever caught. I never did know how my fishing pole was set up. Why would the aliens do that?"

"So what kind of conclusions have you drawn from your experience?" I asked.

"The old men, the elders, have always talked about star visitors. I'm not sure what the spacemen intended to do with me, but one thing I know, it was probably not a friendly visit. I don't believe these are the star people of my elder's generations. Somehow they do not fit the bill of caring, knowledge-seeking travelers."

"Overall, what are your thoughts about your experience?"

"Some people say that age has its advantages. In this case, it did."

I have not seen Emory since our interview, although I travel this route frequently. However, my friend Dylan tells me that Emory's encounter has not prevented him from taking night-fishing trips to the lake.

CHAPTER 23
SNOWMOBILERS WITNESS
A MOOSE ABDUCTION

In 2010, a series of animal mutilations occurred in Wales in the UK. The Animal Pathology Field Unit (APFU) claimed they witnessed two red spheres beaming lights and lasers at sheep in the Welsh Hill farms near Radnor Forest. Several farmers reported that they had either disappearances of animals or deaths caused by strange injuries. Another farmer reported seeing a blimp-like UFO in the vicinity. According to the fifteen witnesses, the lights changed shape and emitted beams of light. Then, at other times, the spheres would morph into different shapes, firing beams to the ground.

The APFU began investigating animal mutilation cases with the intention of providing a logical explanation for the sheep mutilation, but over the years they have researched many mutilations, including ponies, hedgehogs, dogs, badgers, crows, and rats without any conclusions.

In this chapter, you will read the story of two snowmobilers who witnessed the abduction of a moose. They described lights and lasers similar to those reported in Wales.

I met Zane and Roger through a mutual friend in Alaska who suggested they contact me should they want to tell me about their encounter. Zane, who was born in a remote island village, was a Native Alaskan Aleut. At twenty-nine, he was the younger of the two. Roger, a thirty-three-year-old native of Oregon, had gone to Alaska to pan for gold. Influenced by a TV show about gold panning, he arrived in the state with little more than a dream, two hundred dollars in his pocket, and a degree in geology. The two of them met on a boat that took tourists on day fishing trips. Roger, who stood over six feet tall, boasted a bushy red beard and unruly red hair that seemed to end where the beard began. His laugh, which originated somewhere deep in his stomach, was loud and contagious.

Zane, who was about five inches shorter than Roger, was a clean-shaven, soft-spoken man with a gentle, humble manner and a boyish grin. His shoulder-length black hair was parted in the middle and showed premature signs of graying. Both men, who were veterans of Afghanistan, formed a close bond within weeks of meeting, despite their cultural, physical, and personality differences.

The three of us met at a coffee shop in the middle of the village. After we ordered coffee, I brought up the purpose of our meeting: "Sharon told me you had a story to tell. I have been anxious to hear about your encounter. Do you mind if I tape it?"

They looked at each other, shrugged their shoulders, and nodded.

"We don't have a problem with that," Zane said. "If you're going to write our story, we want it written right."

"I promise to tell the story as you relate it to me, and I will keep your identity and place of residence anonymous."

"That's good, but even if you used our names, it is unlikely anyone could ever find us. In fact, we wouldn't even have been in town had it not been our desperate need for some parts for our snowmobiles."

"Yeah, and while we were here," said Roger, "we went to church since it's Easter weekend, and Sharon told us about you. We're heading back to our cabin tomorrow, so it was good timing all around."

"When did your encounter take place?"

"Four months ago," Zane began. "We were checking our trap lines. It's another source of income, trapping for furs, which we hope will eventually lead to total self-sufficiency. Until then, we'll work the fishing season so we can buy the things we need."

"I'm anxious to hear your story," I said.

"We were about twenty miles from our cabin," Roger said, "when both of our snowmobiles shut down. It was weird. One snowmobile might breakdown, but two...what are the odds? It was twenty-four below and snow was falling. It was late in the afternoon, and we decided that we better make camp for the night and try to repair them the next day."

"If we couldn't fix them," Zane explained, "we would have to walk twenty miles, and we weren't looking forward to that. We had some spare parts with us, but the temperature was dropping fast, so we decided it best to make camp. It's not a good thing to get stranded without a contingency plan."

"I gathered firewood," said Roger, "and Zane set up the tent in a clearing that jetted up against a group of Spruce trees. In Alaska you always travel prepared. We made a fire, boiled some water for coffee, and unpacked our smoked salmon and flat bread. The temperature by this time was thirty below, and the snow was coming down steadily."

"As we reminisced about our favorite home-cooked meals," said Zane, "we were suddenly aware of a low, throbbing sound."

"It was a humming sound," Roger corrected.

"Hum, throb, it's all the same," said Zane. "This went on for about a minute, and then all of a sudden a bright light filled the darkness. We watched it move in our direction and hover about fifty yards from where we were sitting. Neither of us moved. The whole air seemed electrified. A strange, unfamiliar odor filled the air. It was overpowering."

"Suddenly these strange balls of lights started flitting around the night air," Roger said. "Occasionally we would see a light beam fall on Earth followed by sharp laser-like spikes of bright blue light."

"How were you feeling at this time?" I asked.

"Our first inclination was to run," Roger said, "but then we were afraid of what might happen if we left the shelter of the trees. So we stayed, not moving, almost fearful of looking around."

"Then all of a sudden," Zane said, "we heard a thrashing sound coming through the trees and a number of moose ran into the clearing. There were maybe fifteen, and that was strange. Moose are solitary animals and don't live in herds like deer. And suddenly, the beam of light fell on the last one, a beautiful bull. And whoosh. It was gone."

"Gone?"

"It was gone," Roger repeated. "They sucked it up. Right into the craft." There was an excitement in his voice that could only be attributed to someone who had seen something that was unbelievable.

"Then all of a sudden," said Zane, "the light withdrew, and we heard the throbbing again. That's when we saw the craft. It was no more than fifty feet above us. It moved west and in a blink of an eye it was gone."

"I'm a private pilot," Roger said. "I flew helicopters in Afghanistan. I have clocked over 20,000 hours of flight time both in the military and privately. I can assure you that I have never seen any craft that maneuvered the way this object did. It was huge, and yet it sped up at unbelievable speeds. I'd always heard stories from other pilots about UFOs, but I'd never seen one. That night I saw one. It turned this skeptic into a believer."

"What did you do when the craft was gone?"

"For a while, we just stood there dumbfounded. After that, we climbed into our sleeping bags, but I didn't sleep much. I could still hear that throbbing in my ears. The next morning, we searched the grounds where the craft hovered, but all we found were ice circles in the snow. The craft had melted the snow and the cold temperatures had frozen it."

"Can you describe the craft?"

"It was a large circular craft. It was huge. It could have covered a football field from end to end."

"There is one other thing," Roger said. "The next morning, our snowmobiles started up immediately. Both of them. We finished our trap lines and were back at our cabin in the middle of the afternoon."

"So do you think the UFO interfered with the operation of your snowmobiles?

"We don't think it, we know it," Zane declared.

"There was a lesson to be learned from all of this," said Roger. "It taught us that you never know what might happen. But I'm curious. Has anyone ever told you a story similar to what we saw?"

"I've heard many stories of animal abductions from crocodiles to buffalo, from cows to horses, even dogs."

"So you think that these aliens mutilate these animals?"

"I only tell the stories others have told me, and, yes, I have been told that animals are mutilated, a form of surgery performed on parts of their bodies."

"What kind of being would do that to a living creature?" Zane asked. "That's inhuman."

"But they're not human. No human flies a craft like we saw," Roger said.

Zane continued: "We decided to tell you our story because we want people to know that these beings abduct animals. We saw it with our own eyes."

"They could abduct people," Roger added, "just like they took that helpless animal. I believe that is what they are doing. I always keep in mind, instead of the moose, it could have been us."

I have not seen Zane or Roger since we first met. My friend gives me a regular report about the two of them each time we talk. They assured me that if they have another encounter, I would be the first to know.

CHAPTER 24
A HUNTER, AN ALIEN, AND
A MONTANA BLIZZARD

It is difficult not to feel that you have left civilization behind once you arrive in the Bear Paw Mountains. One look at the unearthly landscape inspires an association with the supernatural and sacred. The mountains draw holy men who go there for spiritual retreats. Young people frequent the area in search of visions.

American Indian oral tradition tells the story of a lone hunter who went deer hunting and encountered a bear. As the bear held the hunter on the ground, he appealed to the Great Spirit to save him. The Great Spirit filled the heavens with lightning and thunder, striking the bear dead and severing its paw to release the hunter. The paw can be seen at Box Elder Butte, while Centennial Mountain to the south represents the fallen bear. Thus, the name was born: the Bear Paw.

This story is about a hunter who went into the Bear Paw Mountains in search of game for his family. As he tells it, he would not have made it home, except for a chance encounter during the worst Montana blizzard in decades.

I met Cody when he was the best man at the wedding of my friend Charley. He approached me and invited me to join him on the dance floor. During the dance, he told me he had a story to tell. Cody was a handsome man in his early thirties. He credited his black hair and eyes, and almond complexion, to his Chippewa-Cree mother. To his father and grandmother, he attributed the rest. Marrying at the age of thirty to the blue-eyed, blond-haired woman from a neighboring ranch family, he set about immediately putting into practice his degree in animal husbandry and what he had learned from his father about ranching.

The next afternoon, we met at a trailhead about twenty miles from the site of the wedding. When I arrived, Cody had already saddled two horses. He offered me the reigns of a black mare and suggested I follow him. About thirty minutes into the ride, he stopped and dismounted. I followed him through a wooded area until we came to a cliff.

"This is where it happened," he said, as he carefully guided me to the cliff's edge.

"Are you saying this is where your encounter occurred?"

"Yes," Cody said. "It was a year ago this month, when I set off on an annual hunting trip with my buddies. Since we were sixteen, the four of us, Kevin, Abe, Milt, and me went elk hunting. We grew up together and stuck together. We've been friends since the first day of kindergarten. Abe is Blackfeet and Kevin and Milt are breeds like me. Going to a mostly white high school, we discovered we had more in common with one another than with the other students."

"So when you had your encounter, did it happen on the annual hunting trip?"

He did not answer right away.

"A week before the hunting trip, we go to our base camp and prepare everything. Then the next week, we settle in for our weeklong adventure. Each of us travels to the camp individually. We each pack our horse or snowmobile with snowshoes, guns, and food."

He continued: "When I arrived at the spot where we parked our rigs, I was surprised to see that I was the first one to arrive. Abe is always the first, followed by Milt. It is a toss-up between Kevin and me as who will be last. Kevin also has a small ranch and many responsibilities. Milt and Abe are teachers and coaches at the high school."

"So when you parked your pickup, you discovered you were the first to arrive at the appointed spot."

Cody nodded. "It was almost dark when I arrived. Snow had

started to come down heavily, and I entertained the thought that I should go home. But you know how it is, call it macho or whatever, I didn't want my buddies to tease me for the next year if I couldn't handle a little snowstorm. At the time, I didn't realize a major storm alert had been released for the area. So I led Peanuts out of the horse trailer and began packing my saddle bags."

"Did you have any idea where your friends were?"

"No, and I couldn't call. There was no cellphone reception in the Bear Paw so I decided to leave for base camp immediately. Peanuts was agitated, and even though I sensed his reluctance to go into the night with the storm, I paid no attention. After all, we had made the trip dozens of times over the years, and he knew the way. Unfortunately, I should have been keener to his reaction."

"Why did you feel that you had to go this particular night?"

"I'm responsible for putting food on the table. An elk will feed my family for a year. Besides, we had been following the same ritual for fifteen years. There was no reason to think this year would be different."

"So what happened to you once you were on the path to the base camp?"

"The snow was blinding. Fifty feet into the trip, I had no idea where we were. My lanterns and flashlight were worthless. The path had at least a foot of snow. When Peanuts balked, I urged him on until he finally stopped dead in his tracks and refused to go further. I dismounted and walked ahead leading him. That's when I lost my way."

"Why did you not listen to Peanut's instincts?"

"I've asked myself that question a thousand times, but I was determined to get to camp. I planned to build a fire and surprise the guys who always razzed me about bringing up the rear."

"Did you ever get to the camp?"

"Never. I was holding on to Peanuts, leading him in the direction of what I thought was the camp, when suddenly he balked. I pulled on the reigns and he resisted. Suddenly I lost my footing and before I knew it, I was flat on my back about 200 feet down a cliff. I tried to stand up. That's when I realized my ankle was broken. I felt it swelling inside my boot. The snow fell heavier and the wind picked up. I felt around in hopes my flashlight was nearby, but I couldn't find it. It was pitch black. At that moment, I realized I was in serious trouble. I yelled for help even though I knew it was useless. Even if my friends showed up, they would follow the trail. I knew I wasn't anywhere near it. Dawn came the next day and further confirmed the seriousness of my situation. By now, my trail was covered. It would be days before I was found."

"And your injury?"

"I managed to remove my boot from my foot. The bone in my ankle was protruding through my skin. It was a horrible sight."

"What did you do to survive?"

"I had a space blanket in my pocket, and I wrapped myself up in it as best I could. I also had a bottle of water. That was it, but both items were a godsend."

"How did you feel?"

"I was nauseous from the pain. Emotionally I felt hopeless. I prayed to God to look after my wife and children. I didn't think I would make it through another night. The snow continued. No one would be looking for me in a blizzard."

"When did all that change for you?"

"I think it was about midnight of the second night. I was on my back unable to stand or even move. I was praying. By this time, I had accepted my fate as God's will. Suddenly, I saw a blinding light overhead. I was overcome with joy. I thought rescuers had arrived. I yelled, but there was no reply."

"At what point did you realize that your rescuers were not your friends?"

"When the light returned, I thought I saw movement in the trees. I called again and suddenly this strange being appeared at my side. He told me not to be afraid, but that he would help me."

"Can you describe the being?"

"It was dark and snowing. It was impossible to make out characteristics. But I saw a humanoid figure with a strange glow around the edges of his frame. He placed his hands around my ankle, and extreme heat shot through my foot, ankle, and leg. Suddenly I felt myself losing control. The pain was gone, but at the same time, I felt like I was losing consciousness."

"Did the being speak to you?"

"Not that I recall. I knew he was friendly. He told me not to be afraid, that he heard my call for help, and that he was there to help me, but verbal speaking did not occur."

"So what happened next?"

"I must have passed out, because when I woke, I was back at my rig. My ankle was no longer broken. It was totally mended. I looked for Peanuts. He was beside the horse trailer. That's when I saw the craft. I saw it move above the trees, fly toward me, and hover for a few seconds over my pickup. It turned on its side and then zoomed off toward the west and disappeared before my eyes. I put Peanuts in the horse trailer, climbed inside my pickup, and sat there for several minutes trying to wrap my head around the idea that I had been saved by an alien. I knew no one would believe me. I thanked God and the alien, turned the key, the engine started, and I headed for home. All the way I was thinking about how to tell my family about my disappearance."

"Did you tell them?"

"You are the only one who knows. I told everyone that I made it to camp, hung around until the storm subsided, and packed up when no one else showed up."

"Why did you tell me?" I asked.

"I knew you were a friend of Charley's. Before I met you, I read your book about aliens and American Indians, and I knew I had to talk to you. If nothing else, I just needed to tell someone my story who might believe me."

"Thank you."

"There is one other thing. If you have any reservations about my story, I want to show you something." He pulled off his cowboy boot and sock and pointed to a faint, thin scar that stood out against his bronze skin. The scar ran up the side of his foot to an inch or so above his ankle.

"That is the only thing left after the alien used his hands on my ankle. I swear the bone was protruding outside my skin. It is too bad we don't have their medical abilities."

"Did you go to the doctor?"

"There was no need, but I decided to go to see what the doctor would think about the scar. He had no explanation. He took an x-ray of my ankle and confirmed there had been a serious break but had no explanation for the healing. He called it an unexplained miracle."

After he had pulled on his sock and cowboy boot, Cory stood and walked me to my car.

"Your story is very compelling and obviously, it has affected you," I said.

"That means a lot to me. You know if you ever write about this incident, would you let people know that not all aliens are bad? This being cared about me. He saved my life."

"I will tell the story as you have told me."

"It is hard sometimes to keep this secret, but on the other hand, I feel privileged to know there is life out there. Maybe it is true what the elders say. The star travelers do look after us."

I see Cody occasionally. He is still the same devoted father and husband. Every year he takes his hunting trip with his friends, but he does not talk about that night with family or friends. Only the two of us share a secret about what happened the night of the worst blizzard to hit Montana in fifty years.

CHAPTER 25
THEY CALLED ME A DEFENDER

In the 1980s, producer Linda Howe was contacted by a man identifying himself as Special Agent Doty who offered her a film taken of government officials meeting with aliens for an HBO documentary she was developing. The alleged film has never materialized and its existence remains questionable.

In this chapter, you will meet a retired university professor who tells what happened when she threatened to report her abductors to the military.

I first met Janis at an International Bilingual Conference in Denver, Colorado, twenty years ago. We hit it off immediately. Since we were both attending the conference solo, and were the only female Indian participants, we decided to enjoy the city together. One night, we planned an evening at the famous Casa Bonita, a touristy restaurant in the city, which boasted of its mariachi bands, cliff divers, and various other entertainment for diners. When I explained to her that I had to leave early because I had two individuals who wanted to meet with me about some research I was collecting, she inquired about the subject matter. When I told her I collected UFO stories, and the people I planned to meet wanted to share a story of an encounter, she laughed uproariously. She described herself as a "dyed-in-the wool" skeptic and felt anyone associated with UFO encounters were candidates for a mental institution.

At fifty-six, her university offered her a lucrative early retirement package. Recently divorced and in great shape from years of mountain climbing, she decided that she would spend the remaining years of her life dancing "to her own tune." On the day she received her bonus check, she drove to an RV and Recreational Shop and bought a twenty-six-foot Born Free RV.

I had not seen or heard from Janis for several years. Then in October 2013, I received a message from her. She wanted to see me the next time I was in Phoenix.

A couple of months passed before I was in Phoenix again. I sent a message to Janis. I was surprised when I saw her a few weeks later at the Camelback Hotel. At first, I was taken-back by her disheveled appearance and realized I would not have recognized her in a group. She stood as I approached and thanked me for seeing her.

"How are you enjoying retirement?" I asked.

"It has been interesting."

"I saw Beth Forney a few years ago and she told me you were traveling America and writing a book."

"At first, I enjoyed it, but I've decided to give up the vagabond life. I want a home again. I sold my RV last week. I'm trying to decide where to settle. I might move to Colorado. You and I enjoyed Denver, remember?"

"Yes, until you found out that I collected stories about UFOs."

"That's why I wanted to see you. I'm sorry I treated you so badly. You didn't deserve that. In those days, I was an elitist. Being an Indian and a university professor was a big deal. There were not many of us. I didn't want you to ruin your career. In addition, I worried that your hobby would end up getting you fired. Now I know you were doing legitimate research, probably more important than most of the research going on."

"I don't understand."

"I had an encounter," she whispered.

"You can say it out loud, Janis. No one is listening. But before you continue, I must warn you: I tape every story I hear. Is that acceptable?"

"I read your book. I was quite impressed. All I ask is that you keep it anonymous."

"I guarantee it." I pulled the small tape recorder from my bag and placed it on the coffee table in front of us.

"No names."

"Fake names."

"And if you decide my story is worthy of your next book, will you tell it exactly as I tell it? No sugar coating it. Just my story."

"I give you my word."

"I don't know where to begin. You know I was never a believer in such things."

"You mean you never believed in UFO encounters."

"Right." She glanced around the lounge nervously before continuing, dug in her purse and pulled out a pack of cigarettes. Just as she started to light it, a security guard appeared and told her smoking was only allowed on the outside veranda. She put the pack into her purse and looked at me.

"Would you mind if we go outside?" I turned off the tape recorder and followed her. We found an umbrella table near a sidewall and ordered ice tea from the waitress.

"So tell me about your UFO encounter."

"It happened two months ago. I was camping up north in a national park. Their fees are reasonable and since my RV is self-contained, I don't need any hookups."

"In northern Arizona?"

"Yes. When I arrived at the park, there were three other campers. There was a homeless group, just traveling around the country picking up day jobs to buy food." She dug in her purse and retrieved her pack of cigarettes.

"Did something happen that night in the national park?"

She took a long drag on the cigarette and stared blankly at a couple who had entered the veranda. "That night, I sat outside for a while. I built a small fire and roasted wieners. I saw a strange ball of light coming in over the tree line. I heard someone in the distance yell, 'It's a UFO.' I thought of you immediately. I decided it was a helicopter and put out the fire and went to bed. The next morning, I heard all the other campers leave."

"So are you now the only camper?"

"Yes, but that didn't worry me. I stayed in several parks where I was the only camper. I never had a problem. Besides the park center was still open."

"So when did you see the UFO again?"

"I spent the day hiking around the park. Along toward four o'clock I built a fire and grilled a hamburger and made a salad. I went inside the RV after I ate and got a bag of marshmallows. When I returned to the fire, I saw a bright light come in over the trees. But it was different from the night before. The lights vibrated, turning from bright white to red and then back again. I watched it for several minutes, toasted two marshmallows, and then doused the fire. After a few minutes, the ball of light disappeared. I went into the RV, locked the door, took a shower, put on my nightgown, and began a new James Doss novel."

She paused for a moment and then looked at me.

I watched as she put out her cigarette and lit another.

"What I am going to tell you, do you swear to God that you will never tell anyone I told you?"

"Yes, you have my word."

She sighed, took a deep breath, and continued. "Around eleven, I heard thunder. I put my book down and peered out the window. It was dark. No lights anywhere except for the lightning that was turning the whole park into daylight. My mother always warned us when we were kids that if it was sheet lightening, it was not dangerous. Streak lightning strikes down people and trees and sets forest fires."

"I know the kind of lightning. It is beautiful."

"I watched the lightning for maybe thirty minutes, turned off my reading lamp, and went to bed. I had no more than fallen asleep when my RV began to shake. I sat up in bed. I thought someone was outside rocking my vehicle. I reached in the drawer beside my bed and pulled out my handgun. Once it was loaded, I yelled that I had a gun and I was not afraid to use it. I expected I would scare them off, but the RV continued to shake; sometimes violently. Suddenly the whole vehicle was engulfed in a bright light. I looked out the window and saw some red lights. I thought the park rangers had arrived. I got up, unlocked the door, and walked outside."

"And the gun?"

"I had it in my hand. When I got outside there was no park ranger. There was no vehicle, but the red lights were still there. I walked toward them when suddenly a mist fell around me and the red lights turned to white. Out of the mist, I saw a figure. I told him to stop, that I had a gun, but he kept coming toward me. I decided to raise the gun and fire a warning shot, but I couldn't move my arm. That's when I tried to run, but I couldn't move. My feet would not move. My body was frozen to the spot."

"And the figure?"

"He kept walking toward me. I tried to scream, but I couldn't utter a sound. I thought I was going to be raped or murdered."

"Obviously that did not happen."

"No, it was worse."

"Worse than being raped or murdered?"

"This thing, this creature, forced me to go with him. He took me into the woods to the edge of a cliff, and I swear we floated down into a valley. I was terrified even though he assured me I was safe."

"Did he talk to you?"

"Not exactly, but I heard his thoughts telepathically. It was as if he was inside my mind. I knew every word he spoke and he understood my thoughts too."

"Did he take you to a spacecraft?"

"Yes. At the bottom of a ravine, I saw a spacecraft. It was a round machine, like the ones you see in the movies. He guided me inside the craft and led me into a massive room filled with other people. There was a strange smell. I think they used it to dope their victims. Everyone was sitting along the side of the walls. No one was talking. No one was resisting. So I'm sure they were doped. He left me there for quite some time. I looked around for something to defend myself, but there was nothing. Just stone-cold white silvery walls with benches along the side. They weren't exactly benches. They were molded into the craft but it served as a place to sit. I walked up to the largest man in the room and tried to get his attention. I thought he could help me resist these spacemen, but he stared blankly ahead and did not respond. I took my fists and pounded his chest and he did not react. I got so angry, I kicked him in the shins as hard as I could, but he simply walked away."

"Was there any facial response?"

"None. I walked up to another man. The same thing. No response. I tried a third and fourth man, but no reaction. I walked up to several women. I pulled their hair and stomped on their feet and they looked right passed me."

"So while you are beating up on the other victims, where are your abductors?"

"I didn't know, but it wasn't long until I found out. The door slid open and two men came for me. They got me by the arms and took me out of the room. They asked me why I was resisting. I told them I wanted to leave and what they were doing was against the law. I said I would call the military and the government and tell them what happened to me. And that's when I got really afraid."

She paused again and reached for her cigarettes.

"What happened that made you so afraid?"

"They told me the government wouldn't help and the military wouldn't come. They said the government knew about them." She paused and lit another cigarette. "Do you think that's true?"

"I don't know. Some people believe the government allows them to abduct humans in return for advanced technology."

"But do you believe? I want to hear it from your mouth. Is our government in partnership with these creatures?"

"I don't know. I would tell you if I knew. But tell me, what happened to you when they led you to another place?"

"They took me into a room and stood me in the middle of it. A round, long cylinder descended from the ceiling and trapped me inside. I pounded on the sides of the tube and it responded to my blows by correcting any dents I made in it. I think it was an x-ray machine that could take photos of your whole body in 3-D. Occasionally the machine stopped as though it found something of interest and then moved on. They did it three times as they huddled around a monitor that looked like a computer screen."

"What happened after they released you from the tube?"

"They took me to a chair and clamped rings around my hands and feet. They put a metal band around my head. I was paralyzed, but fully aware of what they were doing. They brought forth a needle, a long needle, and penetrated my chest below my neck bone."

She stopped and pointed to the center of her chest just below the neck before continuing with her story. "It was excruciatingly painful. I tried to scream but no sound escaped my lips. I passed out from the pain. When I came around, they asked me why I had not responded to their first treatment. I did not understand their questioning."

"Did they elaborate?"

"Oh, yes. They told me that most of their specimens responded to mind control techniques. One out of tens of thousands did not. I was one of them. They said that most people did not remember their experience, and they didn't worry about those who did, because no one believes them anyway. Do you think that's true?"

"Others have told me similar stories."

"All the time I was with them, I felt their arrogance, their disregard for human life."

"How did that make you feel?"

"Angry. Very angry. I wanted to do something to them, but even though they could not control my mind, they controlled my body through paralysis. They could force me to do whatever they wanted."

"Was that the end of their examination?"

"No. They directed me to a slab along the side of the wall and forced me to lie down. They placed a metal helmet over my head. I cried out and struggled. Another alien, one I hadn't seen before, approached me and told me to be calm. As he talked to me in a robotic manner, my head started to get hot and hotter. It became almost unbearable until a cool breeze engulfed my head and then the helmet was removed. When I demanded to know the purpose of the head contraption, they said they had collected my life's experiences."

"Your life experiences?"

"They said the machine allowed them to view my life from birth. It would help them understand the defenders."

"Defenders?"

"That's what they call those who are not mind-controlled. I was a defender. They were collecting data on all defenders to learn about the differences in their brains that allowed them to resist. At the same time, they were studying the compliers. Those were individuals who did not resist or remember their abduction."

"Did you ask them why they would bother with such an experiment?"

"I did. I told them that we were such a small group of those who resist, why would they bother with such research? They told me they were doing it for my government, the US government."

"Oh, that certainly brings up many questions. Did they conduct any other experiments?"

"None. When they released me, they reminded me that despite my threats, they were not concerned. Their arrogance was nauseating. They knew no one would believe me. I was so angry that I told them about you. I told them you would believe me. I'm sorry. I didn't mean to mention you, but it just came out. I wasn't thinking straight."

"Don't worry. I think that, if they are as omniscient as you think, they already know about me."

"I'm really sorry. I never meant to do it. I had to see you to warn you. They might come for you."

"Don't worry about it, Janis. There is nothing that can be done about it now. It is done."

She lit another cigarette and ordered a vodka and tonic. "I'm so frightened. I'm afraid they will come for me again so I have to move somewhere they cannot find me. Maybe Montana."

"I don't think moving will help. If you want to escape UFOs, Montana is not the place. There are numerous sightings and encounters in Montana. Why don't you move back home to the reservation?"

"That's the last place I'm going. They call me a city Indian and I am. I don't feel at home on the rez anymore."

She paused for a moment and looked at me. "Are you telling me there is no place I can go?" she asked.

"I'm telling you that I believe they have the ability to find you anywhere you go. That is, if they want to."

"I'm sure they will want to. They told me they would see me again." When her drink arrived, she drank it in one gulp and ordered another. "I usually don't drink this early, but I need to settle my nerves. Do you think we could go to dinner tonight like the old days in Denver?"

"I'm having dinner tonight with some old friends, but I could call you and we could go another night."

"I'm leaving tomorrow, but that's okay. I know you have many other friends. Still collecting stories too, I expect."

I looked at her, and for a moment I was reminded of the old Janis, who mocked me for my belief in those who had encountered UFOs. I picked up my purse and headed for the elevator.

She called after me: "By the way, you can add me to your list of believers."

Over the past year, I have received several telephone calls from Janis. She settled in an unnamed survival community in Idaho. She leaves no phone number or no name of the town where she lives. She has not encountered her abductors again and she feels safe in her armed community. As for me, I have not received any alien visitors because of Janis' revelation.

CHAPTER 26
ANOTHER FLATWOODS MONSTER?

In 1952, a fiery object crashed to earth in the town of Gassaway, West Virginia. Within days, an entity appeared in a nearby town of Flatwoods; it eventually became known as the Flatwoods Monster.

Various descriptions of the entity exist. Most agreed that it was at least ten feet tall, had a red face that glowed from within, and a green body. Four young boys who encountered the creature described it as having bulging non-human eyes. The head was described as shaped like either a heart or an Ace of Spades. The creature's body was man-shaped and covered in a dark pleated skirt. Some accounts reported the entity had no visible arms; others describe it as having short stubby arms ending in long claw like fingers. The creature also ejected a thick cloud of dark mist that irritated the eyes and noses of witnesses.

In this chapter, you will meet an elder who tells of a monster from space, but insisted it was not the same as the Flatwoods Monster.

In May 2012, I visited Flatwoods, West Virginia. As I checked into the motel, I asked the clerk if he could direct me to someone who might be willing to talk about the Flatwoods Monster.

"Are you a reporter? We don't talk much to reporters."

"No, I'm not a reporter. I once had an uncle who lived in Gassaway. He told me about the Flatwoods Monster when I was a child. He's passed now, and I just wanted to talk to someone who might remember the event."

"You don't sound like no West Virginian," he said.

"I live in Montana now."

"Montana, huh? I never met anyone from Montana. Do

Indians still live in tepees in Montana?"

"No, they haven't lived in tepees for a long time."

He handed me an ice bucket from under the counter. When he bent over, I saw several patches on his overalls. "Turn it in when you check out or your credit card will be charged seven dollars. By the way, how long do you plan to stay?"

"That depends on whether you find someone to talk to me."

Two hours later, he called my room. "This is Elmer from the desk. I only found one person who is willing to talk, but I'm not sure that old breed knows much. He didn't even live here in the '50s. He said you could stop by around ten tomorrow morning. There's one other thing; he said bring a carton of cigarettes."

"What do you mean, breed?" I asked.

"Half Injun. Don't you know what a breed is?"

I didn't answer his question. I had heard the word "breed" many times in my life, directed at me. I walked to the office and picked up Elmer's hand drawn map to the man's place.

The next morning, I stopped at the grocery store and bought some sweet rolls, a cup of black coffee, and a carton of Marlboros. Thirty minutes later, I pulled into the front yard of a small, unpainted shack perched high on stilts. A huge man dressed in denim, bibbed overalls walked down the steps and greeted me as I exited my car.

"Good morning. You must be the woman from Montana who's looking for the Flatwoods Monster. Oscar Hill at your service, Ma'am."

"I'm the woman." I introduced myself and handed him the carton of Marlboros. "I also brought some sweet rolls."

"You're a woman after my heart," he said. "Come, I'll get you some coffee, and we'll sit on the porch."

I followed him up the steep, wooden stairs. He pointed to a rocking chair and I sat down while he disappeared into the house. I looked around me. A large garden graced nearly half of the front yard. An old tire stood alone in the front yard. It was filled with daisies. A slight breeze came up, and I smelled honeysuckle. As I was taking in the bucolic scene, Oscar reappeared.

He handed me a cracked coffee mug. "Sorry, I don't have cups for company, but it's clean."

I took a sip of the black brew. It was delicious.

"My wife," said Oscar, "she liked to have nice things, but when she died, her sisters came here like a bunch of vultures and took most of her things. I didn't care; I don't take much to fancy things. I been batching it for almost fifteen years now. I'm like an old bull in a china shop around nice things."

He chuckled and examined the box of sweet rolls.

"Before we begin, would you mind if I tape your story?"

"Nope. Don't bother me none. Are you a reporter?"

"No, I'm a writer. I write books."

"Are you writing about the Flatwoods Monster?"

"No, I write stories about UFOs. I remember my Uncle Link talking about the Flatwoods Monster when I was a little girl. He said it came from outer space. I was just curious and wanted to talk with someone who personally knew about the event."

"Interesting. Do you have one of your books on you?"

"I have one in my car. Would you like to have it?"

"Only if you sign it to me. Write something like: To Oscar, the most interesting man I ever met."

He laughed again, and I laughed with him.

"You have a deal," I said. "The book is yours."

He laughed uproariously. His stomach jumped up and down in rhythm with his laughter. He opened the box of sweet rolls, chose a chocolate covered éclair, and balanced the back of his chair against the wall.

"Given that you collect UFO stories, we'll forget about the Flatwoods Monster for the time being. Instead, I'll tell you about my alien friends."

"Have you had an encounter with a UFO?"

"Sure 'nuff."

"Can you tell me about your encounter?"

He settled his chair on the floor with a bang and opened the box of sweets again. He chose a cherry centered roll and took a bite.

"It happened about ten-thirty at night. I always go to the outhouse about that time. I watch the news, go to the outhouse, and then to bed. I'm an early riser. I like to get up around five in the morning, fix my coffee, feed the chickens, and milk the cow, and then work in the garden. Then about noon, I read. The Doc over in Gassaway saves his old *National Geographic* for me. We have a bookmobile that comes around once a month, although there's talk they're gonna stop that. Seems nobody reads anymore. They only go to places where there's a demand for books."

He finished off his roll and reached for the carton of Marlboros, opened a pack and lit one. He took a long drag and smiled. "I love Marlboros. I don't get them often. Mostly I buy generics. Marlboros are too expensive."

"So what happened when you went to the outhouse?" I asked, without referring to the obvious activities.

"I was inside the outhouse when I heard tree branches breaking and a huge gust of wind like a tornado shook the foundation of the building. It was a surprise. I always watch the nightly news, and there was no report of storms headed our way. I sat there until the sound settled down. It felt like several minutes and then as quickly as it started, it quit."

"Did you hear any other sounds?"

"Nope, just silence. I came out of the outhouse and turned to latch the door. That's when I saw the craft. It was jutted up against the hill in the back of the house. I'll take you there shortly. You'll see how the trees are all broken and bent down."

"So there was physical evidence of the landing."

"Yep. They destroyed half of the trees up there. You'll see."

"Can you describe the craft?"

"It was a long, pencil-shaped craft, like a big propane tank only bigger. Maybe about forty feet long and twenty feet around. I estimated that three of me could stand inside three-high with room to spare. Lights came out of the underside. White lights that kind of faded from bright to dim. There was a funny smell. Not a fuel smell, more like burning electric wires."

"Did you see any beings?"

"Not at first. I decided not to look around but headed for the house and got my shotgun. I wasn't going to meet up with an alien without a gun."

"After you got the gun, did you go outside again?"

"Yep, I sure did. I was a little nervous, but I wasn't going to let an alien know that."

"Did you hide and watch the ship?"

"Nope. I walked right up to it and called them out. I told them this was my home, and they were trespassing. I told them I had a weapon and I was going to count to three, and if they didn't show themselves, I was going to fire."

"Did you realize you were dealing with aliens?"

"What else could it be? The US doesn't have any ships like that. Besides, our ships make noise. This one didn't. It just broke trees, and it didn't crash. It just set down on the trees."

"What happened when you ordered them to show themselves?"

"Suddenly they appeared in front of me. Now don't ask me how they did that. One minute there was no one there and the next minute they was in front of me. Just like ghosts."

"Ghosts?"

"Ghosts can appear and disappear. That's what they did. Just showed up out of nowhere."

"Can you describe them?"

"They were more like big lizards than human. Their skin was a scaly, green-brown color. They stood about six feet tall and smelled awful. They told me they meant no harm and would leave soon. They was checking their craft for wear."

"Wear? Did they explain?"

"They said it had to do with atmosphere. They were using different materials and was checking for erosion or corrosion. When I asked them what kind of materials they were using, they said I wouldn't understand. While I was offended by their arrogance, I let it go and just kept them in my sights."

"How did they communicate with you?"

"They talked inside my head."

"Did they make any sounds?"

"Just once when I shined my flashlight toward them."

"Can you tell me about that?"

"I had a flashlight. And when I shined it in their faces, they made a funny sound like a shriek and covered their eyes, but not before, I saw their eyes. They're some kind of demons, I think. They had strange eyes."

"Can you describe them?"

"They were big round eyes. They flashed from red to black. Reminded me of a cat."

"What else can you tell me about them?"

"As I said, they looked like lizards. They had big heads, and I think they had a tail. I'm almost positive because they could swivel around from a standing position. Their arms didn't hang down like human arms. They didn't have the motion we have." He paused and moved his arms up and down. "It was dark. I couldn't make out a lot of details. I wanted to shine my flashlight again to see if they had more arms or legs, but I was afraid I would upset them. They shrieked a deafening sound when I shined the flashlight in their direction. It scared the devil out of me. No need taking another chance."

"How many aliens did you see?"

"You mean, how many monsters? They weren't aliens, like we think of aliens. ETs, you know. They were inhuman, like an animal. A lizard. A big bug. There were four all told. Three that was working; one standing guard."

"After they told you they would leave soon, what did you do?"

"I stood there with my gun pointed at them. Then suddenly they boarded the craft and were gone. The craft moved upward, and I watched it disappear into the sky. Funny thing is, it looked like a slit in the sky opened up, they entered it, and the sky closed around it."

"Have they ever returned?"

"Nope. Never saw them again."

"Did you tell anyone about your encounter?"

"I'm not crazy. The townspeople call me the 'Crazy Breed.' If I told them about the lizard aliens, they'd probably lock me up. I remember how they made fun of the people who saw the Flatwoods Monster. Nosiree. I ain't going to give 'em a chance to ridicule me. And I'm trusting that if you ever write my story, you won't tell nobody where I live or my name."

"You have my word."

"So were you living here during the Flatwoods Monster event?" I asked.

"No. At that time, I was living in Sutton, but I heard all about it. I went out and looked for it. Never found it. I lied to that goofy Elmer. I wanted to meet you. Not too many people come to visit me, and I thought it would be interesting to meet a woman from Montana who was interested in UFOs. Besides I got a free carton of Marlboros."

I looked at him. He was smiling.

Oscar and I spent the rest of the day talking about the Flatwoods Monster, the state of Montana, and current events. He took me on a tour of his garden and he introduced me to his "Cigarette Girls," a flock of chickens who gave him a small income for buying sugar, coffee, and cigarettes. I met Daisy, his pet hog, and Jeremiah, a skunk he called his baby. He showed me photos of Loretta Lynn with him when they were children. He said they were cousins. He took me to the site where the spacecraft had landed and pointed out the broken and bent trees. He had nothing to add about the story of the Flatwoods Monster than what I had read or heard.

Before I left, I got his address and promised to send him a book if I ever told his story. "I've never read a UFO book, but I'm sure going to read yours," he said as I handed him an autographed copy *of Encounters with Star People*. Inside, I wrote, "To Oscar, the most amazing man I have ever met." He looked at the autograph and smiled.

"The aliens I saw were not star people. They were lizards," he said.

I have not seen Oscar since our meeting that day, and while I did not find the Flatwoods Monster, I found a friend for life. Oscar writes me monthly. His letters are mostly filled with stories about his garden and the weather. He always signs his letters, "The Amazing Oscar." He wrote that he loved my book and was eager to read another. I promised to send him one when it was published. Meanwhile, I sent him a copy of this chapter. He approved it wholeheartedly.

CHAPTER 27
A FIERY BALL FROM THE SKY

Kingman, Arizona, was the site of a rumored UFO crash that allegedly occurred near the city on May 20, 1953. In 1973 Raymond Fowler, a UFO investigator, reported an event told to him by a man known as Fritz Werner, a pseudonym for Arthur G. Stancil. Reportedly, Stancil was sent on a special assignment to a UFO crash in Kingman. According to the report, Stancil flew to Phoenix and boarded a blackened-window bus to a secret location northwest of Phoenix. Stancil said he did not know any of the other passengers on the bus, and he never learned their names because they were not allowed to speak with one another.

When they arrived at their destination, they were escorted to a site where a thirty-foot disc was embedded in the sand. The surface of the craft looked like it was made of an aluminum-like material. There was a small hole in the craft that appeared to be the result of the crash.

According to Fowler, Stancil's task was to calculate the speed the craft was traveling when the crash occurred. Once they finished their tasks, they returned to the bus and told never to speak about the incident with anyone. Since Fowler's revelation, several other witnesses have come forth, including a Vietnam commander who has testified to the truth of the story. Other informants have reported a small cabin with tiny chairs inside the craft and the recovery of a body of a small creature about four feet tall.

In this chapter, an elder gives a first-hand account of the event.

I arrived in Kingman on a late Friday afternoon. I had friends in the area who I planned to contact. Anna was the first on my list. A Hualapai by birth, she married a man from the Navajo Nation.

Once settled in my hotel room, I called her. She invited me to her house for dinner that night. I arrived at 7 p.m. and was greeted by three girls, ages twelve, thirteen and fifteen, who were the image of Anna.

"My husband is in D.C. so we have the whole evening for girl talk," she said, as she greeted me. I followed her into the kitchen as she prepared Indian tacos. After dinner and the girls had gone to their rooms, we moved outside and enjoyed the evening breezes.

"Do you ever get lonely living here?" I asked.

"At first, but I was only seventeen when I moved here with my husband. His ways were different from mine. But today, I can honestly say that this is where I belong. It is my home."

For the next several minutes, both of us fell silent as we enjoyed the cool breezes and the beauty of the night sky. "Sometimes I sit for hours and watch the sky," she commented. "There is much to be learned from watching the sky."

"What kind of things?"

"For example, I can predict how hot it will be by watching the intensity of the stars. If they are red hot, the next day will be red hot. If they are white and less bright, it will be a cooler day. If the moon is clouded in mist, we call it a water moon and the next day, it will rain. If the moon is bright orange, it will be a windy day."

"Have you ever seen UFOs?"

"I've seen some strange objects that I couldn't identify. There are frequent intruders on the night sky. One night they're there and the next they're gone. If you look to the south of the Big Dipper, you will notice that bright object. It's moving ever so slowly, almost invisible to the eye, but it's moving. I call it an intruder. It's not normal. It shouldn't be there, but it is. Tomorrow night, if you sit with me, we will see that it's gone. I think it's a UFO, but I'm not a scientist, so what do I know?"

"Probably more than you think."

She laughed and discounted the idea. "My husband calls me his star watcher. Perhaps I am, but I don't expect my amateur observations are worth much."

"Have you ever heard about any UFO crashes in the area?"

"There is one story that my husband's auntie tells. Have you heard of the UFO crash that happened in the '50s?" Anna asked.

"Yes, I've heard of the alleged crash, but UFO debunkers have denied it ever happened."

"They can debunk all they like, but according to Auntie Lucille, she saw the crash."

"Are you telling me she was a witness?"

"That's what she said. She saw it with her father. She was nineteen at the time. She says it has to be the same crash, but then she says she's not sure. So I don't know."

"Do you think I could talk to her?"

"Are you still collecting UFO stories?"

"Guilty."

"I have always been fascinated with the unknown, too, so I admire your interest. I believe, I should say, I know there are many sightings and encounters, but those stories are lost because people will not talk or share their knowledge."

"I would love to talk with Auntie Lucille."

"Auntie Lucille doesn't receive much company now. She just turned seventy and is not in good health. When her husband died, she moved in with her only surviving sister and lives in Kingman. She rarely shows up for family events, but I can ask her. It's still early. She stays up and watches the 10 o'clock news before going to bed. I'll call her. If she answers the phone, I'll ask if she will meet you. Can't guarantee anything. So enjoy the night, and I'll have an answer shortly."

I sat staring at the bright star south of the Big Dipper. When Anna returned, I was convinced it was moving.

"She'll see you tomorrow around noon. Stop by and pick me up. I'll go with you."

Promptly at noon, Anna and I arrived at Auntie Lucille's small house. It was located on a street with endless small houses that were the same; only the paint around the windows was different. One lone chicken pranced around the yard, scratching the desert earth in search of insects.

As we parked, an elderly, round, woman emerged. She wore a long green velvet skirt with a blouse to match. A huge turquoise nugget necklace hung around her neck. She stood under the shade of the porch and lifted an arm in welcome. Anna opened the car door and removed a box of food she had prepared. I followed her as she approached her auntie. After introductions were made, Auntie Lucille welcomed us into her small home.

For several minutes, Anna spoke to her auntie in her native language, explaining my purpose and gaining permission for me to tape her conversation. "She is fine with your taping but amused that you are interested in her story."

"Why does she find it amusing?"

"Because when the accident occurred, no one ever came around and asked questions. Her father had warned her that it could happen and told her never to talk about it."

Auntie Lucille motioned for us to sit at her small wooden table. She placed a teapot on the table and three cups before joining us.

"You can talk with her in English," Anna said. "She understands. Occasionally she may shift to her language. In that case, I will translate."

"Can you tell me what happened that night when you were a young woman and a craft crashed near here?" I asked her.

Auntie Lucille nodded and pointed toward the window. "I was with my father. We had a small grazing plot near here. We had gone in search of a lost sheep. When I gathered the sheep for the night, one was missing. I decided to go look for it even though it was dark. My father went with me. We walked for about half hour when we heard its cry. We headed toward the sound when we saw a fireball the size of this house falling from the sky. It was coming toward us very fast. I was afraid it was going to hit us. I pushed my father down to the ground and fell beside him covering my face. I remember the heat from the object as it flew over us. I felt the earth shake and a loud boom followed. When it became quiet, I helped my father stand. We saw a huge fire about a half mile away.

We approached it carefully."

"How long was it before you got to the scene?"

"Probably fifteen minutes. When we got there, we realized we had never seen such a machine."

"Can you describe what you saw?"

"I saw a round machine. It was tilted on its side. It was smooth and round. There was a hole in the side of it. My father became concerned that we should not be there. He was fearful that disturbing the scene might bring evil. So we moved away out of the light and sat down. My father prayed to divert evil spirits that might be lurking."

"Did you see anyone that was in the machine?"

"I saw no one."

"How long did you stay there?"

"Not long. I heard the cry of my lost ewe, and I told my father I was going to get her and he came with me. We must have walked another hour until we found her. She had become frightened when the machine crashed and kept running away as we came near."

"When you found her, did you return to the crash scene?"

"It was on our way to our pasture so we passed by. The scene was different. I saw several cars and a large truck and trailer parked near the crash. Men were everywhere. Some dressed in military suits and in white suits."

"Did you see a bus?"

"Yes. It was a white bus."

"Was there any writing on it?"

"I don't remember. Besides, I can't read so it would have made no sense to me."

"What were the men doing?"

"They had a machine that lifted the space machine off the ground and placed it on the truck. They covered it with a cloth. The men climbed on the bus and left."

"Did the men see you?"

"No, we hid in the shadows. They didn't know we were there."

"Did you ever hear anything about the crash from neighbors?"

"I remember this one friend of my father talking about seeing the huge flaming ball in the sky."

"Anyone else?"

"No one. My father said it was best to forget about it. He was right. The evil stayed away."

"Why did you agree to talk about it now?"

"Evil spirits only remain for fifty years. After that, they lose interest. It has been more than fifty years."

"And you never told anyone what you saw?"

"No, we didn't trust the *bellagona*. The white man doesn't honor his word. They prosper on lies. It was not our way."

"Is there anything else that you remember about that night?"

"Only one thing. My ewe. She died several days later. She had red sores on her skin. It was sad. We knew it was a warning to keep silent, and we did."

After Auntie Lucille told her story, we enjoyed another cup of tea with her. As we said our goodbyes, she accompanied us to the door, stood on her small porch, and waved until we were out of her driveway. Anna commented that she had never seen her more alive than when she told her story.

While there is no way of knowing whether Auntie Lucille and her father saw Stancil's UFO, there were several similarities that would lead to that conclusion. My friend Anna says Auntie Lucille asks about me every time she sees her. Apparently, she has remembered other things about the crash that she wants to tell me. I plan to visit her on my next trip to Arizona

CHAPTER 28
HE GLOWED

Glowing aliens have been reported over the past several decades.
The most recent account occurred in England on October 23, 2014,
when a man who was a former police officer and pilot reported seeing a
glowing green alien fleeing from his family cottage. Shortly before the
sighting, a neighbor reported a UFO hovering nearby. Inhabitants of
the region frequently report glowing orbs.

In this chapter, an Athabasca Native tells about the time she met a
glowing alien.

Marylou lived in a small village in Alaska. She was a close family friend of a local minister's wife named Carol. When Marylou was a girl, she attended Carol's Sunday school class. Carol said that one day Marylou told her about a strange man from the stars who visited her at the family fish camp on the Tanana River. Carol had comforted the girl, who at first seemed upset, but who later told Carol that she had become friends with the visitor from the stars. After that, Marylou did not offer further information.

Carol told me that her former student had become an accomplished seamstress and often did sewing for her. She offered to contact Marylou, invite her to her house, and ask her if she were willing to share her story.

A day later, Carol called and invited me to breakfast at her house. Marylou wanted to meet me.

When I arrived at Carol's house, I was introduced to a beautiful young woman in her mid-twenties. An Athabasca by birth, she had black hair and eyes to match. Dressed in jeans and a heavy woolen sweater with sealskin mukluks, her exotic looks would have been highly valued by modeling agents worldwide. She was the eldest of eleven children and unmarried.

"I'm sure Carol told you, but I was born on the Tanana River," she said. "My father was taking my mother to the Church when she went into labor. I was actually born on the boat on the river. I've always felt a part of the Tanana."

"Carol tells me that you had an encounter with a star traveler when you were a child. Did that occur on the Tanana?"

"Yes. We have a fish camp on the Tanana River. I met him when I was about eleven." She paused and toyed with a tissue in her hand. "One night a figure appeared out of nowhere at the camp. It scared my whole family. It glowed, lighting up the night like day. We knew it was no ordinary human being. My mother thought it must be an angel, but my father grabbed his gun and threatened the intruder and it disappeared."

She laughed awkwardly and took a sip of the water that Carol had set before her.

"Do you mean it vanished before your eyes, or it disappeared into the forest?"

"It vanished. I know it sounds crazy, but just like a puff of smoke it was gone. My father searched for it, sat up all night with his gun, but it didn't return."

"Did you see it?"

"Oh, yes. The next night it returned. It came across the river like it was walking on water. It terrified my brothers and sisters. My mother was convinced that it was Jesus; my father thought it was the devil. Our dogs fell to the ground and whimpered. My dad grabbed his gun to shoot it, but for some reason the gun jammed. It would not fire. I remember he yelled at me to take shelter, but I ignored him. The glowing man told me not to be afraid. He said he meant us no harm."

"Are you saying that the glowing man talked to you, but not to the rest of your family?"

"Yes. I looked around and no one seemed to hear him."

"You are now calling the entity 'he' instead of 'it'. Do you believe the entity was male?"

"Yes, it was male."

"How did he speak to you?" I asked.

"In my head."

"Can you describe him?"

"I only know that he glowed. I felt good when he was near me."

"Did you approach him?"

"Yes. I looked around and my family had fallen asleep. It was me and the glowing man. He asked me to follow him and I did."

"Were you afraid or anxious? Tell me what you felt."

"I don't remember feeling afraid. I felt at peace with him."

She took another drink of water and hugged herself with her arms.

"What did he want from you?"

"He wanted a place to stay until he could be rescued."

"Rescued?"

"He said he was stranded and alone. I felt his loneliness as he spoke to me. I felt his fear, and I wanted to help him."

"Did you help him?"

"I took him to an old trapper's cabin and told him he would be safe there. Each day for the next two weeks, I would slip away and go visit him."

"How did you know he was stranded? Did he explain?"

"Something happened and he was left alone, but he knew if he could stay hidden his people would come for him. I felt sorry for him, but there were times I believe he controlled me and was forcing me to do something I did not want to do."

"Can you explain?"

"I lied to my parents. I was a Christian girl and I knew it was wrong to keep secrets from my parents and to lie to them about what I was doing."

"What did you tell them?"

"I said I was picking berries."

"Did you pick berries?"

"He helped me pick berries to cover up my lies."

"Why did he need you?"

"He was afraid of humans. He worried my father would alert the authorities. All he wanted to do was survive until his friends came for him."

"Did he ever tell you anything about himself?"

"No. I asked him where he was from and he said far, far away and pointed to the stars. He said they had been traveling three Earth years when they stopped on Earth. He also told me they visited Earth often."

"Did he tell you how he became stranded?"

"He said he strayed from his companions. He felt so happy being on Earth and he missed the exit."

"The exit?"

"He said they were supposed to return to their ship at an appointed time and leave, but he didn't return in time. But he said they would miss him and return for him. He knew they planned to return in a few days for water. From what I gathered, it was about two weeks. He said Earth was the best place for water. It was a guess on my part, maybe because their time is different."

"How do you know this?"

"He told me that at my age, I would be considered an infant on his planet. He said he trusted me because I was mature."

"Did he tell you how his companions would find him?"

"He said he had a tracker inside him, but I didn't understand that. I didn't know what a tracker was, but he pointed to his arm so I suspected it was something that allowed them to find him."

"Were you ever afraid of the star traveler?"

"In his presence, I felt at peace. I felt special that he had chosen me to help him. He told me so. Now that I am older, and I have had years to think about it, I think he told me what he thought I wanted to know. That way he controlled me. I worry that they have the power to control the whole human race or put them to sleep like he did with my family. Can you imagine such a power and what they might do if they wanted to?"

"Can you tell me anything else you remember about your relationship?"

"It was difficult to look at him. He was bright. He told me that they didn't take a form like humans. They were mostly made of light. I didn't understand that when I was eleven, and I don't understand it now."

When Marylou assured me there was nothing left to tell, we spent the rest of the morning talking about her clothing designs, the family fish camp and upcoming celebrations.

I have not seen Marylou again, although Carol tells me she is engaged to be married. I often think of her and wonder if, in her own way, Marylou's worries about the vulnerability of the human race is something that should concern us all.

CHAPTER 29
BALLS OF LIGHT AND LITTLE BOYS

According to Peter Davenport, director of the National UFO Reporting Center, there have been frequent sightings of clusters of red, orange, and yellow "fireballs." There appears to be no adequate explanation for these sightings. The objects clearly are not aircraft, meteors, satellites, weather balloons, or swamp gas.

In this chapter, you will meet a grandmother who has not only encountered the "fireballs," but she reports that her grandsons have engaged them in play.

The first time I met Bethany I knew I would have a life-long connection with her. Our first introduction came when the two of us had been selected as members of a panel addressing issues facing indigenous women in leadership at the First International Indigenous Women's Conference in Leadership held in Washington, D.C. Indigenous women from all over the world attended the event. I spoke about obstacles to American Indian women in male-dominated academic fields at the university level; Bethany represented American Indian women in non-traditional fields such as science and engineering in the workforce.

After our initial meeting, we remained in touch, meeting a couple of times every year at conferences. As our friendship grew, we often visited privately until we formed a bond as close as sisterhood.

In 2011, I visited Bethany in Arizona. Her husband, a local contractor, had finally completed her dream home in the desert about sixty miles from the city. "It's way too large for us," she admitted as she took me on a tour of the sprawling Spanish-style ranch home, "but we're blessed with seven grandchildren that we hope will spend many days with us. We have five-hundred acres. It is our hope that as time passes, our girls will build houses here. My oldest daughter, Jillian, and her husband, Jeff, have already completed a foundation about a mile from here as the crow flies."

"That's wonderful," I said.

"Yes, but I'm worried."

"Why?" I asked.

"I've been suffering from insomnia ever since we moved here."

"Have you seen a doctor?"

"Doctors can't solve my problems. I have to deal with them alone or with the help of my sister." She reached for my hand and squeezed it. "I need your experience to help me sort out things."

"I'm here for you. I'll do anything I can to help."

"Don't laugh at me. I know you have researched the paranormal for years."

"UFO encounters," I said.

"They are the same thing to me."

She paused and shouted for her husband, Mark. She listened for his reply, but there was none. "Good, he's gone to work," she said. "I don't want him to hear what I am going to tell you."

We walked into the massive gourmet kitchen, and I sat down at the long bar. Bethany busied herself making tea as I placed the tape recorder on the counter.

"Mark thinks I'm suffering from depression, but it is not depression, I'm afraid."

"Why are you afraid?" I asked.

"The first night we spent in this house, I couldn't sleep. I attributed it to a new bed and strange surroundings, but there was something in the bottom of my stomach that made me uneasy. I can't explain it. After about two hours of constantly tossing, I got out of bed, slipped on my sweats, and went to the kitchen. For some unexplainable reason, I walked outside and sat down on the veranda. Sometime after that, I was compelled to take a walk."

She paused and walked to the window and pulled back the curtain. "There was a full moon lighting up the night. I began walking down the driveway, and I must have walked a mile or two, when all of a sudden a sense of dread overwhelmed me. I didn't understand it, but I immediately turned around and began my walk back home."

"Did you have any idea why you felt so much dread?"

"No, I'd never been afraid of the dark. As a small child on the reservation, we played in the desert at night. The nighttime was exhilarating."

"Did anything happen on your walk to confirm your fears?"

"As I turned in the direction of the house, I looked over my shoulder, and that's when I saw a red, glowing ball. It was about fifty feet behind me and about twenty feet off the ground. I started to run, and it sped up to keep pace with me. I slowed down, and it slowed."

"What did you make of that?"

"To me, it meant it was guided by intelligence. Otherwise, how would it know to react in such a way?"

"How long did it stay with you?"

"All the way home. When I reached the front door, I turned, and it hovered there on the edge of the house lights and didn't move. I immediately opened the door and closed it behind me. I turned out the lights and looked out the window. It stayed there until my husband walked into the room and turned on the light. He was surprised to find me sitting in the darkened room. When I told him about what I had seen, he walked outside and returned, assuring me nothing was there."

"Did you see it again?"

"Almost every night for two weeks. It hovered outside the house in the trees between midnight and early morning."

"Did Mark ever see it?"

"Never, but Jillian's boys did. That's what makes me so afraid. I was telling you that Jillian was building a house on the property. During her husband's vacation, they brought out their RV, camped, and worked. I went over the second day and offered my help. That's when Darién, the six-year-old, told me about the glowing suns. He had seen them from the window in the camper. He said they were aliens trapped on our planet."

"Aliens?"

"That's what he said. I told him there was no such thing, but he insisted they were aliens."

"You said 'they.' Did he see more than one?"

"He said there were five. He is a smart child. I'm sure he counted correctly."

"Had you ever seen more than one?"

"Only one, and they never communicated with me, but Darién insisted they were trapped here on Earth. He said they would go away soon. They were waiting for the right time."

"You said you saw them for two weeks. Have you seen them since that time?"

"No, but I'm afraid they'll come back. I want to sell this house and return to the city, but I don't want to tell Mark. He built this house out of his love for me, but I don't want to stay here. I'm afraid they will harm the boys."

"Are the boys afraid?"

"No, but they're kids. They know no fear. But they have not returned. Perhaps they did communicate with Darién. They communicated with Dominic too. Dominic is his younger brother. He's five. Darién said they came to earth to explore, and there was some kind of an electrical storm. Their ship was forced to leave them behind to get to a safer place, but when the storm subsided, they would return. They were told not to be afraid."

"Sometimes children are more open to communication with extraterrestrials than adults." I said. "They see things that others don't see."

"That's the other thing. Both of the boys played with them."

"Can you explain?" I asked.

"During the day, the boys said that the balls of light turned into little boys and they would play with them. According to Dominic, they went on adventures together. Darién wouldn't talk about it.

He said it was a secret, but admitted to seeing the little boys."

"Did they describe them?" I asked.

"Nothing, except they were little boys."

"Did the boys believe they were the glowing suns?" I asked.

"According to them, they saw the balls of light turn into little boys."

"Where are the boys now?" I asked.

"They're back in the city. My daughter and son-in-law ran out of money and they want to pay for the house as they build it. Eventually, they plan to move here when the house is completed. Her husband, Jeff, is a contractor too. He'll take over Mark's business."

"Did you ever feel threatened by the orbs?" I asked.

"No, my fear is my own. You have a lot of experience with stories about aliens. Mark thinks I'm nuts. I'm glad I can talk with you."

"What about the boys? Did they tell their mother?"

"They said it was a secret. I have an agreement with the boys. They can tell me anything, and I won't betray them. I planned to tell her, but when they went away, I kept quiet."

"I'm confused. If you were so afraid, why you would keep the secret?"

"I tried to tell Jillian more than once, but every time I tried, I forgot what I was telling her. She thinks I'm showing signs of Alzheimer's."

"I don't think you have Alzheimer's."

"I agree. I think the aliens interfered with my thought patterns and prevented me from telling the boys' secret."

The following year, Bethany spent a week at my cabin in Montana. She had not seen the glowing balls of light since her first encounter. She was now content in her new home even though she keeps her eyes out for the shining balls. Her grandsons, on the other hand, have decided to be astronauts.

CHAPTER 30
THEY TOOK ANTONIO THAT NIGHT

American military men have reported sightings of UFOs since World War II. During the War, both the Allies and the Germans witnessed strange flying objects above their bases and during battles. In 1943, the British set up a special committee to investigate and collect evidence about these objects, commonly referred to as "foo-fighters" at the time. Headed by Lieutenant General Massy, the committee concluded the flying objects were not of German origin.

In this chapter, you will meet an American Indian elder named Sebastian who fought in World War II. He had a most amazing story about an event that occurred on the battlefield, an event that has haunted him all of his life.

I was introduced to Sebastian by his grandson, Jonah, in 2013. Jonah had read my book *Encounters with Star People* and said that he enjoyed it so much he read it to his grandfather. After completing the book, Sebastian requested an audience with me.

I knew of Sebastian. In some American Indian circles, he was regarded as a spiritual man and a protector of the culture. People throughout the reservation sought his advice. At ninety-one, he walked with a cane. His body was bent at the waist, making him appear as though he had a hump on his shoulders. His white hair hung in a wispy, single braid down his back, and his leathery, deeply wrinkled face showed the passing of time. An earring graced his left ear lobe; it was carved from bone and painted to resemble an eagle feather. His eyes had the sparkle of youth and despite his age, he read without the aid of reading glasses, although by his own admission, he preferred to be read to by his grandson.

"I first saw the Star People in 1942," Sebastian began.

"Can you explain the circumstances around your encounter?" I asked.

"It happened during a battle. We were barricaded in what was left of a church. There was no roof but enough walls to provide some protection. My best friend was a man by the name of Antonio. One night a light came from overhead and shined down on me. It struck Antonio, too. He was an Italian from New York, who hung onto me like a leach. He said if he was going to survive the war, it would be with me, and so he stayed by my side. When we saw the light shine down on us, he was sure it was a sign from God and began to pray. It was only after the light moved away, that I saw a huge flying object slide across the sky. It was magnificent. Unlike anything I'd ever seen."

"Did Antonio see the craft?"

"I know he saw the light. It frightened both of us. But when the light was gone, Antonio was gone, too. They took Antonio that night. When it passed over the building, I looked for my friend but he was gone. After that I prayed to the Great Spirit, to Grandfather Sky and Grandmother Earth."

"Are you sure they took him?"

"Yes. The last thing I remember is Antonio calling my name. To this day, he is listed as MIA."

"Did you encounter the spacecraft again?"

"Yes. When I got out of the army in 1945, our first stop in the USA was Denver. We landed there and were processed, and then quarters were arranged while the papers were being completed for our discharge."

"Was that a common practice?" I asked.

"In those days, I believe so. It was a long time ago. I remember we were there for a few weeks. When we got our discharge papers, they gave us our severance pay and bus tickets home. I took the ticket and cashed it in at the bus station."

"How did you get home?"

"I decided to buy a pickup and drive home to the reservation in style."

"Did you buy your pickup in Denver?" I asked, motioning to the faded red vehicle setting alongside his small wooden house.

"Yes. It was a beauty when it was new. I handed the white man cash on the sales lot. She cost me eight hundred dollars and change. I couldn't wait to arrive on the reservation. But along the way, my journey took a different turn."

He paused and stared off into space, as though remembering the events of the past.

"Can you explain?" I asked.

"I left Denver in the evening. It was dark when I put the city lights behind me. I planned to drive all night. I was young then and I learned to stay up all night, sometime for several days, in Europe. I was not worried about my stamina."

"You said that on this trip your journey took a different turn. Can you explain?"

"Somewhere in Wyoming, it happened. I'm not sure of the location."

"Could you elaborate?"

"All I remember was that I had been driving for a few hours. It was dark. Occasionally I would see the light of a ranch in the distance. I remember watching the gas gauge. I was worried I would run out of gas before I found a station to fill up, so I just kept driving. All of a sudden, the entire road lit up. The most unusual thing about the light was that it followed me. When I slowed, it slowed. When I sped up, it did too. It was the same light I had seen that night on that old church."

"So what you saw in Wyoming was the same kind of light as you saw when Antonio disappeared?"

"Yes. I decided to pull the pickup off to the side of the road, thinking it would pass, and I could get a better look, but just as I tried to slow down, I lost control of the pickup and the next thing I knew, I was airborne."

"Airborne?"

"I know it sounds unbelievable but, yes, I was sitting in my truck behind the wheel, the engine is off, and I am being lifted up."

"Can you tell where you were going?"

"Only that I was being pulled upward. I passed out after that. I don't know how long I was unconscious. But when I woke, I was in a room, like a hospital, only it wasn't a hospital. I was there with other people, all in individual beds. The room was filled with a blue light. I couldn't tell where the lights were coming from. There was a mist in the air that gave off a metallic smell. It was not sickening, but it stung my nose. I couldn't move. I cried out to the guy next to me but he didn't hear me. I turned to the guy on my left side and he didn't answer either."

"Did you recognize anyone?" I asked

"No one. I thought I was in a morgue and everyone in the room was dead. I decided I was there by mistake, and no one knew I was alive. I prayed for guidance before I made one last attempt to free myself. And then, just as I started to struggle, I felt my body released."

"Did anyone enter the room to release you?" I asked.

"No. I jumped up and began going from one person to the next. They all appeared asleep. I tried to find a pulse, but I detected no life. I turned to look for an exit, and after that I found myself sitting behind the wheel of my vehicle at a gas station on a four-way intersection. An attendant was knocking on the window. He asked me if I was all right, and I climbed out of the pickup, convincing myself that I must have had a nightmare. But I discounted that idea when I looked at my wrists and saw welt marks on my arms and wrists. I still have them."

He unbuttoned the cuffs of his long sleeve shirt, pulled the sleeves up, and put his arms on the table. "Some people think these are the wounds from a suicide attempt, but I have never been one to end my life. War teaches a man to love life."

I nodded. I knew the marks were not from a suicide attempt. I had seen scars of suicide attempts as a counselor, and these wounds were not wounds caused by cutting. There was no doubt that something had created white scars that stood out like a permanent disfigurement around his wrists and lower arms.

"So now that you are on earth, what do you do?" I asked.

"The first thing I did was try to figure out where I was. Then I tried backtracking. I wanted to figure out where I was taken on board their ship. I was convinced I could find some evidence to prove my story, but I spent a day searching and never found anything."

"What did you do next?"

"After giving up, I continued my drive, but at night, I found a boarding house that took me in for the night. I still wasn't convinced that I had been kidnapped. I kept thinking about the war and that night. I kept thinking I was just feeling guilty."

"Guilty? Why would you feel guilty?"

"I've always felt guilty about Antonio."

"But you should not feel guilty about that."

"I did because I was too afraid to help him. I was so captivated by the enormity of the spaceship, that I never did anything to save him, but the strangest thing happened to me when I was taken on board that ship in Wyoming. They told me they took Antonio because he was destined to die in battle. They told me that I was a survivor. They knew I would survive, but Antonio would not."

"Who told you?" I asked.

"I don't know. I just knew."

"Did they tell you where he was?"

"No, only that he was safe," Sebastian said, thoughtfully.

"Have you ever seen them again?"

"Many times. It's always the same. I'll be in my pickup and they take me and my pickup. When they return me, I'm sitting behind the wheel of my pickup in a safe place. Once they placed me in a rest stop outside Kansas City, and I had to find my way home. Sometimes I wake in my own yard. But I never remember what happened to me."

"But you have kept the pickup all of these years," I commented.

"It's the most dependable vehicle on the reservation," he said. "That is, if you don't care about your destination."

We both laughed and he walked me outside to get a better look at the '46 pickup in collector condition.

I am in contact with Jonah, Sebastian's grandson, regularly. He tells me his grandfather is still active and walks a mile every day. In his last email, he told me Sebastian is requesting another audience with me.

CHAPTER 31
THE STAR PEOPLE HAVE NO NAMES

*According to historian and UFO researcher David Jacobs, abductees
are taken a hundred times a year on average. His research suggests that
abductions are not random at all and that they are intergenerational.
He also believes that these events are planned and repeated throughout
an individual's life.*

*In this chapter, you will meet an individual who maintains that
interaction with star people is a part of his legacy.*

Vernal Looks to the Sky was fifty-eight when I first met him.
He was eighty-eight when he told me the story of his life-
long relationship with the Star People. As a religious leader, Vernal
was responsible for the Sundance revival on his reservation. As a
cultural and language specialist, he served on the Tribal College
Board and taught language classes. After his retirement, he moved
to Denver to live with his daughter. I often stopped to see him
every time I was in the city. Over the years, we became trusted
friends, and near the end of his life he told me there was a story he
needed to tell me before he traveled the Milky Way. His revelation
carried an ominous warning.

"I learned about the Star People from my father," Vernal said.
"My grandfather was called Looks to the Sky. He was born on a
night when hundreds of comets fell to Earth. The elders agreed.
His name would be Looks to the Sky." He paused and took a sip
of ice water.

"So you're telling me, your family has had a lifetime of connections with the Star People, right?"

"Yes, my whole family had that connection."

"Can you tell me about that?" I asked.

"My grandfather was killed in World War I when my father was just a toddler. At his burial ceremony, the elders renamed my father giving him the name of Looks to the Sky in honor of his deceased father. When my father was eight, he was carted off to boarding school. The teachers gave him the name Herbert. He hated that name, but all the way through school, his name was Herbert Looks to the Sky. His old friends from school called him Herbert. They had all been given names, too: Horace, Cleradin, Addison, Hansford, and Oather. Those names stuck and the days of traditional names was over."

"And what about you?"

"My father named me Vernal after his best friend at boarding school. I never knew which name was worse: Herbert or Vernal."

He paused and laughed at the thought of the two names as he shuffled to the stove and picked up a dented coffee pot. He returned to the table, placed two mugs on the table, and filled the cups before continuing his story.

"In the old days the name of a child was important. It could stand for a momentous event, such as the night the comets fell, or it could be the result of a vision by the holy men on the night of the birth. It often foretold the future path of the child. It could be a name to honor a deceased relative or something in nature. Today it is different. The young people name their children after TV characters or names listed in baby books. I hear names like Colt and Cody, Tiffany and Tammy. What kind of names are those?"

Vernal shook his head in disbelief.

"After boarding school, I went to Lawrence, Kansas, and attended the Indian college there. It was mostly vocational, but I learned things there." He paused again and added sugar to his black coffee. "They taught me much English there and the rest I learned in the army."

"Do you think the white kids got a better education back then?"

"The Indian schools were run by nuns. I never knew that religious people could be so cruel. When I think back on it, I believe only the meanest women in the world became nuns." A mischievous smile crossed Vernal's face. "I think they became nuns because they were so mean they couldn't find husbands. I suppose our new names could have been worse. We could be like the Star People and have no names."

"How do you know the Star People have no names?" I asked, but he didn't respond immediately. I watched as he made his way back to the stove, returning the coffeepot to the burner. Even at eighty-eight, Vernal was a strikingly handsome man, and I imagined that in his youth he left behind several broken hearts. He told me once that he had only loved one woman in his life and that she died in childbirth at thirty-one. He never married again and had only one child, his daughter, Dawn and a bevy of great nieces and nephews who fussed over him.

"They told me that names set individuals apart and that in their world, everyone was equal and there was no need to draw attention to uniqueness. When I explained to them that in my world, names were once chosen carefully and determined one's path in life, they considered such practices as similar to theirs."

"What did they mean by that?" I asked.

"When they are born, their direction in life is already planned, but without the name."

"I'm not sure if I understand."

"In their world, the number of births are controlled. A birth only occurs when there is a projected need for a particular job in the future."

"So the birth is determined by society and not the family."

"Oh, yes. That is their way."

"How long have you been in contact with the Star People?" I asked.

"As long as I can remember."

"Are you willing to share your experiences with me?"

"I think it is time I tell my story. I know you have personal knowledge of the Star People, so I think you will understand what I have to tell you."

"Before you tell me your story," I said, "I want you to know that I have written a book about UFO encounters among Indians. I collect stories from tribal people from all over the country and tell their stories."

"I am well aware of that. I read your book. I heard about it from a teacher at the high school. She knew I loved to read and she gave me your book. If you write another book, I would be pleased if you told my story in a book. Deal?"

He raised his hand for a high-five. When my hand joined his, we both laughed.

"I met my first Star Man when I was four or five years old," he began. "It was the year my father took me antelope hunting with him. I remember how proud I was. It was a time of learning for me. My father taught me the ways of the hunter, how to track, how to read signs, how to be aware of the wind and the sounds. It was an important part of moving from boyhood to manhood, and the instruction began early in those days. I was taught only to hunt for food. To be respectful to the animal that gave its life so I might live. He taught me to thank the animal and the Great Spirit."

"Was it on this hunt that you first met the Star People?"

"Yes. We climbed the butte north of our house in darkness. We wanted to get to our destination by daybreak. My father spotted a small herd the day before in the valley below."

He paused and looked at the bottom of his empty cup and walked to the stove and filled his cup again. Once he was settled across the table from me, he began again.

"As we topped the hill, we saw a large spaceship in the valley below, but no antelope herd. My father explained to me the spaceship came from the place where the Star People lived. He took my hand and we descended the butte. The Star Men came forward and greeted him as a friend. He told them I was his son and they took us onboard the ship. Then we were in the air zooming upward in the heavens. I saw the Earth way below us, and that is all I remember, except that when we were back on Earth, we were in the next valley and before us was the antelope herd. My father chose a large buck for our food and he dressed him in the field. After he had completed the task, he made a travois and we pulled it home."

"Did your father talk to you about the encounter?"

"Not at the time. He only told me the Star Men were visitors from the sky, and I must honor them."

"When did you see them again?"

"It became a regular event. As you know, our small ranch was isolated even from the rest of the reservation. It was the home of my grandfather and father. It was where I was born. The Star People have been coming to this place from my grandfather's day. Looks to the Sky was a fitting name for him."

"So are you telling me that over the years you have had regular contact with the Star People?"

"As you know, I lived on the ranch for a good part of my life. In the 1980s, there was a movement to restore our language and culture in the schools. I was invited to be a part of that so I moved to town. My work was there and my brother lived there. I had a room in his house. I could watch my nieces and nephews grow up. But I always knew when the Star People were returning. I would come here to meet them."

"How did you know they were coming?"

"Somehow they sent me a message. I just knew."

"Why did they come to Earth?" I asked.

"They seeded the Earth. They have seeded many planets, and they return to check on them."

"Have they ever told you anything about their world?"

"They tell me there are many worlds, some similar to Earth. Some that are very different."

"Have they told you anything about the beings that inhabit those planets?"

"I learned there are several hundred. Some are humanoid or resemble humans. Others are not."

"Can you elaborate on that?"

"Some are more like animals. I know it is hard for us to accept the idea the Great Spirit created entities that are so different from man. Some people think that the idea of non-human beings destroys the idea that God created man in His image, but not me. The Great Spirit can create anything. He may have created man in his own image, but that does not mean he did not create others."

"Did they tell you anything about the non-human entities?" I asked.

"Only that they are to be avoided. They hold humans in contempt and are aggressive toward them. Although they are advanced technologically, their evolutionary process has stagnated. They believe they can speed up that process using humans."

"Are you telling me that they are the ones abducting humans?"

"They have human-like collaborators, who are scientists and have no moral codes that guide them. Together they commit horrible atrocities, not only against Earth humans, but other humanoid populations in the universe as well."

"Do you think we have anything to fear from them other than the abductions?"

"There is no question that they are more advanced technological than us. They can breathe in our atmosphere, but it is limited. If they ever develop the means to breathe safely on Earth, then we might have to worry."

"What do you think would happen to humans?"

"I don't think the human race would survive."

The next time I saw Vernal, he was in the hospital. Age-related problems with diabetes complications took him the night after I arrived. I was grateful that I had a chance to say good-bye to my friend of some thirty years. His warning is always foremost in my mind as I continue to search out stories about UFO encounters.

CHAPTER 32
SOMEWHERE IN MONTANA

Several UFO investigations believe that encounters with large rabbits, little people, or angelic girls may be linked to the UFO phenomenon. These stories often tell of individuals, generally children, lured into play by a rabbit, a bird, or a small child, and then led onboard a spaceship.

In this chapter, you will meet a woman who told of her first encounter where she danced and played with two girls, who called her sister, before being taken onboard a spacecraft.

Stephanie, a twenty-two-year-old graduate of a prestigious eastern university with double major in aeronautical engineering and astronomy, remembered the day she was taken onboard a space ship. "I went into the mountains with my grandmother to pick huckleberries. It was my birthday and Grandma promised to make me a huckleberry cake. I loved huckleberry cake; still do." She smiled broadly.

Stephanie had recently completed the Air Force's Officer Candidate School and held the rank of Second Lieutenant. A self-assured young woman, she was scheduled to report for duty in ten days.

"Did you encounter the UFO on your birthday?"

"Yes," she said, pausing as she rummaged in her purse. "I was wearing my turquoise cowboy boots with embroidered purple roses. It was a gift from my grandmother for my twelfth birthday. I was so proud of them."

She paused, pulled a See's lollipop out of her purse, and held it up like a treasure. "It happened on the reservation at my grandmother's place. We picked huckleberries for about an hour, and then decided to split up. I headed to the top of the hill and my grandmother went around the base. We planned to meet in two hours. If we missed each other, we would go directly home."

"So you were alone when you encountered the UFO."

"Yes. As I topped the hill, I watched a craft shaped like a toy top land in the meadow. I stood on the mountain looking down, mesmerized by it."

She paused, unwrapped the See's lollipop, and stuck it in her mouth. "I don't know why I was drawn to it, but it drew me like a magnet."

"How big was the craft?" I asked.

"Not too big. Maybe forty feet in diameter. It was dull silver. There were three levels. At the top were retractable windows they used when they wanted to see something. Otherwise they kept them shuttered to give an outward appearance of a single piece of metal."

"Did you see any activity around the craft as you approached it?"

"No, not at all. I remember feeling joy. I felt no fear. I felt like jumping and dancing for joy."

"Can you explain the reason for this joy?" I asked.

"No, I have no explanation. It was coming from deep inside me. I had no control over it."

"Did you ever see any of the occupants of the craft?"

"I did. In fact, the next thing I remember was seeing two girls, my age, coming toward me. They were wearing silver, slinky pajamas. I wanted a pair of pajamas like that so badly. They pointed to my boots. They liked my boots."

"What did they look like?"

"At first, I focused only on their pajamas. I was so spellbound by them. I know it sounds crazy, but remember, I was only twelve years old. Not a child, but not a woman either. Grandma called me her baby. I lived with her after my mother ran off with a cowboy. Shortly after, she and her boyfriend were killed on an icy highway outside Steamboat Springs, Colorado."

She plopped her lollipop in her mouth, took it out, and examined it.

"Did you remember any of the features of the girls in the slinky pajamas?"

"They had shoulder-length blond hair. It was thin when compared to my thick Indian hair. When I reached out to touch them, they were pale next to my skin. They called me sister, and I felt loved even though I knew they were too pale to be my blood. They had the biggest black eyes I had ever seen. They were round like a quarter."

"Anything else?"

"They held out their hands to me, and we began to dance." She picked up the lollipop again, got up and walked to the kitchen sink. She ran water for a few seconds, filled a glass and drank.

"After we danced, they led me to a doorway on the opposite side of the craft. My next memory is standing in a field looking at Grandma's house. My grandmother saw me and ran toward me. I could tell she was upset. She demanded to know where I had been. All the time, I'm trying to find my clothes."

"Your clothes?"

"Yes. I was naked. I was still wearing my cowboy boots but nothing else; I was so ashamed when I saw my grandmother. There was no place to hide and no clothes."

"Where were your clothes?"

"I have no idea. I tried to tell my grandmother about the girls in the spaceship. She looked at me firmly and said never to speak about them again. She took off her sweater and wrapped it around me. Later I learned she had been looking for me for four hours."

"Do you think she believed you about the spacecraft?"

"She confided in me that she saw the spacecraft just before I appeared in the field, so yes, she believed me."

"Your story is different from any I have ever heard," I said.

"But that was not the end. Since the first meeting, I saw the same girls many times. They appeared at the most untimely and unexpected times. It was always the same. We greeted one another, and then I followed them into the spacecraft."

"Do you have any recollection of any details in your subsequent meetings?"

"Many memories. I was always with the two girls."

"Did they age the same as you?" I asked

"At first, I thought so." She paused and picked up her purse again. She found a package of chewing gum and offered a stick to me.

"Can you explain what you mean about their ages?"

"I discovered over the years that they had the ability to look my age, but I don't think they were girls at all. Sometimes I saw other things."

"Can you describe them?"

"Big heads, strange eyes."

She shook her head as though in disbelief and continued. "But I know what I saw. I am not crazy or delusional."

"Do you have any memory of what they did with you?"

"None. Now that I am more mature and no longer fascinated by the two girls, I think they are devious creatures."

"Can you explain?"

"I think they have the capacity to control our perceptions of them. I worry about that. If they ever invaded this planet, I fear that they could control our thoughts and could overtake us without resistance. When I was able to concentrate on something so they could not enter my mind, I could see them for what they really were."

"What do you think they really are?"

"Obviously, they are alien. I don't think they are friendly, nor do I think they care for humans at all. I think they are kidnapping us to test their power. They present themselves as friends, but I don't believe that."

"Did you learn anything else from them?"

"I once asked them where they came from and they showed me a star system. Because of them, I studied engineering and astronomy. One day I plan to visit them."

"How do you plan to do that?"

"My plan is to become a pilot. That's why I joined the Air Force and one day, I plan to be the first female Indian astronaut."

"That's a wonderful goal. Have you ever met John Herrington?"

"I heard him speak at my high school when I was sixteen. We were all in wonder of a Chickasaw Indian that became an astronaut. I hope to follow in his footsteps."

"Can you tell me about anything you might have learned about the aliens' planet?" I asked.

"They took me on a simulated tour of their home planet. It was a holograph tour. Their planet looked like earth. There were rivers, oceans, valleys, mountains, deserts. But there again, I never trusted what I saw because I knew their power. They could be deceiving me."

"Did they ever tell you why you were chosen?"

"Only that I was alone and seemed to need a friend. Now does that make sense to you? Sometimes when I think of their evasiveness, I get angry. Once I saw them approaching, I tried to run from them. But there was no way. They can paralyze you on the spot. There is no escape."

"Do you believe they conducted tests on you?" I asked.

"Of course, why else would a twelve-year-old girl end up without any clothes. I would not have taken them off. I was a shy. I was too shy to undress in front of my female cousins. It was just something I refused to do. I got in trouble in school for not wanting to take community showers after P.E. Yes, I do think they experimented on my body, but I don't remember anything. It's probably a good thing. I'm still modest. If I knew the truth, I may not be able to live with it."

"Is there anything else you remember?"

"Their spaceship. It reminded me of a top I had as a child. It gave off this warm and welcoming feeling, almost like my grandmother's arms around me. I felt warm and loved. Like a comfortable nest."

"Did that feeling change over time?"

"Even though I felt warm and loved, the spaceship was cold to the touch."

"Did you ever see other abductees?" I asked.

"Never. I was always alone and I felt alone."

"Do they still come for you?"

"No. My grandmother passed the summer I graduated from high school, and after that the visits stopped. I got several college offers. I became something of a math whiz kid and couldn't get enough of science. I think it was because of them. I guess that's one good thing that came out of my abduction. From the moment I met them, I knew what I wanted to do. So when I was offered a full scholarship, I went away and I never looked back. I might be a city Indian now, but the reservation is still in my soul. I keep in touch with my cousins on Facebook, but so far, I haven't gone back."

Stephanie keeps in touch by email and an occasional phone call. She is living her dreams. She is a pilot now and from her emails, it appears that she is well on her way to reaching the stars.

CHAPTER 33
THE JOINER

In the realm of the paranormal, stories about "walk-ins" are those that involve two souls swapping places. In other words, a walk-in occurs when the original soul of a human leaves a person's body and another soul takes over. Some walk-ins can continue life within the personality of the original soul. Other walk-in personalities overwhelm the host body and dramatic changes have been known to occur, including divorce, name changes, and abandonment of current life course.

In 1979, Ruth Montgomery presented a collection of accounts of walk-ins in her book, Strangers Among Us. *Afterwards, a belief system grew up around this phenomenon. New Agers began talking about channeling and telepathic contact with extraterrestrial intelligences as walk-in experiences as well.*

In this chapter, you will meet a woman who adds another term to the identity change. She calls them "the joiners."

Della heard of my interest in UFOs and Star People through friends and contacted me by email. She explained that she had a story to tell, but felt uncomfortable writing about it in an email and invited me to meet her the next time I was in Billings.

Having left the reservation as a young woman, married twice, and divorced, Della lived her life in relative solitude. She was a small woman, standing only about five feet tall. Her long black hair was prematurely peppered with gray. Her pockmarked face made her look older than her declared thirty-eight years.

"I fit no place," she said, as I sat down at her kitchen table. "I fled the reservation in my early twenties to get away from the old ways, the limits on my life, the ignorance, or at least what I regarded as ignorance." She paused as she set a cup of black coffee in front of me and joined me at the table. "Now I know that I was the ignorant one, but it's too late to go back."

"Perhaps you should begin at the beginning," I suggested, as I set my tape recorder on the table between us, "and tell me what happened to you that makes you feel so alone."

"I don't want any notoriety," she said, as I hit the record button. "I'm only seeking others who might have had similar experiences. Maybe after you hear my story, you can give me some guidance."

"I will be happy to do that, if I can help," I replied.

"I visit the reservation about twice a year. My mom and two aunties still live there. There're some cousins, too, but I'm not close to them. In December [2014] I decided to visit my mom for Christmas. I worked at the local Walmart part-time for a while and picked up some presents for her and my aunties through-out the year. Not much, but more than they have. So I felt good about going and delivering presents. I knew they would be thrilled. Mom had decorated a fake Christmas tree and had some lights around the doorway. My aunties had moved in with her since it was cheaper to live together with the economy cutting many jobs on the reservation. My old room was occupied by the two of them. That was okay with me. I wanted to sleep on the couch anyway. I often woke up in the middle of the night, fixed tea, and watched TV. I preferred the couch."

"But you mentioned that you had a story to tell."

"I'm getting to it. You asked me to start at the beginning, and this is the beginning."

"I apologize. Of course, I wanted you to start at the beginning."

"You see, it was on this trip that I met the Joiners."

"I'm not sure I understand who 'The Joiners' are," I said.

"The aliens, the Star People, as you call them."

"Please go on and tell me your story."

"My mother's house was located on five acres on an unpaved reservation road. She received the land through a tribal transfer of 126 acres of obscure land to the tribe. She built a small two-bedroom house there and paid for it with her income from her tribal job. She was thirty minutes from the small town on the reservation where she worked and less than an hour and a half from the nearest off-reservation city." She paused, offered to refill my coffee cup, and lit up a cigarette. "I hope you don't mind," she said. "It settles my nerves."

"It's fine," I said.

"Anyway, I unloaded all the presents when I arrived and put them under the tree. It was warm that day. I had never seen it seventy degrees on the prairie in the winter. At night, it was still warm; around forty degrees or so."

She stubbed out the cigarette in the ashtray, stood and peered out the kitchen window. She pounded on the window. "I hate magpies. They steal food from little chickadees that come to my bird feeders." She pounded on the window again. Satisfied the magpies were gone, she sat down again and continued with her story.

"I woke in the middle of the night to bright lights shining through the picture window. I opened the door and walked outside. I saw two lights in the distance. Thinking they were headlights, I waited. But as the lights got closer, I realized it was not a car or truck. The lights became one and moved closer. That's when I saw the outline of a circular craft. I stood there in the front yard, mesmerized, paralyzed, and unable to move. I felt both excitement and fear. I wanted to run inside, but I couldn't."

She paused again and lit another cigarette.

"That's when a beam of light came out of the craft and took me onto the craft. I tried to free myself, but there was no hope. When I found myself on board the craft, they told me they were the Joiners. They said they come to Earth and choose individuals who live different lives and join with them so they can experience life on this planet. They had chosen me for their dual existence."

"Do you mean they wanted to occupy your body?"

"Yes. They said it would be temporary, but that they often chose humans for such an experience."

"What was their purpose?"

"They explained that they wanted to experience life as humans. It was an experiment."

She paused and took a deep drag on her cigarette, letting the smoke out slowly. "At the time, I thought it sounded okay, but I wasn't sure I wanted to participate and I told them so. They told me I had been chosen because I was suicidal, and that I had no choice. They said my new joiner would help me put those thoughts behind me and I would be a new person."

"So did the joiner enter your body?"

"I don't remember how or why, but the next morning, I remember waking around 8 a.m. I had a renewed sense of purpose. I made pancakes, bacon, and eggs for breakfast. I was filled with energy. I felt great. While I remembered the night before, because they said I would remember, I did not feel any different than a sense of ambition. During the next few days, I helped Mom paint the living room. We repotted her plants; I washed windows inside and out, and scrubbed the bathroom and repainted it. I was aware the joiner was with me. Sometimes she would talk to me at night."

"What did she say? Was your joiner a female?"

"Yes, I believe it was a female entity. She said I had more important things to do than wash windows and paint rooms. She wanted me to leave and go back to the city."

"What did you do?"

"I ignored her demands at first, but then on New Year's Day I left and drove back to Billings."

"What other differences are you noticing at this time?"

"Several. At first, I noticed only the energy, but then I began realizing I was losing time. I would go to work and wake up the next morning, but I couldn't remember anything beyond leaving work. I felt lost. I had no idea what was happening after work and I was tired, very tired. I didn't even know what time I went to bed."

"So you believe that once you left work, the joiner took over your personality."

"Yes. I even contacted Kevin. He was a friend of my ex-husband's. I asked him to follow me and find out what I was doing.

He thought I was crazy, but he agreed to do it. He said he tried five times to follow me, but I was so illusive he lost me. So obviously the joiner knew he was following her and could elude him."

"Is your alien joiner still with you?"

"No. She has been gone for about four months now. It is a relief."

"Did you learn anything from the experience?"

"There were times that I thought I saw her memories. I saw flashes of a city that I had never seen. I saw creatures I had never seen."

"Can you describe them?" I asked

"As I said, I saw only flashes…a city with trees growing up the walls of the buildings and a cat-like creature that was enormous."

"Can you describe the city?"

"Lot of circular skyscrapers. The whole city was circular. It appeared crowded. I saw no cars. No people. But it felt crowded."

"Anything else?"

She shook her head no and then added, "There is life out there."

I have visited with Della a couple of times since our first meeting. She is happy to report the joiner has not returned. She recently graduated from college and has been hired as a counselor in a diabetes prevention program for American Indians. She is excited about her future and says that she no longer thinks of suicide. On the weekends, she volunteers at a call-in center for those contemplating suicide. She believes her new-found outlook on life is related to the impact the "joiner" had on her life.

CHAPTER 34
AN EVENT IN THE EVERGLADES

In March 1965, James Flynn, a rancher from Fort Myers, Florida, took his swamp buggy, camping gear, and four dogs, and set out for the Everglades, about eighteen miles east of the Big Cypress Indian Reservation. On Sunday night, the dogs jumped a deer and ran off. He waited until about midnight, but when his dogs did not return he got in his swamp buggy and headed in the direction where he saw them enter the swamp.

About an hour later, Flynn spotted a huge light in the sky above some cypress trees. The object descended about four feet off the ground. Flynn drove closer, got out his binoculars, turned off the light on his swamp buggy, and watched the craft. It was an unusual object. He estimated that it was about 30 feet tall and twice as big across the bottom as it was high. Roughly eight feet from the top was a row of windows, below which were three more rows of the same size—about two feet by two feet. The craft was cone-shaped.

After a few moments, he cranked up his buggy and approached the craft. He walked to the edge of the lit area, raised his arm, and waved. He got no response. After waiting about 30 seconds, he walked about six feet into the lit area, raised his arm, and waved again. Suddenly a "short beam" of light erupted from just under the bottom of the windows and struck Flynn on the forehead. He fell unconscious. He woke about twenty-four hours later and made his way to the home of a Seminole Indian friend. By this time, he had only partial sight in his left eye and was blind in his right eye.

According to people who checked out Flynn's account, there was a huge burned area on the ground. A dozen twenty-five-foot cypress trees were scorched on top with scrape marks on the trunks about four feet off the ground, and all supported Flynn's account.

In 2012 Billy Joe, a Seminole Indian, told me an equally compelling story.

I met Billy Joe when I contracted with him to take me on a tour of the Everglades. When no one else showed up for the tour, he took me on his Airboat as a solo passenger. Before the trip began, I told Billy Joe I was interested in the site where James Flynn had encountered a UFO.

"I know the James Flynn story," he said. "My father told me about it when I was a boy. I was both frightened and intrigued by the story. Seeing mysterious lights is a common event in this part of the country."

"Have you ever had an encounter?" I asked. He looked at me pensively and walked past me without responding. "I collect stories about encounters from American Indians and other indigenous people. I write books about those encounters. If you have had an experience, I would love to hear it."

He pushed the boat away from the dock. "So you can include me in your next book?" he asked. "No thanks."

"I'm sorry to hear that. I never disclose the identity of those who share their experiences with me. I respect that many people do not want to come forward."

He did not respond.

We traveled nearly a half hour before the engine slowed and Billie Joe jumped down from his perch and joined me on the bench seat.

"Flynn's encounter was in that area," he said. I followed his arm and looked in the direction he was pointing. "I don't think it's a good idea to get off the boat. But this is the general location. I don't want to run onto an alligator." He laughed but avoided looking at me.

Billy Joe was a short man nearly as broad as he was tall. He wore ill-fitting Levis that he tugged at every time he stood. His stomach hung over his belt.

"Do you swear that no one will ever know?" he asked. "I don't want the publicity and I don't want people coming to Big Cypress [referring to the reservation] asking questions. My elders would not approve."

"I understand."

"It's common to see mysterious lights over the Glades. There's hardly a month that goes by there is not a sighting. Most of them never make the news. We don't talk much about them. They are just a part of the landscape."

"What has been your personal experience?" I asked.

"A few months ago, I got a call from Ben, a friend of mine, asking me to come to his rescue. He is in the tour business, too. He said that he had taken his sons out for the evening and his boat engine died. He couldn't get it started despite trying several repairs. I agreed to come to his rescue. Within minutes, I headed to his rescue. I estimated that I would locate him within an hour."

"How did he call you?"

"We have shortwave radios and cellphones. There was much static on the line, and it broke up a couple of times, but I learned enough that I knew his boat was disabled."

"Did anything happen on your way to meet him?"

"Two things. I tried calling him once I was headed in his direction, and I got no response. Then my cellphone went dead and my GPS malfunctioned. But I know the Glades and that did not worry me. It was only when a light, a beam of light, appeared above me that I became concerned."

"Did you know the source of the light?" I asked.

"I knew it had to be aerial since it was coming from overhead, and at first I thought it was a searchlight, perhaps from a helicopter. But there was no sound so I immediately discounted that. That's when the searchlight moved to the south and I saw the shape of the craft. It was enormous. I saw the searchlight disappear and in its place blue and red lights appeared outlining a circular object. Suddenly it rose and disappeared."

"Could you describe the craft in any other way than it was

circular?" I asked.

"No. I saw the outline of the ship. It was perhaps fifty feet across. It was outlined in blue lights. In the center were red lights that throbbed."

"Did you ever find your friend?" I asked.

"Once the craft was gone, I found him within minutes. But that was the strange part. When I arrived at his boat, I found him sound asleep and his boys were missing."

"Missing?"

"They were nowhere in sight. After much shaking, my friend woke up. At first, he seemed delirious. He didn't know where he was, and he didn't know where his kids were. I gave him some coffee and left him."

"Why did you leave him?" I asked.

"He was weak and in no condition to search for his boys. This is alligator country and time is important. I had to find the boys. I began by circling his boat and gradually increasing the circle, moving slowly and widening the circle. Many times, I stopped and called out to them. No answer. Just as I was about to give up, I heard a faint cry. I headed toward the voice and there on a small island, no bigger than this boat, I saw the boys huddled together. They were naked."

He paused, poured coffee from his thermos into a Styrofoam cup and offered it to me.

"Where were their clothes?" I asked.

"I never found them, but I didn't spend a lot of time looking either. I got the boys into my craft, gave them some blankets, and headed back toward their father. He was still disoriented but more aware of his surroundings. He kept talking about a spacecraft and praising God for returning his boys to him. The boys kept assuring him that they were okay."

"Did you ever find out what happened to the boys?" I asked.

"I stayed with them until the sun came up and then accompanied them back to their dock. By that time, the father appeared to have made a full recovery. He told me that they saw a spacecraft hover overhead, shining a spotlight on them in the boat. He tried to outrun them, but couldn't. After his engine died and he tried repeatedly to repair it, he called me for help. Then he remembered the craft shining a spotlight on the three of them, taking his sons upward on the beam of light. After that he fell unconscious."

"And the boys?"

"They had no recollection of what happened to them. They didn't know what happened to their clothes, but both of them had a large circular red mark on their necks and a small red mark on their shoulder."

"How big was the mark on their necks?"

"About the size of a silver dollar."

"Did they remember where they got it?"

"No recollection."

"What about the mark on their shoulder?"

"It was a perfect mark about an inch long. Both in the same place. Neither boy had knowledge of how they got the mark. It was strange. It reminded me of a welt I once got when my father whipped me for drinking beer."

"What do you think happened to your friends?"

"I think they were abducted by aliens. I believe they disabled Ben and then they abducted the boys. There is no other explanation."

I have not returned to the Everglades since I met Billy Joe, but I often think of the story he told me. Others have reported being abducted while a loved one is rendered unconscious, so his story is not that unusual. The fact that it happened in a remote location is not uncommon, nor are the marks found on the boys' bodies. Perhaps these events occur more often than we know, but because of the encounters take place in isolated areas, the stories are never revealed.

CHAPTER 35
CAT EYES

In 1967 a police sergeant Herbert Schirmer saw red lights along Highway 63 near Ashland, Nebraska. Thinking that it was a disabled truck, he approached and shined his high beams toward the lights. Instead of a truck, he discovered a disk-shaped object hovering above the road. He described it as a shiny, polished aluminum disk with a catwalk around it. Blinking red lights and windows completed his description. The UFO was about six to eight feet above the road, and was hovering in the air with a slight tilt. He noted that when the object began to rise, it made a siren-like noise and issued flames from underneath. Sgt. Schirmer watched the UFO pass overhead. Then suddenly it shot up and out of sight.

Later, under hypnosis, Schirmer recalled how humanoid beings, about four to five feet tall, escorted him from his car and into their ship where he was given a tour. Schirmer maintained that the event forever changed his life.

I recently talked to a truck driver from Wyoming who told me about an encounter in Nebraska that changed his life forever, too. This is his story.

"I've never given much thought to UFOs," Solomon began, as we sat at a rest stop in Bozeman, Montana. "My grandmother believed. She always talked about the men from the stars. She raised my sister and me after our mom died. She warned us to be home before dark; otherwise, we might be captured by the men from the stars. She's a fan of yours. She read your book *Encounters* and suggested I contact you. Since I often travel through Bozeman, I decided to email you. Thanks for meeting me."

"It's my pleasure. I'm always willing to meet someone who wants to share a story with me."

"I haven't talked about my experience to anyone except my grandmother. I live with her and take care of her. She only has me and my sister, who looks after her when I'm on the road."

"Did you tell your sister?" I asked.

"No one. No one except my grandmother, and now, you. I wouldn't want anyone at work to know. They might think I'm not fit to drive, and I need my job."

"What are your travel routes?"

"I deliver goods throughout the Northwest and sometimes to the Dakotas, Kansas, and Nebraska for Walmart. I'm based out of Salt Lake City, so I work non-stop for twelve days and then take a week off."

"You wrote in your email that you had your encounter near Aurora, Nebraska. What can you tell me about it?" I asked.

"It was one of the rare times I was sent to Lincoln, Nebraska. I had been driving most of the night. It was close to 3 a.m. when up ahead I saw some bright flashing lights on the highway and figured there was an accident. As chance would have it, there was a turnoff on the right hand side of the road and I took it. I decided to grab a few winks and wait until the highway was cleared. It was better than sitting in traffic, and I was ahead of schedule and thought I could sleep a couple of hours and still arrive in Lincoln on time."

"Where did you park once you were off the Interstate?"

"There was a viaduct over the road. I parked beneath it to avoid lights from the highway. At least I thought so. I had no more than settled down, and I heard noise outside the truck. I climbed outside to investigate when I came face to face with these creatures. They had cat-eyes—almost amber in color. I saw six fingers. I knew they weren't of this earth. I tried to run, but something stopped me dead in my tracks. My resistance was in vain. I called out into the night, but there was no one to help. The strangest thing, the traffic on the Interstate was gone. Not a single car was moving. They led me onto their craft, and the next thing I know, we were in space. I knew that because I felt sick to my stomach. It reminded me of the times when I used to ride in the back seat of the car when my mom would drive the reservation roads to town. I always got sick. Too many curves. This space ride was the same."

"What happened to you once you were onboard?"

"They led me to a brightly lit room and signaled that I should stay there and left. I felt cold and the light bothered my eyes. I decided to get out of there, and just as I reached the entryway, they reappeared. They told me they weren't going to hurt me, but that I needed to follow their directions."

"Were they talking as you and I talk?"

"No, I just understood in my mind what they were saying. I told them I had a job and I had a schedule. The strangest thing, they seemed to know that I had to be in Lincoln and they told me not to worry, I would make my schedule."

"Can you describe them?"

"They were what we call weaklings. No muscles. Just thin, very thin, and yet they had a forceful grip. They had cat eyes, they changed color from amber to yellow and they didn't blink the way humans do. They wore very tight dull silver suits, but their hands were covered with gloves. There was an insignia on their uniforms."

"What about their faces?"

"I'm not sure. I think they wore helmets."

"How could you see their eyes?" I asked.

"I saw them through the helmets."

"Can you describe the insignias?"

"They were octagon-shaped with a small ball near the center. Black dots appeared at three sides of the octagon. The patch was black but the dot in the center was red. I asked them about the symbols and they said the small dots represented the planets from their system, and the red ball was symbolic of leadership."

"Do you have any recollection of what happened to you while you were onboard?"

"They examined me. They asked me about my job and why

humans were still using this method for transporting goods. I told them we did not know any other way. They told me there were much simpler ways. When I asked them to tell me about them, they said the tunnels. When I told them I did not understand, they said all worlds have tunnels. I told them if there were tunnels, I would lose my job." He paused and laughed. "Sounds stupid, doesn't it? But at the time, that's all I could think to say."

"Do you remember anything else?"

"There was one thing that I thought strange. They took my blood and then asked me questions about the differences between Indians and other races on the planet. They told me that on their planet, the people were all the same and treated equally. They worked as a community. I told them that in the old days, the Indian people lived the same way. When one ate, everyone ate. When one went hungry, so did the rest."

"Did they call you Indian?"

"Yes. They asked me what my race was called. I told them Indian, so they used Indian, too."

"They did ask me why there were so many different Indians. I told them we came from different places."

"Do you remember anything else?"

"The strangest of all is they said they thought as one. Everyone was connected. All I could think about was those Aspen trees in Colorado that are said to be the largest living organism on the planet. Can you imagine a world where everyone thinks as one? They look alike and think alike. Not a world for me."

"Anything else?"

"I only remember them assuring me I would not be late for my delivery in Lincoln. I kept looking at my watch, but it didn't move. It had stopped at 2:24 a.m. and never moved. I had to buy a new one when I got to Lincoln."

"How did you get back to Earth?"

"Strangest thing. I have no memory of that. I woke up in Lincoln just blocks from the Walmart parking lot. I have no memory of how I got there. I couldn't believe it. Do you think they were right about the tunnels?"

"I'm not sure. What do you think?"

"I don't think. For me there is no answer."

I hear from Solomon about once a month by email. He has since read Encounters with Star People *and tells me he feels better about the men from the stars. He told he has not made the trip back to Lincoln again and has asked not to be sent that way. He told the dispatcher that he wanted to avoid bigger cities, and so far, he simply drives the northwest. The next time Solomon comes to Bozeman, he plans to buy me lunch.*

CHAPTER 36
IT HAPPENED IN THE BEAR PAW

One of the most remote breathtaking landscapes in Montana is the Bear Paw Mountains backcountry in north-central Montana. The area includes several, isolated mountain ranges that reach 7,000 feet and is home to abundant wildlife.

In this chapter, you will read a story of a UFO encounter that occurred in the Bear Paw, not once, but several times over the years during an annual family camping/hunting trip.

In May, I drove to Havre, Montana, to visit a friend who asked specifically that I make the visit before the month of June. Havre, which is located about ten miles from the Bear Paw Mountains, is a town that's about ten percent American Indian, mostly Chippewa-Cree. My friend Macie had moved from the reservation after marrying and had remained there after her divorce.

I arrived at Macie's house around 4 p.m. Her granddaughter greeted me and led me through the house to a small dimly lit bedroom in the back of the house, "Grandma's been waiting for you. I'm worried about her. She talks about little green men and UFOs. Maybe she has Alzheimer's."

As soon as I entered the room, Macie sat up and smiled. Despite her smile, Macie's health had declined dramatically. She no longer dyed her hair; it was almost white. It appeared as though she had lost almost half her weight. She looked tired.

"Took you long enough to get here," she said in a soft whisper as I walked to her bedside and took her hand. "Help me sit up," she said, directing her orders to her teenaged granddaughter. "Have you met Cheyenne?" Macie asked.

"We met," I said. "You're lucky to have such a beautiful and dutiful granddaughter."

"Yes, I am. She's a good girl, too. She's been reading your book to me," she said, pointing to a copy of *Encounters with Star People* on the nightstand near her bed.

"Why didn't you tell me you were interested in UFOs? All of these years I've known you professionally and as a friend, and you never mentioned your UFO research."

"I thought you knew. Didn't your friend Buddy call me the UFO lady?"

"Yes, Buddy, God rest his soul, did call you the UFO lady. I thought it was because you had seen one. I never knew it was because you were collecting stories."

She paused when Cheyenne reappeared in the room with a pot of tea. I watched as she removed my book from the nightstand and replaced it with two mugs.

"Cheyenne mentioned you have been talking about little green men. Are you interested in UFOs?" I asked.

"Oh, yes, in fact, I have a story," she said as she smoothed the blankets across her lap. "But I wanted to make sure that you would come to see me and not come because of my story. So I didn't tell you that I have a story."

She laughed.

"You don't need a story to get me to come visit you," I said. "I'm happy you invited me. I've been looking forward to reliving the old days."

"First of all, let's get something out-of-the-way." She paused for a moment and wiped her eyes. "The truth is I'm dying. The old cancer is throughout my body. It hasn't destroyed my brain yet, but the docs know my days are numbered on this earth."

She paused again and I watched her fight back the tears. I reached for her hands and held on tight. "Now don't feel sorry for me," she said. "I've made my peace with the Great Spirit and the Catholic priest for good measure. I have both the medicine man and the priest on call. I've had a good life. It's more than I can say for most."

She paused, laughed weakly, and took a sip of the hot tea.

"You and I have had some great adventures together," she continued. "Remember the time we decided in the middle of the night to drive to Browning in a blizzard?" She smiled. "Well, let's remember that tomorrow. I was telling you about my Star People. We need to do that first."

"Before we do that," I said, "I want to know: Did you get a second opinion about your cancer?"

"I've had several. There's nothing anyone can do, and if you come to my funeral, I want you to wear red. I want colors at my funeral, not black. Okay?"

"I promise."

"Now, I want you to get this story right. I may not be around to critique it."

I pulled out my tape recorder. After I showed her how to start and stop the recorder, she looked at me. "Ready?" she asked.

"I'm ready, if you're sure you want to continue."

"I'm ready. I might be dead tomorrow."

"I doubt that. You're too feisty to die."

She laughed weakly and pushed the start button. "I was about six years old the first time I was abducted. My father used to take the family up in the Bear Paw on extended camping trips in the summer. We'd set up camp on the St. Mary and fish. We'd trap and hunt, even though it was often out of season. Sometimes we'd stay a month or two. Dad built a smoker and we dried fish. He always killed a couple of deer. It was our basic food supply in the winter. There wasn't much work for Indians. We survived on hand-outs from the Catholic Church, government commodities, and the meat my father was able to bag."

"Did you enjoy those summers?"

"Mostly. But I got lonely. My brother was older than me by seven years, and Dad expected him to fish and hunt like a man. My mother was busy with cooking and drying meat. When she wasn't doing that, she was washing clothes in the river or fishing alongside my brother. So I was left alone much of the time. I knew better than to whimper or to try to get attention. So I'd wander around, pick flowers, search for berries. Mom told me to stay within shouting distance, but every day I wandered further from camp."

She paused and picked up her teacup.

"And you were only six years old?"

She nodded and offered the teacup to me for a refill.

"It was on one of my excursions that I came across a little boy. At least, at the time, I thought he was a little boy. He wasn't much bigger than me, but he ran and played with me. We climbed trees. We sang. We waded in a stream and looked for baby fish. We danced. I picked flowers and he helped me. After that, he invited me to follow him. He said he had something to show me. I followed thinking I was going to his camp. Instead, he took me to a big dollhouse that was hidden in the trees. He welcomed me inside. I was frightened and ran home."

"A dollhouse? Please explain what you saw."

"It looked exactly like the dollhouses in the Sears and Roebuck catalog. It was amazing. A two-story structure. It was pink with white shutters."

"Did you see the little boy again?"

"The next day, I looked for him, and sure enough he showed up again. We played for a while and then he invited me to follow him. This time I went into his house. It was so clean inside. So bright. Two other people welcomed me. I thought they were his parents, even though they looked different."

"Can you describe them?"

"All I remembered at the time was that they were small, not tall like my mom and dad and they had strange eyes."

"Tell me about that."

"Like any six-year-old, I asked them about their eyes, and they told me the light hurt their eyes and that they had to wear special glasses. I asked them if I could have a pair of those glasses, but they said they were medical and a little girl shouldn't wear the glasses."

"When they spoke to you, were their voices oral? Could you hear them?"

"When I was six, I guess I didn't realize that their voices were in my head. Later, I discovered that their communication was in my brain—telepathy, isn't that what they call it?"

"Yes. You were telling me about the house before I interrupted you. Can you elaborate?"

"I remember it was cool inside. I was thirsty and they gave me a blue drink. It was tasty. I drank about half of it, but when I tried to set the glass down, they said I should drink all of it. Suddenly, I felt sleepy. I told them I had to return to my camp that my family would be worried. They told me I should lie down and rest and they lifted me onto a high bed. After that, I fell asleep, I guess, because the next thing I remember, I was back in my camp."

"Did you tell your parents about the little boy?" I asked.

"I did, but later I heard my mother tell my father about my imaginary friend. I never saw the little boy again that summer, but he reappeared the next year. This went on for several years. By the time, I was ten or so, I knew he was not a little boy. He was a little creature, I think. His skin looked smooth, but when I touched it, it felt spongy like the mushrooms that grow around old trees in the forest. And the color. It was strange."

"Do you mean the color of his skin?"

"Yes. It was like ashes in a burn-barrel. Not white, not brown like me, but a grayish/whitish color. It was not like the white kids' skin in school."

"When did you learn they were from the stars?"

"I was in the fifth grade. The teacher gave us a *Weekly Reader*. It was a weekly newspaper for children. One issue had photos of possible spaceships that would take us to the stars. One of the spaceships was circular like a silver dollar. It was just like their traveling machine."

"I thought you said they took you to a dollhouse."

"Yes, that was the first time. But after that, they showed me their spaceship. I told the teacher I had seen one just like that. The whole class, including the teacher, laughed at me. I learned my lesson that day. I never spoke of my friends from the stars again. It was my secret."

"Did you ever tell anyone?" I asked.

"Not really. I told Cheyenne about them, but she thinks I'm fading in and out of reality. But I'm not. I wanted you to hear my story. Otherwise, the truth would die with me."

"When did the visits with the Star People end?"

"When I married. Until then, I always joined my parents for their annual campout, even when I was in college. After I married, I no longer went with my parents. It was strange. I told the Star People I was getting married and wouldn't be returning to the forest. They don't marry so I spent some time explaining marriage to them. They don't bear children either. Everything was different on their planet. I asked them not to come for me again. I explained that my husband would not understand. The Star People agreed. They said their work was completed."

"Many people report a history of visitations, just like you," I said.

"From the time I was six until I was twenty-six they came for me. That's over twenty years. I thought of them as a second family. I know I wasn't the only one they took to the stars. Over the years, I saw many others. No other Indians, just me."

She paused and took another sip of her tea. Cheyenne entered the room and asked her grandmother what she would like for dinner. She turned to me and said. "Remember the last time you were here. We went to the China Garden. I wish I were well enough. We could go there tonight."

"Maybe Cheyenne could go to the China Garden and pick up some food," I said. "I love their orange chicken and crab puffs." We made a list, I gave Cheyenne cash and sent her to the restaurant to pick up the food. "If you can't go to the China Garden," I said, "we will bring it here."

Macie smiled approvingly.

"How long have we been friends?" she asked.

"About thirty years," I replied.

"In all of those years, we never had a fight. You are my only friend who never fought with me. The Star People often talked about how humans were violent. We are a violent people in general, but I've only seen you mad a couple of times. But you always forget and forgive. I have a hard time forgiving."

I refilled her teacup and she took a sip.

"What else did the Star People talk about?" I asked.

"Different things at different times. When I was younger, they often asked me to play games and solve puzzles. They would put two or three of us in a room with puzzles. I think they wanted to see how fast we could complete them. I always won. When I got older, the tests were harder, but I tried to keep up. When I was a teenager, I had solved all the problems they gave me. They said I was of superior intelligence."

"I could have told them that."

Macie laughed out loud.

"You said you competed with others," I said. "Who were the others?"

"Other children. I didn't know them. They weren't Indian."

"Did they ever take you to their planet?"

"No, but they took me into space. I saw the earth from space. I saw other planets, too, but they said it was too far to take me to their planet."

"Did they perform tests on you?"

"Yes, but they never hurt me. They were kind to me."

"Can you talk about that?"

"In the early years, it was a physical examination every year. They measured everything: my height, weight, hair, blood, and my mind. They ran a machine over my body and checked my internals. At least that's what they told me. When I became a teenager they began taking my eggs."

"Your eggs?"

"It must have been. Why else would they open my legs?"

"I guess I never thought about that."

"It was okay. I learned to trust them. They didn't want to hurt me. In fact, they made me believe in myself. They made me feel special. I shudder to think of the things I could have done with my life, but it was the Star People who intervened."

"What do you mean by that?"

"They told me I was of superior intellect. I knew from them I could go to college. They gave me the confidence I needed. If it hadn't been for them, I might have ended up with a very bad life. The day I got married, I knew I made a mistake. I stayed for two years and had Marybeth. She was only one-year-old when I packed up the car, and Marybeth and I left for college. I didn't look back. I credit the Star People with my courage and belief in myself."

When Cheyenne returned, the three of us sat on the bed and ate. Macie ate a crab puff and then said she would eat more later. Around eight p.m., she decided she was tired and wanted to go to bed. She wanted me to return the next morning to complete the interview. I checked into a motel around nine p.m. after I was sure that Macie was settled for the night.

When I returned the next morning, she had lapsed into a coma. Cheyenne called an ambulance and admitted her to the hospital. Two hours later, I checked in with the family, but the doctors were not hopeful. I spent three nights at Macie's bedside, but she never regained consciousness.

Finally, I returned home.

Macie passed three weeks later. Cheyenne told me that on the night of her death, a bright light appeared in the sky. Several people at the hospital saw it, but everyone had a different opinion of what they saw. For a few minutes, Macie regained consciousness and told Cheyenne and her daughter, Marybeth, goodbye. The priest and medicine man were at her side.

The day of the funeral, a light rain fell. I covered my red sweater and denim skirt with a black raincoat, but wrapped a bright ruby-red scarf around my neck and wore my red cowboy boots. Macie and

I had bought identical pairs at a western store in Dallas many years ago. I knew if Macie was watching, she would smile. As the coffin was lowered into its opening, I placed a red rose on it. When I turned to leave the burial site, Macie's medicine man pulled me aside and told me that Macie wanted me to know the Star People had come for her. I think she was right. After all these years, they returned to take her home.

CHAPTER 37
MY DNA IS CLOSE TO THEIRS

In 1996, Dolly—a cloned domestic sheep—was presented to the public. The field of genetic engineering is a heated topic of discussion in today's society with the arrival of stem cell research, genetically modified food, and gene therapy. After cloning was successfully demonstrated through the production of Dolly, many other large mammals were cloned, including deer, pigs, horses, and bulls. Today DNA has multiple uses, including criminal investigations, courtroom proceedings, parental identification, and the diagnoses of potential health risks.

But long before Dolly entered the picture, UFO researchers received reports from individuals allegedly involved in human/alien experimentation and human-hybrid cloning.

In this chapter, you will read about the collection of DNA from an abductee.

Bertha was a great-grandmother. I met her on her ninetieth birthday. I had stopped off in Cheyenne on my way to Denver to meet a former student who told me she had something special to share with me. When I arrived, she suggested that I go with her and Bertha to the Elder Center for lunch. When we arrived, it immediately became obvious the lunch was a birthday celebration for Bertha. Slab birthday cakes were brought into the dining hall on trolleys. Bertha walked to the front of the room aided only by a cane. An elderly holy man rose and addressed the group. A silence fell over the celebration as he prayed for Bertha and for her continued health. Afterwards a drum group began to sing a traditional song, and the cafeteria workers rushed forward and cut the cakes. After each elder and family member was served, everyone else formed a line, received a piece of cake, stopped and kissed "Grandma Bertie," and wished her a happy birthday.

I watched the scene unfold from the sidelines. As the day wore on and more community members came, a buffet was laid out and the elders ate together. Then the dance began and the young and the old joined in several group round dances. Shortly after lunch, Grandma Bertie turned to me.

"My granddaughter calls you the UFO lady," she said.

"I'm not sure about that. I collect stories about UFOs."

"I have a UFO story, and I doubt you've heard anything like it. Let's go home. I will talk to you."

We arrived at her house about twenty minutes later. Bertha led me into the kitchen. While her granddaughter made tea, Bertha invited me to sit at her kitchen table. She unwound a bun at the back of her neck and pulled her thin white hair across her shoulder. She was a small woman, weighing less than a hundred pounds, I suspected. Before she began her story, two cats entered the room and climbed upon her lap.

"This is Huckster," she said pointing out the black and white cat. "This one is Abigail. I rescued both of them one night on my back porch in below zero weather. I think they are brother and sister. Been with me sixteen years now." She smiled as she continued to pet the cats.

I placed the tape recorder on the table. "I hope you won't mind if I tape your story." She shook her head and began.

"I was abducted by a UFO in 1942," she said. "At the time, I didn't know nothing about UFOs. I thought it was the Nazis capturing me."

"The Nazis?"

"Yes, we were in the middle of World War II, and I thought they were Nazis."

"Could you tell me about it?" I asked.

"I was picking chokecherries down by the stock pond. It was a hot day, so I waited until evening."

"Where was the stock pond?"

"It was at my Dad's ranch, about twenty miles west of here. When the craft came over the pond, I was so scared I couldn't run. I was frozen. When I finally gathered my senses about me and tried to run, I couldn't. I couldn't move."

"Is that when they took you on board?" I asked.

She nodded and watched as her granddaughter poured tea into two cups. "I found myself in a cold room. It was barren. Nothing was in the room. I was scared to death. Then two creatures appeared at the door and told me to follow them. I wanted to resist, but I had no will of my own." She paused and put two teaspoons of sugar in her tea and took a sip.

"You used the word, 'creatures,'" I said. "Can you describe them?"

"They were like wooden machines, but they had this blue-gray pasty skin and six fingers. They never talked that I could hear but they made me know I was to follow them. When I saw their fingers, I realized they weren't Nazis. When they moved, it was strange. They didn't walk; they scooted across the floor. I still think they were machines. Although I suspected they weren't from Earth, I was confused because they weren't the Star People of the old ones' stories."

"Can you describe their faces?"

"I know it sounds unbelievable, but I never got a good look at their faces. It was like they were wearing masks. I'm not sure, but I saw nothing human about them."

"Did they do anything to you?" I asked.

"They took some of my hair. They checked my teeth, and they took some blood. That is all I remember. The next thing I know, I am sitting on the steps of my house with a bucket of chokecherries. My mother was so happy that I had found so many berries that I didn't spoil it by telling her what happened to me."

"Did you see them again?" I asked.

"Not for a long time. I got married and had a daughter. When she was six, they came for the both of us. She does not remember the event. But it was the same. We were berry picking and they came. I don't think it is the berries that attract them; I think it was because the places we picked berries was isolated. It was a good place to kidnap us."

"Has it happened again?"

"Three more times. Every time I had a baby girl, we were taken. It was always the same. They came when Vicky was six, and together they examined us and took samples of hair and skin. Finally, it was more than I could take. I told them that I was no longer going to cooperate. I told them they had no right to take me. I fought and struggled, and that's when four different men entered the room. They looked human, at least more human than the mechanical men and the gray paper men."

"Can you describe them?" I asked.

"They were taller, maybe close to six feet. I remember they had high foreheads and even though their hair was long, it was thin. They looked a lot like Indians. They were darker than white men."

"Did they say anything to you?" I asked.

"When I repeated that they had no right to take me, they agreed. In fact, they apologized, but they said that the molecules in my body were closest to theirs. I told them I did not understand, and they said I would someday. They explained that molecules were responsible for the development and function of life. They said 'your scientists call it DNA,' and that my DNA was closest to theirs, and they needed my hair and blood. They said my DNA would help them. I never understood what they meant. At the time, I did not know what DNA was. I didn't even know what a molecule was. I still am not sure I know what it is, but I have heard about DNA on *The Maury Show* and *CSI*. I went home and wrote molecule and DNA down in a notebook hoping I could learn about it." She got up and opened a drawer near the refrigerator. She pulled out a tattered spiral book, leafed through it, found her note and pushed it across the table to me. "There it is. I wrote this back in 1974. "Do you see the date?"

I nodded. Before me in handprint form, she had written: "dna, maulecule."

"I asked people about DNA and no one knew what it was," she continued. "Now I guess everyone knows, although I still don't know for sure. Did you know about DNA in 1974?"

"I don't think so," I replied.

"Do you know what it is now?"

"I believe DNA is the hereditary material in the human body. Every cell in the body has the same DNA. That way, if a man denies a baby and he is the father, a scientist can tell if the baby is his from the DNA. The baby will inherit both the father and mother's DNA. It is the same with a crime. If someone leaves blood during a struggle or hair, the police collect the DNA of the killer."

"So if my DNA matched the aliens, that means we are related," she said.

"It would seem so."

"Why didn't they tell me that in the first place? Those mechanical men scared me. If only I had known the truth."

"Do they still come to you?"

"I haven't seen them since my last girl was born." She paused and walked to the stove and returned with the teapot. "I told you my story was different. Have you heard another one like it?"

"I haven't heard a story like yours," I assured her. "I probably never will."

Over the past three years, Bertha's health has suffered. Her oldest daughter, Linda, recently moved in with her mother to care for her. Bertha insists that she will never go to a nursing home; it is not a common practice among American Indians. Extended families care for their elders in their homes. I visited Bertha two months ago. Although she spends most of her time in bed, she sat up for two hours and talked with me. She has finally broken her silence and told her daughters about her encounters.

CHAPTER 38
ALIENS ON ARCHULETA MESA?

Archuleta Mesa, which rises a few thousand feet over the small, rural community of Dulce, New Mexico, is the hub of the Jicarilla-Apache Indian Reservation. The Mesa is well known in the UFO community. Some UFOlogists claim that the Mesa is the site of a massive underground facility operated by the U.S. government and one or more alien races. There are some reports that the Mesa contains a seven-story complex that connects to Nevada's Area 51 and Los Alamos National Laboratory in New Mexico. Others believe it is simply a Cold War era fallout shelter.

But in 1979, Thomas Edwin Castello, who claimed to be a senior security guard at the Mesa's secret underground base, described a research facility with an ominous sixth level, dubbed Nightmare Hall, where both humans and aliens conducted appalling operations and experiments. He claimed alien abduction victims were used for crossbreeding and fertilization

UFO researchers mention reports of strange lights and cattle mutilations in the area. The residents of Dulce acknowledge that there is something out of the ordinary at Archuleta Mesa, but most are reluctant to talk about it.

In this chapter, you will read a firsthand account about a strange event that occurred on the Mesa.

I first met Harlyn in the 1970s at a National Indian Education Association (NIEA) Conference in Minneapolis, Minnesota. We were seated in an auditorium waiting for the keynote speaker to arrive. We struck up a conversation and afterward attended various events together. Over the years, our friendship continued, and we always looked for each other at the annual conference. After the internet became popular, we kept in touch on a more regular basis.

Harlyn had a stocky build and the shoulders of a bear. Over the next thirty years, I had watched his coal black hair become peppered with gray, while his bronze skin, devoid of signs of aging, disguised his age. Now, he seemed to have aged ten years in the past year. The two of us admittedly had watched the years pass, suffered tragedy and celebrated successes, and provided support as our friendship grew. Over the years, I had visited Dulce twice and had come to know his wife and children.

During my last trip to NIEA, Harlyn introduced me to his granddaughter, Chelsea. As she scurried off to get coffee, Harlyn leaned over and spoke in a stage whisper. "This might be my last trip to NIEA. I have cancer, diabetes and COPD. The triple threat. Probably from my years as a smoker. I don't want Chelsea to know how serious it is. She loves her Poppie. But I've had a good life. No regrets. I now live in Albuquerque, just to be closer to doctors and the hospital."

When Chelsea returned with two black Starbucks coffees, the two of us moved to a secluded section of the hotel lobby and spent some time recounting our life's experiences. As the discussion waned, I changed the subject: "I've always wanted to ask you about Archuleta Mesa."

Harlyn nodded. "I'm not surprised. Strange things happen on the Mesa."

"I heard there was a Navajo woman who was found wandering naked around the Navajo River. Rumor has it that she escaped from an underground facility in the mountain. What do you know about that?"

"Exactly what you know," he said. "According to the man who found her, she kept asking where she was repeatedly. She told him they were experimenting on people inside the mountain and that she had escaped. As strange as her story was, there was no investigation. Rumor has it that a man showed up claiming to be her husband and took her away. She was never heard from again. Many people think the government silenced her. We never did know her name."

"Since she didn't know where she was, how did she get there?"

"She was abducted and taken inside the mountain, at least that's what she told the man who found her."

"Is that what convinced you that something was going on there?"

"No, there were a series of things. I'd seen the lights in the sky that vanished. Hell, I'd seen the mutilated cattle. Then the naked Navajo woman set me to thinking. Before I saw these things, I didn't believe. One night, after my wife and I divorced, I was feeling low. I bought myself a pint of whiskey and headed toward the Mesa. I took the Seguro Canyon Road. It is a rugged, four-wheel drive road, and it only goes part way. If you want to get to the top of the Mesa, it is a good six-hour hike."

"Before you continue, did you drink the whiskey?"

He laughed. "Never got a chance to drink it."

"What happened?"

"That was the night I became a true believer." Harlyn paused, took a drink of his coffee, drew a long breath, and looked at the ceiling for several seconds as though he was trying to formulate in his mind the story he had to tell.

"I drove up the Canyon Road just to get away and think," he continued. "I had been married for thirty years. There were no other women in those years. Even though Betty and I argued a lot, I still loved her. It never occurred to me that she would want a divorce. I was thinking about this, when suddenly I heard a helicopter overhead. I quickly turned out the lights on my pickup, parked, turned off the engine, and got out to get a better look."

"What time was this?"

"It was after midnight. I know that because I was in town at midnight. Probably around 2 a.m."

"Do you have any idea what the helicopter was doing near the mountain?"

"It flew back and forth as though scouting for something, and then another helicopter appeared. They had floodlights and were shining them in all directions as though looking for something. Twice I ducked when their lights came near me. Together the two helicopters flew back and forth, shining spotlights toward the mountain."

"How long did they continue this activity?"

"About fifteen minutes. Then suddenly, I saw the outline of a UFO heading toward the Mesa. The helicopters took a stationary position, and I saw the UFO fly between them and go inside the mountain."

"Inside the mountain?"

"I swear. That's exactly what happened. Until this time, I always assumed that the military was doing some things up there, but was not sure about the alien connection."

"Even with the story of the Navajo woman?"

"Even with that story. She could have been dumped off by an irate boyfriend or husband, but this not only gave credence to her story that aliens were involved at Archuleta, but I saw it with my own eyes. I sat there most of the night watching. As soon as the UFO disappeared, the helicopters flew away. I stayed there until daybreak, but never saw the UFO again."

Harlyn shrugged his shoulders and laughed.

"Can you describe the UFO?" I asked.

"It was a circular craft. As it approached the mountain, a strange thing happened. It seemed to condense."

"What do you mean by that?" I asked.

"I really can't explain it, but it seems like it got flatter as it approached the mountain. It was very strange."

"Have you seen other UFOs since that event?"

"Twice. I go to the mountain occasionally. I have even climbed the mountain but have found nothing to show there is an opening. But I know what I saw."

"Tell me about the other two sightings."

"I saw them from my front yard. They come in low over Dulce.

They wait until it's very early in the morning, when most of the tourists and gamblers are asleep. They make no noise and they fly toward the mountain and disappear."

"Have you ever seen any beings?"

"Never. Only the crafts, but I can't help but wonder if they have abductees on board. I try to stay positive and not think about it, but I have to admit it is something that keeps me up at night. What if it was your brother or sister or your mother? I feel guilty remaining silent. Maybe you can tell my story when I'm gone."

Harlyn passed eleven months after our last meeting. From my home in Montana, I picked up a friend in Denver, and we drove to Dulce for his funeral. Dulce is a small, Jicarilla Apache town that enjoys tourists hoping to see a UFO and gamblers dreaming of hitting a jackpot at the Best Western Tribal Casino. None of them know of Harlyn, a man who knew the truth about the Archuleta Mesa but was too afraid to tell it. Instead, I am his voice, as he hoped I would be.

CHAPTER 39
A STRANGE ENCOUNTER
AT JOE'S PLACE

According to a storeowner in Arizona, a man once entered his store who looked rather uncomfortable in his body. He walked stiffly and was unable to turn his head from left to right. He would turn his whole body to see what was beside him. When the stranger left, the storeowner watched him struggle as he climbed into his car. Since the man had parked directly in front of the store, the owner was curious about how he would back out of the parking lot since he could not look behind him or to the side. However, according to the storeowner, the man's eyes moved around his face to the back of his head and he backed out. While the storeowner admits that not too many people believe his story, he knew what he saw and he believed this stranger was not from Earth.

In this chapter, you will read Joe's story, which has similar elements to the encounter in Arizona.

Joe owned a small convenience store on the edge of the reservation, which included a pizza shop with a dining area and one gas pump. On any given night, the place was full. It was a regular hangout for teenagers who ordered milkshakes and French fries, listened to the latest music on the jukebox, and did their homework. The weekends were reserved for family groups who came from throughout the region to Joe's Place to eat pizza, which reportedly was the best in the state.

Joe described himself as a Heinz 57 Indian. His mother was a quarter Lakota, one fourth Northern Cheyenne, and the rest of her blood came from the Arapaho, Chickasaw, Cherokee and Choctaw; his father, according to Joe was a "hybrid-white" of French and Irish descent. Despite growing up on the reservation and having at least one-half Indian blood, Joe was unable to enroll as a tribal member because of his lack of Indian blood in any one tribal group. In school, the non-Indian boys were his friends.

When he was fifteen, Joe was arrested for killing his father. His friends and relatives rallied to Joe's defense. Even his teachers testified that Joe had been the object of abuse by his father since the first grade. His frequent trips to the hospital served as proof, and the federal judge hearing the case set Joe free. For the next several years, Joe lived in Des Moines, Iowa, with an aunt, the sister of the father he had killed. In his thirties, he returned to his birthplace and opened his store.

I heard from Jonas, the son of one of my best friends, that Joe's Place had been the site of an unusual encounter with an alien. One night at dinner, Jonas had told me about the event he had witnessed.

So on a Friday night around 11 p.m., I made my way to Joe's and ordered a supreme pizza. Realizing he would close at midnight, I ate slowly and watched as the other patrons left, all wishing Joe goodnight. When the last of his customers left, Joe locked the door.

"Take your time," he said. "I have to clean up, so I will be here for a while."

"Thanks," I replied, "but I really came here to talk with you."

He turned and looked at me. "What about?" he asked, as he continued cleaning tables. I watched as the overweight, barrel-chested man in Levis, wearing a Hawaiian sport shirt and an apron, bussed the tables with the precision of an experienced waiter.

"I heard that you had an alien encounter at this establishment a few weeks ago. I wondered if you would tell me about it?"

Joe set down the dishes he was carrying and approached my table.

"Who are you?"

After introducing myself and explaining that I wrote books about UFO encounters, Joe appeared unimpressed.

"Perhaps I could come back another time," I said. "I know you are busy."

"No. It's fine. You're fine. I just never thought the encounter, as you call it, would create so much interest."

He pulled out a chair and sat down opposite me.

"What do you mean?" I asked.

"You are the third person in the past two weeks who has come here to ask me about that night."

"Would you tell me about the others?"

He shrugged his shoulders and stood. He walked to another table and wiped it down. "The first one was a reporter. I don't know how she found out about what happened that night, but she did."

"What did you tell her?"

"Nothing. I didn't want this place overrun by curiosity seekers. I told her I knew nothing about it, and she went away."

"What about the others?"

"Two men came. They said they worked for the government, and they were following up on a visit I might have had. They described the stranger, but I told them I knew nothing of such a stranger."

"Why not?"

"They were suspicious looking characters. I mean, the day they came here it was a hundred degrees in the shade, and they walked into this place wearing wool suits and hats. How could I possibility trust men who dressed like that? No one wears suit coats in that weather. Besides, anything that looks like government or smells like government is not to be trusted."

"Can you describe them?"

"Yeah."

He scratched his head, reached in his pocket, and pulled out a cigarette. "I hope you don't mind," he said.

I shook my head and watched the flame of the match sizzle as it met the end of the cigarette.

"There was just something about them. They looked like twins. Wore black hats, black pants and jackets, black ties and white shirts. And I almost forgot black glasses. They never took them off. They flashed a badge, but I never got a good look at it. They were white, very white. Like they never were in the sun. That's about it."

"And you never told them anything?"

"One other thing: when I told them I didn't know of such a stranger, they told me that I could go to prison if it was discovered that I was withholding important information." He shrugged and took a long drag on his cigarette.

"Did that bother you?" I asked.

"Nope. I just stared them down. I don't talk more than I have to. Besides, I never met a government man I trusted."

"Would you feel like talking to me about what happened?"

"Did you say that my buddy Jonas told you about it?"

"Yes. He's Terry's son. I'm visiting her."

"Jonas is a good kid. He helps me out on the weekends and holidays. He is dependable and honest, so if he sent you, you're okay in my book." He paused and looked around the room. "Besides, you look like a breed. I trust breeds. We've all been to hell and back."

He stood and picked up some trash from the floor.

"I'll help you clean up," I offered. "I know it's late and I really appreciate you taking the time to tell me your story."

"I've got time," he said. "On Saturdays, I don't open 'til noon. That's my late night. I stay open 'til 2 a.m." Joe got up and returned to the table with a box. "For your pizza," he said as he sat down again.

I placed the pizza inside the box and put a twenty-dollar bill on the box. Joe pocketed the twenty.

"Do you mind if I record your story?" I asked.

"As long as you don't use my real name, it'll be okay. As I said, I don't want any curiosity seekers around here. They'll run away the regulars. I don't need my business hurt."

"I guarantee you I won't tell anyone."

"On a stack of Bibles?" he asked smiling.

"On a stack of Bibles."

He smiled and pulled out another cigarette.

"It all started around nine o'clock, as I remember."

"P.M.?"

"Yes." He walked behind the counter and returned with an ashtray.

"I remember the dining room was full, and there were several people sitting in their cars waiting for tables. Sheri, my cousin, always helps on Saturdays. She's the waitress, the cashier, and the hostess. When someone leaves, she clears the table, goes to the door, and tells the next person to come in. People always respect each other and take their turns. We trust them and they trust each other, but this night it was different."

"How different?" I asked.

"Just as she opened the door, everyone from the parking lot headed inside. They crowded around the counter, all talking at once. They said that a UFO had just passed over the building. No one inside heard anything, but they said that it was no more than fifty feet overhead. They described the craft as circular, and so big that it not only covered the building but the parking lot as well. One of my Saturday-night regulars said that when it passed over, his radio blasted static and then went out. A woman named Jo who comes from an off-reservation town to eat pizza said the same thing happened in her car. She said she was going to call the military base and report it."

"Did you see the UFO?"

"No, I didn't see it. But there were at least eleven people who did. I don't want to say their names. They may not want anyone to know their names."

"Jonas mentioned he wanted anonymity."

"That's the way it is. Nobody wants to talk about it."

"Was Jo an Indian?"

"No, she just likes my pizza," he replied, smiling. "I have several customers from off the reservation."

"So what happened after that?"

"The only thing I remember was about the same time the people in the parking lot reported trouble with their radios, the lights flickered and I said a few Hail Mary's willing the electricity to stay on. When it did, I thought my prayers had worked."

He paused and lit another cigarette from the one in his hand. "Is that it?"

"No. About an hour later, a stranger walked into the place. His very presence was shocking. He was tall, at least six feet six and maybe taller. I'm six feet two and he was taller than me. He wore pale blue coveralls with an insignia on the right arm. There was a jacket of the same color over the coveralls. His boots, too. The only place I had seen someone dressed like that was on the ski hill, but he didn't strike me as a skier, and we don't have a ski hill around here."

"Can you describe the insignia?" I asked.

"It was a diamond shaped with some kind of odd figures underneath it. I didn't recognize them. They made no sense to me."

"Can you describe the figures?"

"I really can't. It could have been writing for all I know."

"What about the man's features? Can you describe them?"

"His hair was a white blond, if you can imagine that. Not quite blond, but not quite white. He also had the bluest eyes I had ever seen, but they appeared strange to me because they were larger than normal eyes."

"Did he sit at a table?"

"Not at first. He walked over to the counter and sat on that stool. Sheri uses it when she's not waiting on customers or manning the cash register."

He pointed toward the stool and I looked over my shoulder toward the counter. "When he entered, Sheri asked him what she could do for him. She knew he was a stranger because he had not waited in the parking lot like other customers. He walked over and sat down on her stool. He spoke only one word, but it sounded strange to her. She thought he wanted tea."

"Sheri brought him tea and set sugar and cream on the counter. He looked at it cautiously. He picked up the spoon and ate the sugar. Afterwards, he drank the boiling hot tea. It would have burned blisters on the mouth of any human."

He stopped and shook his head. "Sheri ran in the kitchen and told me what she observed. I took out a hot teapot, poured him another cup of hot water, and placed a tea bag beside it. I swear to you, he downed the hot water like it was ice cold."

"Did he ever say anything except 'tea'?"

"He nodded when I asked him if he wanted a pizza. I asked him what kind and he pointed to the one at the top of the marquee menu. When it was ready, he took a table in the back of the room." Joe stopped and pointed to a back booth. "Everyone in the dining room started calling for boxes or began leaving. Each of them voiced his strangeness and how he sat there and stared at them. One customer said she felt he was putting thoughts in her mind. Another said when she stood she was momentarily paralyzed. When she caught herself on the table, she looked at him. She thought she heard him say, 'I can control you.'"

"Did you ever feel any of these things?"

"Only when he left. I heard a voice in my head that said I wouldn't remember him."

"What exactly did you hear?"

"You will not remember this night. That is exactly what I heard."

"Did he pay for his pizza?"

"No, but he didn't eat it either. I put it in a box since I was due to close at midnight. I was hoping he would take it and leave. But he left without it. I gave it to some of the homeless guys near the bridge."

"Did you ask him to pay?"

"No. I was glad he left. He was very strange. Like he was not really human."

"Did anything else happen after you heard the voices?"

"I locked the door after he left and turned off the lights. In the darkness, I watched him leave the parking lot. That was the strangest part of all. Instead of backing out of the parking lot, I saw the car levitate about two feet off the ground, turn around and then lift upward. Then, I heard the back door slam. Sheri came running in. She had seen it too. She was out back putting garbage in the dumpster and saw it. She was sure he did not see her."

"Once he turned the car around, what did he do?"

"Sheri and I ran out into the parking lot and watched as the vehicle lifted upward and then it disappeared in the night sky."

"So do you think he was from the UFO?"

"Do you have another explanation?"

"Tell me about the car? What model was it? What color? Was it new or older?"

"I don't even know. When I think about it, I often wonder if it was a car at all. Maybe it was an illusion. Perhaps he had that ability to create an illusion so he could mingle with humans."

"What do you mean?"

"I mean, just think about it. He was tall, taller than any human I have ever seen. He wore a strange suit with an unrecognizable symbol. He drank boiling water and ate a bowl of sugar. He could get inside people's heads and paralyze them. He levitated a vehicle off the ground and flew it upward to the sky. All of this happened two hours after a UFO was seen."

Joe paused and lit another cigarette.

"What do you think about the event?" I asked

"I never paid much attention to all this stuff about UFOs. But I do believe this man was not human. He scared the hell out of the people in my dining room. He scared the hell out of me, but I fooled him. I remembered what happened. And not only that, Jonas remembered. And my regular farm lady from down the road, she must have called the newspaper and the base. That would explain the journalist and the government men. No, he was wrong about us. His power doesn't work on everyone."

I have seen Joe a couple of times since our first meeting. He has not had an alien visitor since that one fateful night, nor has anyone reported a UFO in the area. He told me that none of his patrons have ever mentioned that night. Perhaps the power of suggestion had worked on most of the clientele, and only Jo, the farm lady, and Jonas remembered the event. In any event, I have become a regular customer when I am in the area. There is no doubt in my mind, Joe's Place definitely serves the best pizza in the state, but more importantly it is the site of an alien visitation. If you did not know better, you would think it was just another non-descript pit stop on a rural two-lane road.

AFTERWORD

I have more credible reports of UFO encounters from American Indians, both living on and off the reservation, than I could fit in two books on the subject. To date, more than fifteen hundred individuals, people who neither sought nor desired to profit from their encounters, have convinced me of the veracity of their experiences. That does not take into account the three hundred plus individuals I have never met who have contacted me through email about what happened to them.

But what do these encounters actually say to us?

The contact experiences are extensive, and those of off-reservation participants are quite similar to those living on the reservations. Although there were more cases of physical evidence presented to back up the testimony of urban American Indians, most of their stories were similar to those of reservation-living American Indians. Both groups told of stories involving different types of aliens. Furthermore, individuals in both groups described the rage, pain, joy, and fear they experienced. But I found that younger individuals who live off the reservation were more accepting that UFOs exist than those on the reservation, which may be due to their increased exposure to the media coverage of such events. Those who were abducted relate similar stories of physical manipulations, including the collection of fluids and hair. Both groups reported that their abductors communicated that their memories would be suppressed, and both groups reported telepathic communication with the aliens. All the individuals I interviewed recollected their encounters without the intervention of hypnosis. However, the off-reservation group appeared more fearful of the purpose of the aliens; they were fearful that the aliens had the power to not only conquer humans, but to do with the

Earth whatever they chose to do.

While the UFO phenomenon is certainly not just found among American Indians, I believe that the encounters with Native people should teach us that we should approach this phenomenon with more humility, a sense of humbleness, and openness to the potential that alien life forms exist on Earth and are engaging humans more often than we know.

ACKNOWLEDGMENTS

I wish to acknowledge the individuals who shared their stories with me. You know who you are, and I am honored and humbled that you chose me to tell your stories. I will never forget you.

I also want to thank Randy Radke, Seth Hartman, and Phil Van Gorden. While you are my biggest critics, you are also my biggest supporters. Thank you for your friendship.

And as always I want to thank my husband, Kip, who accepts canceled dinners, delayed holidays and celebrations, unscheduled trips and impromptu interviews, countless telephone calls and emails, and time alone to allow me to tell these stories. Thank you for your love and understanding.

And last but not least, I want to thank Patrick Huyghe, my editor. You are the best; more than I could ever have hoped for and probably better than I deserve.

BIBLIOGRAPHY

—, "1953: Kingman Arizona UFO crash," *Think About It*. http://www.thinkaboutitdocs.com/1953-may-20-kingman-arizona-ufo-crash/.

—, "Barrow, Alaska," *Alaska Travel Guide*, http://www.travelguidebook.com/index.cfm?inc=place&place_id=1705

—, "Known Types of Alien Races," *The Watcher Files*, http://www.thewatcherfiles.com/alien_races.html.

—, "List of alleged extraterrestrial beings," *Wikipedia*, https://en.wikipedia.org/wiki/List_of_alleged_extraterrestrial_beings.

—, "Monster Bird with Red Eyes May Be Crane," *Gettysburg Times*, Dec. 1, 1966.

—, "Reptilians & Aliens Abductions & Encounters: The Weirdest Story of All," *Meta Tech*, http://www.metatech.org/reptilian_alien_abductions_encounters.html

—, "Stephen Hawking: alien life is out there, scientist warns," *The Telegraph*, November 22, 2015.

—, "Unidentified Flying Objects," *Grolier's Book of Knowledge*, Volume 20, 1952.

—, "Underground Alien Bases," *UFO Hunters*, 3/25/2009, http://www.dailymotion.com/video/x19mw9g_underground-alien-bases-ufo-hunters-aliens-extraterrestrial-paranormal-documentary_tv.

—, "Walk-Ins," *Crystallinks*, http://www.crystalinks.com/walk_ins.html.

—, "Walk-In," *Wikipedia*, https://en.wikipedia.org/wiki/Walk-in.

Appelle, Stuart. "The Abduction Experience: A Critical Evaluation of Theory and Evidence," *Journal of UFO Studies*, 6, pp. 29–78, 1995/96.

Bader, C., "Supernatural Support Groups: Who Are the UFO Abductees and Ritual-Abuse Survivors?" *Journal for the Scientific Study of Religion*, 2003.

Barker, Gray. "The monster and the saucer," *Fate*, January 1953.

Bishop, Gregory J., *Project Beta: The Story of Paul Bennewitz, National Security, and the Creation of a Modern UFO Myth*, Paraview Pocket Books, 2005.

Bourke, Lee, *Death Valley Men*, Macmillan Co., 1930.

Bryan, C. D., *Close Encounters of the Fourth Kind: Alien Abduction, UFOs, and the Conference at M.I.T.*, Knopf, 1995.

Byrne, Holt. "The Phantom of Flatwoods," *Sunday Gazette-Mail*, March 6, 1966.

Bullard, Thomas E., "The Rarer Abduction Episodes," in: Pritchard, Andrea & Pritchard, David E. & Mack, John E. & Kasey, Pam & Yapp, Claudia, *Alien Discussions: Proceedings of the Abduction Study Conference*, North Cambridge Press, pp. 72–74, 1994.

Bullard, Thomas E., "The Variety of Abduction Beings," in:

Pritchard, Andrea & Pritchard, David E. & Mack, John E. & Kasey, Pam & Yapp, Claudia, *Alien Discussions: Proceedings of the Abduction Study Conference*, North Cambridge Press, pp. 90–91, 1994.

Clark, Jerome, *Extraordinary Encounters: An Encyclopedia of Extraterrestrials and Otherworldly Beings*, Visible Ink Press, 1997.

Clarke, David, *The UFO Files: The Inside Story of Real-Life Sightings*, The National Archives, 2009.

Carroll, Robert T., "Cattle Mutilation," *Skeptic's Dictionary*, http://www.skepdic.com/cattle.html.

Clifford, James, "Varieties of Indigenous Experience: Diasporas, Homelands, Sovereignties," in Marisol de la Cadena & Orin Starn, *Indigenous Experience Today*, Berg Publishers, 2007.

Clifford, James, *Returns: Becoming Indigenous in the Twenty First Century*, Harvard University Press, 2013.

De Lafayette, Maximillien, *Dulce: Greys' Hell in America: Aliens' Factory of Human Bodies' Parts (Hybrids & Human Beasts)* Times Square Press, 2015.

Everett, Allen and Roman, Thomas, *Time Travel and Warp Drives,* University of Chicago Press, 2012.

Farish, Lucius, and Titler, Dale, "Mysteries of the Deep," *UFO Magazine*, Vol. 2, No. 3, May 1977.

Feschino, Frank C., *The Braxton County Monster: The Cover-Up of the Flatwoods Monster Revealed*, Quarrier Press, 2004.

Ford, L. H.; Roman, Thomas A., "Quantum field theory constrains traversable wormhole geometries," *Physical Review* D 53 (10): 5496–5507, 1996.

Getches, David H., Wilkinson, Charles F., and Williams, Robert L., *Cases and Materials on Federal Indian Law,* Thomson/West, 2005.

Good, Timothy, *Alien Contact: Top-Secret UFO Files Revealed,* William Morrow & Co., Revised edition, 1993.

Hardy, Chris H., *DNA of the Gods: The Anunnaki Creation of Eve and the Alien Battle for Humanity,* Paperback, Bear & Company, 2014.

Hendry, Allan, *The UFO Handbook: A Guide to Investigating, Evaluating and Reporting UFO Sightings,* Doubleday, 1979.

Hopkins, Budd, *Intruders,* Random House, 1987.

Hopkins, Budd, *Missing Time,* Ballantine Books, 1988.

Howe, Linda Moulton, *Alien Harvest: Further Evidence Linking Animal Mutilations and Human Abductions to Alien Life Forms.* Linda Moulton Howe Productions, 1989.

Jacobs, David M., *Walking Among Us: The Alien Plan to Control Humanity,* Disinformation Books, 2015.

Jain, S.P.S., "What're close encounters of the first, second, third, fourth and fifth kind?" *The Times of India,* March 22, 2003.

Jones, Richard, "Unexplained sheep attacks caused by aliens in UFOs, farmers claim," *The Telegraph,* April 5, 201.

Joyce, Judith, *The Weiser Field Guide to the Paranormal: Abductions,*

Apparitions, ESP, Synchronicity, and More Unexplained Phenomena, Other Realms, 2010.

Keel, John, *Operation Trojan Horse*, IllumiNet Press, 1996.

Keyhoe, Donald E., *Flying Saucers from Outer Space*, Henry Holt, 1953.

Khatsymosky, Vladimir M., "Towards possibility of self-maintained vacuum traversable wormhole," *Physics Letters B* 399 (3–4): 215–222, 1997.

Kirsch, I., and Lynn, S., "Alleged Alien Abductions: False Memories, Hypnosis and Fantasy Proneness," *Psychological Inquiry 7 (2): 151–5, 1996.*

Krasnikov, S., "The quantum inequalities do not forbid spacetime shortcuts," *Physical Review* D 67 (10): 104013, 2003.

Lamb, David, *The Search for Extraterrestrial Intelligence: A Philosophical Inquiry*, Routledge, 2001.

Levengood, W. C, "A Study of Bovine Excision Sites from 1993 to 1997," Pinelandia Biophysical Laboratory, 1997.

Lewis, Tyson & Kahn, Richard, "The Reptoid Hypothesis: Utopian and Dystopian Representational Motifs in David Icke's Alien Conspiracy Theory," *Utopian Studies,* 16 (1): 45–75, Winter 2005.

Mack, John. E., *Abduction Humans Encounters with Aliens* (Revised Edition), Ballantine Books, 1995.

Marika, K., *Werewolves, Shapeshifters and Skinwalkers*, Sherbourne Press, 1972.

Mars, Jim, *Alien Agenda: Investigating the Extraterrestrial Presence Us,* William Morrow Paperbacks, 2000.

Mathis, Brandon, "Do you believe? Archuleta Mesa's aliens inhabit a prime chapter in UFO mythology," *The Durango Herald,* April 29, 2014.

McClleland, Mike, "Judy Carroll, Grey Aliens and Owls," *Hidden Experience,* http://hiddenexperience.blogspot.com/2012/11/judy-carroll-gray-aliens-and-owls.html.

McClleland, Mike. *The Messengers: Owls, Synchronicity and the UFO Abductee,* Richard Dolan Press, 2015.

Metcalf, R. Warren, *Termination's Legacy: The Discarded Indians of Utah,* University of Nebraska Press, 2002.

Moffitt, John F., *Picturing Extraterrestials,* Prometheus Books, 2003.

Montgomery, Ruth, *Strangers Among Us,* Fawcett, 1984.

National Urban Indian Family Coalition (NUIFC), "Urban Indian America: The Status of American Indian and Alaska Native Children and Families Today," The Annie E. Casey Foundation; National Urban Indian Family Coalition; Marguerite Casey Foundation; Americans for Indian Opportunity; National Indian Child Welfare Association, 2008. Online at http://www.aecf.org/KnowledgeCenter/Publications.aspx?pubguid={CCB6DEB2-007E-416AA0B2-D15954B48600s.

O'Brien, Christopher, *Enter the Valley,* St. Martin's Press, 1999.

Oehlerking, Jerry. "The Dick Williams Story: If Bear Butte

Would Speak," *South Dakota Conservation Digest*, March/April 1977.

Parker, Barry, *Alien Life: The Search for Extraterrestrials and Beyond*, Perseus Books, 1998.

Pratt, Bob, *UFO Danger Zone*, Horus House Press, Inc., 1996.

Steiger, Brad, *Strangers from the Skies*, Award Books, 1966.

Swords. Michael, "Fear, Sanity, and Crossing the Line," *International UFO Reporter*, 2007.

Thornton, Russell, in *Changing Numbers, Changing Needs: American Indian Demography and Public Health*, National Research Council, 1999.

Thorne, Kip S. *Black Holes and Time Warps*, W. W. Norton, 1994.

Treurniet, William C. "Is covert-technology used to create balls of light in the sky?" *UFO Digest*, http://ufodigest.com/article/covert-technology-used-create-balls-light-sky.

Turner, Mark, "Couples See Man-Sized Bird...Creature... Something," *Point Pleasant Register*, November 16, 1966.

Walters, Edward and Bruce Maccabee, *UFOs Are Real: Here's the Proof*, Avon, 1997.

Weinstein, Dominique F., "Unidentified Aerial Phenomena: Eighty Years of Pilot Sightings," *National Aviation Reporting Center on Anomalous Phenomena (NARCAP)*, February 2001.

Wunder, John R. (ed), *Native American Sovereignty*, Taylor & Francis, 1999.

ABOUT THE AUTHOR

Dr. Ardy Sixkiller Clarke brings to the field of UFOlogy degrees in history, English, psychology, and educational leadership, as well as a background as a teacher, university professor, junior college and university administrator, licensed therapist and psychologist, and social science researcher. As a Professor Emeritus at Montana State University and former Director of the Center for Bilingual/Multicultural Education, Dr. Clarke has worked with indigenous people for most of her career.

Her first book in the field of UFOlogy was the best-seller *Encounters with Star People: Untold Stories of American Indians* (Anomalist Books). Her second book, *Sky People: Untold Stories of Alien Encounters in Mesoamerica* (New Page Books), was published in 2014. She is also the author of twelve children's books and the best-selling academic text *Sisters in the Blood: The Education of Women in Native America*.

She lives in the middle of the Rocky Mountains in Montana with her husband and her beloved Lhasa Apso, Prairie Rose, and her Maine Coon rescue cat, Rez Perez. Dr. Clarke is currently working on a new children's series: *Noqisi: A Rabbit from Planet Alesii*. Her website www.sixkiller.com provides the latest information on her appearances and writing. You may contact her at: ardy@sixkiller.com.

Printed in Great Britain
by Amazon

40461019R00187